BEYOND BOUNDARIES

Cooperation in the BIMSTEC Framework

BEYOND BOUNDARIES

Cooperation in the BIMSTEC Framework

Editors

Vinod Anand

Prerna Gandhi

Vivekananda International Foundation

PENTAGON PRESS LLP

First published in 2025 by
PENTAGON PRESS LLP
206, Peacock Lane, Shahpur Jat
New Delhi-110049, India
Contact: 011-26490600

Typeset in Adobe Garamond, 11 Point
Printed by Aegean Offset Printers, Greater Noida

ISBN 978-81-987484-2-3

www.pentagonpress.in

Contents

PART III
MARITIME COOPERATION AND REGIONAL SECURITY

PART IV
CLIMATE, ENVIRONMENT, AND WATER GOVERNANCE

PART V
TECHNOLOGY, CRIME, AND NON-TRADITIONAL SECURITY

Foreword

Dr Arvind Gupta, Director VIF

BIMSTEC's security landscape is undergoing a profound transformation amidst shifting geopolitical dynamics, deepening economic interconnections, and the rise of non-traditional security threats. In this context, unity among member states is paramount to overcoming persistent implementation gaps and realizing tangible progress. As the global order fractures and regional alignments evolve, the Bay of Bengal—home to nearly 1.7 billion people—stands at a critical crossroads. With the Indo-Pacific gaining strategic prominence, BIMSTEC, often underutilized in the past, now offers a unique platform for shaping a shared regional future. *Beyond Boundaries: Cooperation in the BIMSTEC Framework* is a timely and significant contribution, reflecting the urgent need for BIMSTEC nations to collaborate across strategic, economic, technological, environmental, and cultural domains.

BIMSTEC's distinctive strength lies in its ability to bridge South and Southeast Asia—connecting landlocked Himalayan states with dynamic coastal economies and encompassing a diversity of political systems, levels of development, and civilizational legacies. Since its inception in 1997, BIMSTEC has often operated in the shadow of larger groupings like SAARC and ASEAN. However, as SAARC stagnates and the Indo-Pacific discourse ascends, BIMSTEC is increasingly seen not as a fallback, but as a forward-thinking, issue-based compact capable of delivering pragmatic cooperation. The essays in this volume embody this ambition. Drawing on the expertise of diplomats, scholars, and sectoral experts, this book offers a blueprint for reimagining regionalism in the Bay of Bengal.

The policy recommendations presented across these chapters underscore the need for enhanced institutional capacity and leadership within BIMSTEC, emphasizing the importance of political will, inclusive leadership, and addressing regulatory inefficiencies. While India's leadership role is pivotal in advancing regional integration through infrastructure development and digital connectivity, this volume stresses the need for inclusive leadership to avoid perceptions of dominance and ensure that all member states are equally engaged. A strong push is made for fast-tracking the BIMSTEC Free Trade Agreement (FTA) and fostering regional cooperation in key areas such as MSMEs, green energy, and digital transformation. The development of both "hard" connectivity (infrastructure for roads, railways, ports, and energy corridors) and "soft" connectivity (cultural, academic, and people-to-people exchanges) is essential for strengthening regional ties.

In the realm of maritime security, the volume advocates for institutionalizing cooperation through BIMSTEC, IORA, IONS, and multilateral naval exercises. Key steps to address regional maritime security challenges include enhancing Maritime Domain Awareness (MDA), real-time intelligence sharing, and establishing a BIMSTEC Maritime Security Forum. Fisheries cooperation is also highlighted, with proposals for shared research and data harmonization to ensure sustainable marine resource management.

On environmental issues, the volume calls for tailored climate policies suited to the unique vulnerabilities of BIMSTEC nations. Recommendations emphasize cooperation in energy, disaster resilience, and technology transfer, aligning climate action with sustainable growth and poverty alleviation. A coordinated BIMSTEC Water Cooperation Mechanism is proposed to manage transboundary water governance, along with diplomatic engagement for greater transparency in water flow management. The volume also advocates leveraging BIMSTEC's collective diplomatic influence to engage China on water governance issues.

To strengthen security cooperation, particularly in counterterrorism and transnational crime, the chapters suggest improving intelligence sharing, legal frameworks, and technology-driven initiatives. Special emphasis is placed on addressing cybersecurity challenges through a unified framework for AI regulation and combating cybercrime, as well as tackling narcotics trafficking and organized crime through legal harmonization and modern surveillance techniques.

Finally, the volume proposes formally including "women-led development" as a sector of cooperation, addressing gender disparities and promoting inclusive growth. Integrating gender perspectives into climate adaptation policies and leveraging digital technology to empower women are also critical recommendations. BIMSTEC's shared cultural heritage, particularly its Buddhist traditions, should be harnessed to foster regional cooperation, preserve cultural heritage, and promote cultural tourism.

Taken together, these policy recommendations aim to address the challenges facing BIMSTEC while unlocking its potential as a resilient regional platform for connectivity, security, and sustainable growth. The chapters argue for a paradigm shift: BIMSTEC should no longer be viewed as a secondary platform, but as a primary arena for addressing the 21st-century challenges of the Bay of Bengal. Although challenges remain—such as capacity gaps, political transitions, and differing priorities—the value of BIMSTEC lies in its ability to harness diversity and forge a community of committed partners.

This volume serves as both a mirror and a map, reflecting the current state of regional cooperation while offering tools for a more integrated future. Policymakers, diplomats, analysts, and development professionals will find not only diagnosis but direction in these pages. In an era of fractured globalization and rising multipolarity, the question is no longer whether regionalism matters, but what kind of regionalism will endure. *Beyond Boundaries* points towards a regionalism that is adaptive, inclusive, cooperative, and rooted in the shared aspirations of both people and states. The Bay of Bengal deserves no less.

Let this volume, and the ideas it presents, catalyze a more resilient and collaborative regional future within BIMSTEC and beyond. We invite readers to engage actively with these insights and contribute to shaping the Bay of Bengal's shared destiny.

Editors' Note

Vinod Anand & Prerna Gandhi

Beyond Boundaries: Cooperation in the BIMSTEC Framework offers a timely and comprehensive exploration of the evolving dynamics within the Bay of Bengal Initiative for Multi-Sectoral Technical and Economic Cooperation (BIMSTEC). In an era marked by global challenges, this book provides a valuable analysis of BIMSTEC's potential to shape the future of South and Southeast Asia.

The contributions from a diverse range of experts and practitioners offer fresh perspectives on key themes such as strategic outlooks, economic integration, maritime security, environmental sustainability, and non-traditional security threats. Each chapter provides an in-depth examination of a specific area of cooperation, highlighting both the challenges and opportunities within the BIMSTEC framework.

From fostering economic connectivity and sustainable development to addressing transnational crime and promoting cultural ties, this volume emphasizes the importance of cross-border collaboration in building resilience, stability, and shared prosperity. With contributions from both governmental and academic experts, the book provides insights that are both practical and visionary.

The book also delves into the growing significance of non-traditional security issues, such as climate change, cyber threats, and social empowerment. It calls on BIMSTEC nations to unite not only in confronting shared challenges but also in leveraging their collective strengths. In today's rapidly changing global landscape, *Beyond Boundaries* is an essential read for policymakers, academics, and practitioners seeking to understand the strategic, economic, and societal potential of BIMSTEC, while envisioning a future of cooperation that transcends borders and promotes sustainable, inclusive growth for the region.

Part I: Strategic Outlook and Institutional Trajectory sets the stage by analysing BIMSTEC's evolution, institutional recalibration, and strategic potential. It emphasizes that regionalism is not just about trade and infrastructure but also about building a shared strategic framework. BIMSTEC's modular, less formalized structure could offer resilience in the face of global uncertainty. This section also acknowledges persistent challenges such as institutional weaknesses and political transitions that require sustained political will.

Part II: Economic Integration and Connectivity delves into the practical aspects of regional synergy. As global supply chains shift post-pandemic and amid great power rivalry, BIMSTEC countries must deepen trade integration, invest in secure and sustainable infrastructure, and create interoperable port ecosystems. These efforts are not merely economic but strategic imperatives for long-term resilience.

Part III: Maritime Cooperation and Regional Security explores one of BIMSTEC's most urgent and promising domains. The Bay of Bengal is both a shared commons and a zone of competing interests, with growing external involvement and security challenges such as piracy and illegal activities. Contributors call for a layered maritime strategy—spanning naval coordination, legal frameworks, and sustainable fisheries governance—anchored in co-creation and regional ownership.

Part IV: Climate, Water, and Agriculture addresses environmental interdependence, now central to both security and development. The essays highlight the need for integrative responses, such as climate-smart agriculture and transboundary water governance, to embed environmental foresight into regional planning.

Part V: Technology, Crime, and Non-Traditional Security focuses on emerging borderless risks like cybersecurity, narcotics, radicalization, and financial crimes. Contributors advocate for "networked responses"—shared legal frameworks, interoperable technologies, and regional intelligence systems—to address these asymmetric challenges. This section also references recent 2025 cyber security initiatives, underscoring BIMSTEC's role in addressing emerging technological threats.

Part VI: Societal and Cultural Linkages shifts focus to people-to-people connections, emphasizing the rediscovery of cultural ties, promotion of women-led development, and fostering of societal cohesion as pillars of a more enduring, people-centric regionalism.

It is hoped that this book will contribute to the ongoing dialogue within the BIMSTEC framework, helping to strengthen regional ties and create a brighter future for all member states.

Rahul Mishra traces BIMSTEC's evolution from a subregional initiative bridging South and Southeast Asia into a vital platform for connectivity, economic growth, and security, as discussed in Chapter 1. He highlights its geopolitical relevance amid SAARC's decline, China's expanding influence, and India's strategic eastward outreach. Despite progress in trade, connectivity, and counterterrorism cooperation, BIMSTEC faces institutional weaknesses, Myanmar's political instability, and limited intra-regional trade. Mishra emphasizes BIMSTEC's potential to shape a resilient, rules-based Indo-Pacific order through initiatives like SAGAR and the BIMSTEC FTA. He argues that crises present opportunities for deeper cooperation, urging stronger collective resolve to transform vision into sustained regional integration, as noted in Chapter 1.

In "Region Building in BIMSTEC: Understanding the Geo-economics of Trade and Connectivity," Faisal Ahmed and Vinod Anand argue that BIMSTEC's region-building potential hinges on its geo-economic promise, with trade and connectivity at the core, as highlighted in Chapter 2. They trace BIMSTEC's evolving institutional architecture and policy agendas, noting India's leadership in advancing regional integration through physical infrastructure, digital public goods, and cross-border linkages. However, they caution that poor connectivity, high transaction costs, and asymmetrical capacities hamper progress. Advocating for an FTA, MSME integration, and multimodal transport networks, they underscore the need for political will, inclusive leadership, and institutional reforms to realize BIMSTEC's transformative potential, as discussed in Chapter 2.

In Chapter 3, Sanjay Chadha argues that BIMSTEC, despite its strategic location and economic scale, remains underutilized due to political inertia, regulatory fragmentation, infrastructure deficits, and geopolitical tensions. He emphasizes BIMSTEC's untapped potential in digital transformation, green energy, diversified supply chains, textiles, and pharmaceuticals. Chadha advocates for fast-tracking the FTA, investing in connectivity, forging a unified investment framework, engaging the private sector, and mitigating geopolitical risks. He offers a pragmatic five-point action plan and showcases recent positive developments as proof of latent potential. His central message: BIMSTEC must evolve from a vision to an actionable platform to become a regional economic powerhouse, as noted in Chapter 3.

In Chapter 4, Xavier and Sinha argue that for BIMSTEC to emerge as a cohesive regional bloc, it must develop both "hard" and "soft" forms of connectivity. "Hard connectivity" refers to secure, multimodal infrastructure—roads, railways, ports, and energy corridors—essential for economic integration but currently hindered by regulatory inefficiencies and coordination failures. The authors advocate a corridor-based strategy, enhanced policy harmonisation, trade facilitation, and India's proactive development cooperation. "Soft connectivity" involves fostering a shared regional identity through people-to-people exchanges, academic collaboration, and cultural linkages. They emphasize building institutional memory, investing in public outreach, and reviving the Bay of Bengal's historical community ethos, as discussed in Chapter 4.

In Chapter 5, Shitesh Ranjan argues that robust port cooperation is essential for unlocking BIMSTEC's potential as a dynamic economic and strategic bloc. He underscores India's pivotal role in enhancing maritime connectivity, modernising infrastructure, and ensuring maritime security. Through projects like the Kaladan Corridor, Chattogram upgrades, and Trincomalee Port, India is positioning itself as a regional anchor. Ranjan stresses the need for policy harmonisation, joint investments, and capacity building to overcome infrastructure gaps and regulatory hurdles. By leveraging its institutional strengths and promoting green, inclusive practices, India can catalyse regional integration, counter external influence, and transform BIMSTEC ports into engines of prosperity, as highlighted in Chapter 5.

In Chapter 6, Anurag Bisen argues that the Bay of Bengal, despite its strategic location, rich resources, and pivotal role in Indo-Pacific connectivity, remains undermined by overlapping developmental, environmental, and security challenges. The region is home to vulnerable coastal communities, suffers from territorial disputes, IUU fishing, climate risks, and rising extra-regional contestation, particularly between China and the U.S. Bisen emphasizes the urgency of institutionalizing maritime cooperation through BIMSTEC, IORA, IONS, and multilateral naval exercises. He underscores India's leadership in promoting maritime domain awareness, disaster resilience, and connectivity, advocating enhanced regional frameworks to address the BoB's complex maritime security landscape holistically, as noted in Chapter 6.

Soumya Tiwari and Faisal Ahmed argue that maritime security in the

BIMSTEC region is shaped by interlinked geopolitical, economic, and ecological dynamics, as discussed in Chapter 7. The Bay of Bengal, a strategic hub connecting South and Southeast Asia, faces rising complexities due to India-China rivalry, SLOC vulnerability, and geopolitical spillovers from the Indo-Pacific and BRI. While perspectives differ—from economic integration to strategic competition—member states converge on enhancing Maritime Domain Awareness (MDA). The authors advocate for real-time intelligence sharing, joint naval drills, stronger legal frameworks, port resilience, and a BIMSTEC Maritime Security Forum. Ultimately, holistic cooperation is key to ensuring sustainable, resilient, and inclusive regional maritime stability, as outlined in Chapter 7.

In Chapter 8, Pandian Krishnan, Murugesan SriHari, and Rajdeep Mukherjee argue that fisheries cooperation offers a unique and urgent opportunity for BIMSTEC to address poverty, food insecurity, and climate vulnerability in the Bay of Bengal region. Highlighting the centrality of fish to livelihoods, nutrition, and trade, they underscore the ecological threats from overfishing, IUU fishing, and climate change. The authors propose a collaborative, fisheries-centric framework involving shared research (via initiatives like BIMReN), data harmonization, and a BIMSTEC-Coast Guard Consortium to curb IUU fishing. They stress that regional trust, integrated governance, and policy-level cooperation are essential for sustainable marine resource management, as highlighted in Chapter 8.

The authors, Sukrit Joshi and JR Bhatt, argue that BIMSTEC nations must pursue climate action and sustainable growth independently, considering their unique vulnerabilities and developmental needs, as discussed in Chapter 9. They emphasize the region's rich biodiversity and cultural heritage, advocating for tailored climate policies rather than a one-size-fits-all approach. The authors highlight the importance of regional cooperation in energy, disaster resilience, and technology transfer, urging developed countries to honour their climate commitments. They stress that economic development and poverty alleviation should remain priorities while addressing climate change, as noted in Chapter 9.

In Chapter 10, the author Suhas P. Wani emphasizes the need for enhanced cooperation among BIMSTEC countries to address agricultural challenges. The main arguments focus on the importance of collaboration to tackle issues like poverty, malnutrition, climate change, water scarcity, and land degradation. The author highlights the increasing population and urbanization, which strain agricultural productivity and sustainability. The nuances include the need for integrated water management, efficient use of green water, and adoption of innovative technologies like AI and IoT. The author also stresses the importance of holistic solutions, public-private partnerships, and empowering small farmers to achieve sustainable food and nutrition security.

P.K. Khup Hangzo argues that BIMSTEC must play a more assertive role in transboundary water governance amid escalating water insecurity driven by population growth, climate change, and China's upstream control over key rivers like the Brahmaputra and Mekong, as discussed in Chapter 11. Highlighting the stark water dependency ratios of member states, the chapter underscores the geopolitical and ecological risks posed by China's unilateral dam-building and refusal to join legally binding water-sharing frameworks. Hangzo calls for a coordinated BIMSTEC strategy—through a Water Cooperation Mechanism, scientific collaboration, and integration of water issues into broader negotiations—to enhance resilience, ensure equitable flows, and diplomatically pressure China for greater transparency, as noted in Chapter 11.

Sudhir Saxena's chapter examines BIMSTEC's evolving role in countering terrorism and transnational crime, as highlighted in Chapter 12. Security cooperation, particularly in counter-terrorism (CT), has become a focal point for member states since the group's inception, driven by events like the 9/11 and 26/11 attacks. Saxena outlines BIMSTEC's multi-tiered CT framework, including sub-groups on intelligence sharing, legal issues, money laundering, and cyber threats. Despite efforts to harmonize national laws, challenges remain, such as differing domestic priorities and resource limitations. Saxena suggests enhancing cooperation through technology-driven initiatives, intelligence sharing, and better data processing to address contemporary transnational threats effectively.

The authors, Jiten Kumar Jain and Saroj Kumar Rath, argue that BIMSTEC member states are intensifying their collaborative efforts to address complex cybersecurity challenges and capitalize on emerging technological innovations, as discussed in Chapter 13. They emphasize the importance of identifying, monitoring, and reporting cross-border fraudulent mobile numbers involved in cyber scams to enhance regional protective measures. Additionally, they highlight the need for a unified framework for regulating Artificial Intelligence (AI) to mitigate the threat of deepfakes. The authors also discuss the critical challenge of illicit call centre operations in Thailand and Myanmar, where

BIMSTEC citizens are forcibly abducted and forced to execute digital scams. They advocate for the systematic dismantling of these illegal enterprises to preserve BIMSTEC's reputation as a resilient, cyber-secure regional bloc.

Anurag Sharma's chapter on the nexus of narcotics trafficking and organized crime in the BIMSTEC region underscores the significant security and socio-economic challenges posed by drug trafficking, as highlighted in Chapter 14. The region's proximity to the Golden Triangle and porous borders facilitates the production and movement of synthetic drugs like methamphetamine, with Myanmar at the center of production. These illicit activities are closely tied to organized crime, including human trafficking, insurgency, and arms smuggling. Despite efforts like the BIMSTEC Convention and enhanced cooperation, disparities in national enforcement and corruption hinder progress. The paper calls for stronger regional coordination, legal harmonization, and modern surveillance to combat this growing threat.

Shubhamitra Das discusses BIMSTEC's potential in addressing both traditional and non-traditional security (NTS) threats in the Bay of Bengal region, emphasizing the importance of sub-regional cooperation for broader Indo-Pacific integration, as mentioned in Chapter 15. The chapter highlights issues like climate change, transnational crime, IUU fishing, and the Rohingya crisis, all of which hinder regional stability and economic growth. India's leadership in BIMSTEC, aligned with its "Look East" and "Neighbourhood First" policies, focuses on disaster management, maritime security, and cross-border cooperation. The author stresses the need for stronger regional frameworks, enhanced connectivity, and expanded membership to ensure sustainable, cooperative growth and resilience against NTS challenges.

The author, Dr. Cchavi Vashisht, argues that the Bay of Bengal Initiative for Multi-Sectoral Technical and Economic Cooperation (BIMSTEC) should formally include "women-led development" as a distinct sector of cooperation, as highlighted in Chapter 16. This inclusion could address gender disparities and foster inclusive regional progress. The chapter highlights the persistent barriers women face, such as unequal access to education and health, limited economic opportunities, and exclusion from leadership roles. The author emphasizes the transformative potential of women-led development in addressing these issues and promoting gender equality. The chapter also discusses the importance of integrating gender perspectives into climate adaptation policies and leveraging digital technology to empower women across BIMSTEC nations.

The author, Saudiptendu Ray, explores the historical and cultural connections among BIMSTEC nations, emphasizing the role of Buddhism as a unifying force, as discussed in Chapter 17. The article highlights the ancient trade routes and cultural exchanges around the Bay of Bengal, which facilitated the spread of Indian cultural traits to Southeast Asia. The author underscores the significance of Buddhism in shaping the cultural and social fabric of BIMSTEC countries. The article also discusses contemporary efforts by BIMSTEC nations to leverage their shared Buddhist heritage to promote cultural tourism, strengthen regional cooperation, and preserve cultural heritage. The author concludes by acknowledging the challenges faced by BIMSTEC but remains hopeful that shared Buddhist values can foster greater socio-economic development and mutual understanding.

अजीत डोभाल, कीर्ति चक्र
राष्ट्रीय सुरक्षा सलाहकार
Ajit Doval, KC
National Security Adviser
Tel : 23019227

सत्यमेव जयते

प्रधान मंत्री कार्यालय
नई दिल्ली–110 011
PRIME MINISTER'S OFFICE
NEW DELHI - 110 011

MESSAGE

I congratulate the Vivekanand International Foundation (VIF) for bringing out the book titled "Beyond Boundaries: Cooperation in the BIMSTEC Framework" during the 4th Track 1.5 BIMSTEC Security Dialogue in New Delhi in May 2025. It is an opportune moment to take forward discussions on BIMSTEC's core founding principles of security, commerce, connectivity, energy and people-to-people exchanges.

We are witnessing increasing uncertainty and tensions in the global geo-political environment. Digital dependency and use of advanced technologies for perpetuating cyber-crimes and financial frauds are impacting people across international boundaries. Rising populations and energy needs are accentuating the pressure on trans-boundary water systems like the Ganges, Brahmaputra and Mekong. This has increased the salience of regional cooperative mechanisms.

BIMSTEC has emerged as a significant platform for fostering regional cooperation, economic integration and connectivity. Improved intelligence-sharing mechanisms, cooperation in predictive and emerging technologies and establishment of joint task forces are essential to mitigate the challenges of drug and human trafficking, gun running, money laundering and cyber-crime. Additionally, resilient trans-national mechanisms for preparing and responding to natural disasters is gaining urgency.

In the above backdrop, this book contains several valuable suggestions to deepen regional trade and commerce, deal with traditional and non-traditional security threats. I am sanguine that the book will enhance awareness and complement governmental efforts to boost intra-regional cooperation through the BIMSTEC Framework.

I compliment Director VIF and his team for their dedicated efforts in publishing the book and organizing this Track 1.5 Dialogue. I wish the participants all the best in their endeavor to strengthen BIMSTEC.

(Ajit Doval)

BIMSTEC

Secretary General

Secretariat
Bay of Bengal Initiative for Multi-Sectoral Technical and Economic Cooperation (BIMSTEC)

Message

The Bay of Bengal Initiative for Multi-Sectoral Technical and Economic Cooperation (BIMSTEC) has emerged as a vital platform for regional collaboration in Bay of Bengal region, aimed at fulfilling the shared aspirations of its member States for peace, prosperity and sustainable development. Since its inception in June 1997 as a regional platform for technical and economic cooperation, there has been expansion in BIMSTEC's Agenda for regional cooperation, reflecting the developmental priorities of the member States. It has now its own Charter and well-established institutional mechanisms, including Summits and Ministerial mechanisms. BIMSTEC works on the basis of consensus amongst its member States and it has ensured equal role for all the member States through adopting the unique system of making its member States as Lead States for forging cooperation in specific sectors. BIMSTEC's commitment to staying away from political issues has enabled it to stay focused on developmental agenda of the member States and achieve significant progress in forging regional cooperation. The success of BIMSTEC is evident in conclusion of a number of Conventions and Agreements, setting up of specialised Centres and Facilities and delineation of sector specific Action Plans for expanding and deepening cooperation in various agreed areas on BIMSTEC's Agenda.

02. I am very happy over publication of this Collection of very informative and thoughtful essays "Beyond Boundaries: Cooperation in the BIMSTEC Framework". It is very comprehensive in its scope and presents a vivid picture of BIMSTEC in its various dimensions. It is very timely as it is being published just after the 6th BIMSTEC Summit (04 April 2025, Bangkok), which has provided a new momentum and direction to BIMSTEC, with adoption of, besides the Summit Declaration, BIMSTEC Bangkok Vision 2030, which envisions a prosperous, resilient, and open BIMSTEC region, and the Report of the Eminent Persons' Group, which recommends specific steps to overcome institutional challenges. The signing of the Agreement on Maritime Transport Cooperation at the Summit is being seen as a new milestone in boosting connectivity in Bay of Bengal Region. BIMSTEC has also taken initial steps to forge external partnerships with regional and international organisations such as IORA, IFPRI, WB and UNODC apart from expanding its long-standing partnership with ADB.

House # N.W.(I)-06, Road # 53, Gulshan-2, Dhaka-1212, Bangladesh
Telephone: +880-2-222290096, 222287391; Fax: +880-2222287565
E-mail: sg@bimstec.org, communications@bimstec.org, Website: www.bimstec.org
:BimstecInDhaka :BimstecInDhaka :bimstec_secretariat

03. In the context of the ongoing churn in global politics and economy, including upheavals in global trade, the salience of regional organizations for realization of shared security and developmental goals has been recognised. The importance of BIMSTEC as a platform, which acts as a bridge between South Asia and South East Asia, for enhancing regional cooperation to deal with the contemporary security and developmental challenges in Bay of Bengal region has been underscored. I am confident that, with the ongoing reforms and revitalization and the abiding political commitment of its member States to its success, as expressed by BIMSTEC Leaders at the 6th Summit, BIMSTEC is set to emerge as a dynamic and vibrant regional organisation.

04. The need for a broad discourse on the future direction of BIMSTEC, with a view to redefine its priorities to deal with the new and emerging challenges, has been widely felt and I am confident that this Collection of essays "Beyond Boundaries: Cooperation in the BIMSTEC Framework" will serve this purpose very well. I wish it success in realizing this goal.

05. The BIMSTEC Secretariat is committed to work with the member States and other stakeholders in order to make regional cooperation in Bay of Bengal under BIMSTEC a great success.

(Indra Mani Pandey)

Contributors

Dr. Rahul Mishra is Associate Professor at the Centre for Indo-Pacific Studies, School of International Studies, Jawaharlal Nehru University, New Delhi, and Senior Research Fellow at the German-Southeast Asian Center of Excellence for Public Policy and Good Governance, Thammasat University, Thailand. He was previously Director of the Centre for ASEAN Regionalism Universiti Malaya (CARUM) and Coordinator of the European Studies Programme at Universiti Malaya. His past affiliations include the Foreign Service Institute (MEA), East-West Centre, IDSA, ICWA, and RSIS, Singapore. He specializes in Indo-Pacific politico-security affairs, ASEAN-EU regionalism, and comparative regionalism, and is Book Series Editor of the Palgrave Series in Indo-Pacific Studies.

Faisal Ahmed is a Professor of International Business at the FORE School of Management, New Delhi, and a geopolitical expert on China and the Indo-Pacific. His research spans international trade, political economy, and regional integration. He is the author of the book The Belt and Road Initiative: Geopolitical and Geo-economic Aspects (Routledge), which explores the multifaceted implications of China's BRI on global and regional systems. Dr. Ahmed frequently contributes to policy and academic forums, offering strategic insights on India's role in the Indo-Pacific and global trade order. His work bridges geopolitical analysis with international business and development studies.

Vinod Anand is a Senior Fellow and Research Coordinator at the Vivekananda International Foundation (VIF), New Delhi. His research focuses on strategic studies, India's Act East Policy, and China's Belt and Road Initiative. With deep expertise in the Asia-Pacific, his work also explores development and security issues in Southeast Asia. At VIF, he contributes to policy research on regional connectivity, geopolitical competition, and India's strategic engagements with East and Southeast Asian countries. He writes regularly on military and diplomatic dimensions of regional affairs and closely follows evolving dynamics in Indo-Pacific strategic thought and India's foreign policy trajectory in the region.

Sanjay Chadha is a seasoned Indian Trade Service officer who served as Additional Secretary in the Ministry of Commerce and Industry, Government of India. With decades of experience in international trade negotiations, he played a key role in shaping India's foreign trade policy. He was actively involved in India's engagements at the WTO and FTAs and led trade negotiations with the UK and EU. Chadha has contributed to strategic trade frameworks across Asia and the Indo-Pacific, represented India at various multilateral trade forums, and remains a respected voice in trade diplomacy, economic policy, and global economic governance discussions.

Constantino Xavier is a Senior Fellow in Foreign Policy and Security Studies at the Centre for Social and Economic Progress (CSEP), New Delhi. He is also a non-resident fellow at the Brookings Institution, Washington DC, and Visiting Professor at Ashoka University. His expertise includes India's regional role, security, connectivity, and democracy in South Asia and the Indian Ocean. He also researches India-EU and Indo-Pacific relations. Dr. Xavier holds a Ph.D. from Johns Hopkins SAIS, an M.Phil. and M.A. from Jawaharlal Nehru University, and a B.A. from Nova University Lisbon and Sciences Po Paris. He has published extensively on India's foreign policy.

Riya Sinha is an Associate Fellow in the Foreign Policy and Security vertical at CSEP. She was the 2024 Maitri Fellow at the United States Studies Centre, supported by the Centre for Australia India Relations. In 2022, she served as a Visiting Fellow at the Stimson Centre in Washington DC. At CSEP, she coordinates the Sambandh Regional Connectivity Initiative, conducting data-driven research on India's economic and strategic links with neighbouring countries. Her core interests lie in regional economic connectivity in South Asia, with a particular focus on trade, logistics, infrastructure development, and border management in India's neighbourhood.

Shitesh Ranjan has had a distinguished career in shipping and maritime administration. He holds a B.Tech in Naval Architecture & Ocean Engineering from IIT Madras, an LLB from the University of Mumbai, and an LLM with distinction from IMO International Maritime Law Institute (IMLI), Malta. As Deputy Director General of Shipping, he leads maritime policy reforms and advocates for sustainable, globally aligned maritime practices. He has represented India at the IMO, ILO, BIMSTEC dialogues, and various bilateral forums. His expertise covers maritime safety, environmental and international maritime law, reflecting his commitment to strengthening global maritime frameworks and regional maritime collaboration.

Anurag Bisen is a veteran submariner of the Indian Navy with over 35 years of service, including command of a Kilo-class missile submarine. He served eight years in the National Security Council Secretariat, contributing to maritime strategy, boundary law, Indo-Pacific issues, and India's Arctic Policy. A graduate of DSSC Wellington, he holds master's degrees in Defence & Strategic Studies and Telecommunication & Electronic Warfare, an LLB, and a diploma in Russian. UGC-NET qualified and pursuing a PhD from JNU, he is an expert at Lomonosov Moscow State University and Adjunct Faculty at NMF.

Dr. Pandian Krishnan is Director of the Bay of Bengal Programme Inter-Governmental Organisation (BOBP-IGO) in Chennai. With over 20 years of experience, he has worked at ICAR-NAARM, NCSCM, and CIARI, specializing in fisheries science, environmental law, and coastal resource management. He has authored 90+ peer-reviewed papers, 15 books, and multiple policy documents. Dr. Krishnan has received several national awards, including the Fakhruddin Ali Ahmed Award and Rajendra Prasad Puraskar, for his outstanding contributions to fisheries and coastal governance.

Mr. Murugesan SriHari is a BOB Fellow at the Bay of Bengal Programme Inter-Governmental Organisation (BOBP-IGO) and is affiliated with the College of Fisheries, Central Agricultural University, Tripura. His research focuses on fisheries policy and sustainability in the Bay of Bengal region. As a BOB Fellow, he collaborates on thematic research, contributes to policy development, and participates in capacity-building initiatives aimed at strengthening regional fisheries governance.

Mr. Rajdeep Mukherjee is a Policy Analyst at the Bay of Bengal Programme Inter-Governmental Organisation (BOBP-IGO), Chennai. His work focuses on sustainable fisheries management and fostering regional cooperation among Bay of Bengal nations. He plays a key role in policy analysis, advocacy, and the development of strategies aimed at improving the livelihoods of small-scale fishers and strengthening the resilience of coastal communities through informed and inclusive policymaking.

Soumya Tiwari is a doctoral research scholar in international business at the FORE School of Management, New Delhi. She also serves as Chair of the Asia and Oceania Standing Research Committee (SRC) at the International Association for Political Science Students (IAPSS), where she contributes to global academic collaboration and research leadership in political science and international affairs.

Sukrit Joshi is an expert in energy, environment, and sustainable development, with research interests at the intersection of development, climate change, and energy security. He is currently associated with Energy Infratech, a leading engineering consultancy in the energy and environment sector. Previously, he worked at the Research and Information System for Developing Countries (RIS), an autonomous organization under the Ministry of External Affairs, New Delhi. Prior to that, he served as a researcher at The Energy and Resources Institute (TERI), New Delhi. His work spans policy, research, and practical solutions for sustainable energy development.

Dr. J. R. Bhatt is an internationally recognized expert on climate change and biodiversity. He represented India at over 90 international meetings, advocating sustainable development, equity, climate justice, and technology transfer. Twice extended post-superannuation in 2020 by the Appointments Committee of the Cabinet, he currently serves as Member of the Supreme Court's Central Empowered Committee, Distinguished Fellow at VIF and RIS, and Adjunct Professor at NIAS, Bengaluru. He was India's National Focal Point to the IPCC and UNFCCC, co-authored India's first Biodiversity Action Plan, and led key national climate reports. He continues to mentor research on climate and biodiversity.

Dr. Suhas P. Wani, former Director – Asia and Founding Director, IDC at ICRISAT, served as Visiting Professor at the University of Alberta, Edmonton. He was on Unilever UK's SAAB, boards of JSW Foundation, and several academic institutions across India. An international consultant to ADB, FAO, and IFAD, he co-authored six strategy papers for the PMO, including on DFI, DBT, pulses, and digital agriculture. He has published over 600 research papers and received multiple awards from India, China, and Vietnam. Recognized among the 50 Most Impactful Leaders in Water & Water Management, his work focuses on sustainable agriculture.

P. K. Khup Hangzo is an Associate Fellow at the Vivekananda International Foundation (VIF), focusing on climate change and border security, particularly the geopolitics of transboundary rivers. His research explores the link between environmental change and regional security, emphasizing India's strategic vulnerabilities and responses. Prior to VIF, he was a researcher at the S. Rajaratnam School of International Studies (RSIS), Nanyang Technological University, Singapore. At RSIS, he specialized in non-traditional security issues including food and water security, internal armed conflicts, and transnational crime. His work bridges environmental policy and regional geopolitics in South and Southeast Asia.

Sudhir Saxena currently serves as Senior Fellow at the Vivekananda International Foundation (VIF), specializing in National Security, Counter Terrorism, Technologies, and Strategic Programs. He is also an experienced Systems Developer and has served in various arms of the Government of India for over 35 years.

Jiten Kumar Jain is a renowned cybersecurity specialist with expertise in AI-driven global order and cybercrime forensics. He is CEO of Indian Infosec Consortium and Director of Voyager Infosec, advancing cybersecurity solutions and public policy. Jain plays a pivotal role in combating emerging cyber threats and promoting digital resilience in an interconnected world. His work focuses on proactive strategies to protect critical infrastructure and democratic institutions. He regularly contributes to national debates on cybersecurity, shaping policy frameworks and operational responses to evolving digital challenges at both national and global levels.

Saroj Kumar Rath is a distinguished scholar of South Asia's security history. He authored the critically acclaimed *Fragile Frontiers: The Secret History of Mumbai Terror Attacks*, recognized as an "All Time Great Book on Terrorism." Currently, he serves as faculty at the University of Delhi, contributing to academic research on terrorism and regional geopolitics. Rath's work provides deep insights into state and non-state actors, intelligence failures, and the evolving threat landscape in South Asia. His research also informs broader discussions on global security, policy responses, and strategic narratives shaping the 21st-century security order.

Anurag Sharma completed his MPhil in Politics and International Relations (International Security) at Dublin City University in 2018. His thesis was titled "The Islamic State Foreign Fighter Phenomenon and the Jihadi Threat to India." His research interests include terrorism and the Internet, Cybersecurity, CVE, Radicalisation, Counter-terrorism, and Foreign Fighters. Prior to joining VIF, he worked as Research Assistant at the Institute for Conflict Management. He is a Junior Researcher with TSAS (Canada) and an Affiliate Member with AVERT (Australia). He also holds an MSc in Information Security and Computer Crime from the University of Glamorgan, UK.

Dr. Shubhamitra Das is an Associate Professor at the Centre for Indo-Pacific Studies, School of International Studies, JNU, New Delhi. She holds MPhil and PhD degrees, with research expertise in Australia, the South Pacific, and Indo-Pacific regional dynamics. Dr. Das has led international consultancy projects on child labour, public health, and governance in India, supported by global NGOs. She authored a book on Australia's defence policy and published widely on gender, poverty, and foreign policy. Her multidisciplinary approach brings strategic depth to regional cooperation and inclusive development in the Indo-Pacific.

Dr. Cchavi Vasisht is an Associate Fellow at the Chintan Research Foundation. She earned her PhD from the Centre for South Asian Studies, School of International Studies, Jawaharlal Nehru University (JNU), New Delhi, and was awarded the UGC-NET Senior Research Fellowship. She also holds an MPhil and MA in Sociology from JNU. Her research interests include South Asia, Southeast Asia, and Gender issues. She has co-edited the book *Revisiting Myanmar: Present Through Past* with Brig Vinod Anand. Her academic work reflects a multidisciplinary approach to regional studies and socio-political developments across the Asian landscape.

Saudiptendu Ray is a Research Associate at the Vivekananda International Foundation, New Delhi. He holds a Master's in Modern Indian History from the University of Delhi and another in Museology from the National Museum Institute. He graduated in History from Kirori Mal College. With nearly seven years of museum experience, he has worked on the Prime Minister's Museum Project at NMML and documented over a hundred oral histories at the Partition Museum. At the National Museum, he conducted in-depth research on firearms technology. His interests include oral history, Indian military history, and scriptwriting rooted in historical narratives.

PART I

Strategic Outlook and Institutional Trajectory

1

BIMSTEC: Trends and Trajectory

Rahul Mishra

The BIMSTEC (Bay of Bengal Initiative for Multi-Sectoral Technical and Economic Cooperation), earlier known as BISTEC (Bangladesh-India-Sri Lanka-Thailand Economic Cooperation), has evolved substantially over almost three decades, converting itself into a leading sub-regional cooperation mechanism for littoral states around the Bay of Bengal.

BIMSTEC has not only become a pillar of multilateral cooperation but also acted as an institutional bridge between countries in South Asia and their Southeast Asian partners, viz., Myanmar and Thailand.

From its formation as a complementary and alternative regional cooperation mechanism to the South Asian Association for Regional Cooperation (SAARC), today BIMSTEC has emerged as the mainstay of regional cooperation in South Asia.

It is a crucial platform fostering collaboration between its seven member states—Bangladesh, Bhutan, India, Myanmar, Nepal, Sri Lanka and Thailand.

Initially conceptualised as BISTEC in 1997, the name of the grouping was changed to BIMSTEC following the inclusion of Myanmar in 1997 and Nepal and Bhutan in 2004.[1]

This sub-regional grouping, spanning South and Southeast Asia, represents a population of approximately 1.73 billion people and an estimated collective GDP of around USD 5.2 trillion.[2]As it observes its three decades of existence, its role in enhancing regional economic growth, connectivity and security has become more significant, particularly with regard to India's broader geo-political and economic strategies.

Rationale for BIMSTEC

During the pre-colonial era, the Bay of Bengal area was one of the thriving maritime routes, with important Indian, Burmese, Thai and Indonesian ports acting as key nodes of international and regional maritime trade. Under British colonial rule, these ports were exploited for resource extraction. After independence, the Bay of Bengal turned into one of the most underutilised sub-regions in terms of developing maritime trade linkages, collective utilisation and protection of natural resources, besides enhancement of physical and digital connectivity.[3]

Turbulence in India's northeastern states, inward-looking dictatorial rule in Burma and India's tense relations with Pakistan, which until mid-December 1970, had East Pakistan under its control, did not work in favour of these waters. The rise of the Liberation Tigers of Tamil Eelam (LTTE) and the resultant political upheaval in Sri Lanka complicated the situation further.

With Thailand launching its "Look West" policy, complementing India's "Look East" policy in many ways, both countries tried to turn the situation around.[4] The BISTEC, thus was a blend of "Look East" and "Look West" policies of India and Thailand. The proposal to establish BISTEC came from Thailand in 1994, which India supported, but not without expressing apprehensions about its efficacy on the security front.

One of the major reasons why India supported BIST-EC/BIMSTEC was its concern for its landlocked northeastern states. The only outlet for the seven northeastern states was the Bay of Bengal, which could function as its gateway to the world of maritime trade and commerce.

A major advantage of BIMSTEC has been that even though some of the littoral states have been marred by political instability and domestic upheavals, unlike the neighbouring South China Sea, there are no mutually overlapping territorial claims and resultant clashes in the Bay of Bengal. In the South China Sea, China being the biggest littoral state, has been exercising its hegemonic influence, and staking a claim to a large number of islands and Exclusive Economic Zones (EEZ), which is in complete contrast with the Bay of Bengal and India's policy as the biggest littoral state. V. Suryanarayan points out:[5]

> India has settled its maritime boundaries with all of its Southeast Asian neighbours. Agreements were signed with Indonesia in 1974 and 1977, with Thailand in 1978, with Myanmar in 1987, and the trijunction among India, Thailand and Indonesia in 1978. As far as South Asia is concerned,

> the maritime boundaries with Sri Lanka were demarcated by maritime agreements in 1974 and 1976. These agreements were based on the principle of equidistance, though in the case of Sri Lanka and Myanmar, New Delhi made some concessions in the interest of good neighbourly relations.

The absence of any intra-regional territorial disputes between India and its littoral Bay of Bengal neighbours is an advantage that remains to be utilised.

At the time of BIMSTEC's launch, India and Thailand were the only two economically significant nations. However, over the years, Bangladesh has established itself as one of the fastest-growing economies in Asia. Despite the recent political turmoil and ongoing uncertainties about the country's political future, the country has shown its economic potential.

Over the past 28 years, BIMSTEC has crossed several milestones and strengthened cooperation among the Bay of Bengal littoral states. The growing salience of BIMSTEC is a testimony to several key developments in the Bay of Bengal sub-region.

BIMSTEC and Major Power Politics

With China's strategic and economic footprints going deeper into the sub-region, particularly in Myanmar, Nepal, Bangladesh and Sri Lanka, a greater focus on BIMSTEC makes more sense for India. The BIMSTEC Summit was recently held in Bangkok where partner countries agreed to move their joint cooperation to the next level.[6]

India is mindful of the challenges posed by China's Belt and Road Initiative (BRI) and its attempts to deepen its strategic footprint. (Mentioned at beginning of para)

Through its BRI, China has increased its strategic presence in South Asia. China's formidable control of Hambantota (Sri Lanka),[7] Kyaukphyu (Myanmar),[8] and growing presence in Chittagong (Bangladesh),[9] have certainly increased its economic and strategic profile.

India, too, is trying to tap its underutilised potential in the Bay of Bengal sub-region through its SAGAR (Security and Growth for All) and IPOI (Indo Pacific Oceans Initiative),[10] upgraded to MAHASAGAR during Prime Minister Modi's recent Mauritius visit, which saw the signing and launching of a range of bilateral and mini-lateral connectivity initiatives. The growing role of Japan, the US and Australia, makes it evident that the Bay of Bengal sub-region is a theatre of considerable economic and strategic importance, the potential of which still remains underutilised.

However, reviving the Bay of Bengal dynamism is a task easier said than done. For one, this sub-region is one of the biggest sources of humanitarian crises in the Indo-Pacific region, which primarily emanates from the Rohingya crisis and the domestic political upheavals in Myanmar.[11]

The domestic political and economic crisis in Sri Lanka also demands a more proactive role for BIMSTEC, particularly India, which has proposed to act as the "security pillar" for the group.

It is often said that moments of crisis lead to the birth of new transnational initiatives. Just as several crises have led to the greater consolidation of the European Union of ASEAN during and after the Asian Financial crisis. Similarly, the economic crisis in Sri Lanka, the humanitarian crisis in Myanmar and the political upheaval in Bangladesh present an opportunity for Bay of Bengal littorals to learn their lessons and manage the crises. For India and its Indo-Pacific partners—the US, Australia and Japan, there cannot be a better moment than this to strengthen BIMSTEC and realise the Indo-Pacific vision of a free, open and rules-based order.

Economic Integration and Trade Cooperation

Trade and economic cooperation are central to BIMSTEC's objectives. The Bay of Bengal region is home to some of the world's fastest-growing economies, notably Bangladesh and India, which have witnessed robust economic expansion in recent years. However, intra-BIMSTEC trade remains relatively low, accounting for only seven percent of the member states' total trade volume. Addressing this requires greater harmonisation of trade policies, reduction of tariff and non-tariff barriers and the establishment of efficient supply chains.

India has been actively pursuing trade agreements with several global partners, including the UAE, Australia, the UK and the European Union. However, its decision to opt out of the Regional Comprehensive Economic Partnership (RCEP) in 2020, has necessitated the need for alternative regional trade arrangements. In this context, BIMSTEC provides India with a viable framework to enhance trade ties with its eastern neighbours. The ongoing negotiations on the BIMSTEC FTA hold promise for bolstering intra-regional trade and investment flows.

Connectivity as a Cornerstone of BIMSTEC

Connectivity is a fundamental pillar of India's engagement with BIMSTEC. Enhancing transport and digital connectivity between South and Southeast Asia is crucial for regional economic integration. India has undertaken several initiatives to improve infrastructure linkages, including:

- BBIN Motor Vehicles Agreement (MVA): This agreement between Bangladesh, Bhutan, India and Nepal facilitates the seamless movement of passenger and cargo vehicles across borders, improving regional trade and mobility.
- India-Myanmar-Thailand Trilateral Highway: This ambitious project aims to establish a direct road connection between India and Southeast Asia, boosting trade and people-to-people ties.
- SAGAR (Security and Growth for All in the Region): India's maritime security initiative prioritises the Bay of Bengal as a key strategic and economic hub.
- Expansion of cross-border railway and air connectivity: India is investing in rail links with Bangladesh and Nepal, while exploring direct flights between Indian cities and major Southeast Asian destinations.

These initiatives align with BIMSTEC's Master Plan for Transport Connectivity, which seeks to enhance multimodal transport networks and integrate regional markets.

Security Cooperation: Counterterrorism and Transnational Crime

India has consistently advocated for stronger security cooperation within BIMSTEC. The organisation's focus on counterterrorism, transnational crime and maritime security has gained prominence in light of growing security threats in the region. India serves as the lead country in BIMSTEC's Counterterrorism and Transnational Crime (CTTC) sector, underscoring its commitment towards combating terrorism and organised crime.

The Bay of Bengal region faces significant security challenges, including:

- Cross-border terrorism: India has long sought regional cooperation to counter state-sponsored terrorism and prevent extremist networks from exploiting porous borders.
- Human trafficking and drug smuggling: Myanmar's political instability has exacerbated illicit trafficking routes, necessitating collective regional efforts to address these issues.

- Maritime piracy and illegal fishing: Enhancing maritime domain awareness and naval collaboration among BIMSTEC states is critical to safeguarding regional waters.

India has called for enhanced intelligence-sharing mechanisms and joint counter-terrorism exercises to bolster regional security cooperation. Additionally, the adoption of the BIMSTEC Convention on Mutual Legal Assistance in Criminal Matters marks a step forward in strengthening legal frameworks to combat transnational crime.

Humanitarian and Disaster Relief (HADR) Cooperation

The Bay of Bengal is highly vulnerable to natural disasters, including cyclones, tsunamis and rising sea levels due to climate change. BIMSTEC's disaster management framework emphasises regional cooperation in disaster preparedness, response, and mitigation.

India has played a proactive role in disaster relief operations, extending assistance to BIMSTEC nations in times of crisis. The Indian Navy and Air Force have been instrumental in delivering humanitarian aid during natural calamities, including Cyclone Amphan in Bangladesh (2020) and the Rohingya refugee crisis in Myanmar (2017). BIMSTEC's Disaster Management and Climate Change Working Group aims to enhance collaborative efforts in building climate resilience across member states.

The Road Ahead

With the sixth Summit held in Bangkok, Thailand, in April 2025, BIMSTEC has also launched its BIMSTEC Bangkok Vision 2030 and PRO BIMSTEC 2030, which stands for Prosperous, Resilient, and Open BIMSTEC. These are positive developments, which indicate the organisation's promising future. However, despite its potential, BIMSTEC faces several challenges that hinder its effectiveness:

1. Institutional Weaknesses: The organisation lacks a robust institutional framework, limiting its decision-making capabilities and implementation of agreements.
2. Political and Economic Divergences: Member states have varying economic priorities and geopolitical alignments, which often slow down consensus-building processes.

3. Myanmar Crisis: The ongoing political instability in Myanmar following the military coup of 2021 poses a significant challenge to regional stability and cooperation.
4. Funding Constraints: BIMSTEC relies heavily on contributions from member states, necessitating greater financial commitments to sustain its initiatives.

To address these challenges, BIMSTEC must undertake structural reforms to enhance its institutional efficacy. Strengthening the Secretariat, expediting the implementation of agreements, and fostering deeper economic integration will be key to maximising the organisation's potential.

BIMSTEC has emerged as a critical regional platform that aligns with India's strategic vision of a connected, secure and prosperous Bay of Bengal region. India's leadership in trade, connectivity, security and disaster management underscores its commitment to regional cooperation. However, realising BIMSTEC's full potential requires sustained political will, enhanced institutional mechanisms and deeper economic integration among member states.

As India continues to champion BIMSTEC's growth, its ability to navigate regional complexities and foster an inclusive, development-driven agenda will determine the organisation's success in the coming decades. With a dynamic economic landscape and evolving geopolitical shifts, BIMSTEC has the opportunity to play a transformative role in shaping the future of South and Southeast Asian cooperation.

NOTES

1 According to Ambassador Ranjit Gupta, the initial plan mooted by Thailand, had just India, Thailand, and Sri Lanka as its members, giving it the acronym ISTEC. However, after much deliberation, Bangladesh was included, and it became BISTEC.

2 Bhuyan, Aroonim (2025), "Why BIMSTEC Matters: India's Strategic Bet on Regional Cooperation", *ETV Bharat,* https://www.etvbharat.com/en/!international/india-strategic-bet-on-regional-cooperation-bimstec-enn25033104726#

3 Mishra, Rahul & Hashmi, Sana (2017), "Can India take the lead on BIMSTEC?" *East Asia Forum,* https://eastasiaforum.org/2017/09/23/can-india-take-the-lead-on-bimstec/#:~:text=Can%20India%20take%20the%20lead,East%20Asia%20Forum September 23.

4 Mishra, Rahul (2012), "Growing ties with Thailand Gains from India's Look East policy", *The Tribune,* April 7, 2012, https://www.tribuneindia.com/2012/20120407/edit.htm#4

5 Suryanarayan, V. (2000), "Prospects for a Bay of Bengal Community", *Seminar LOOKING EAST a symposium on the need to refocus our foreign policy,* 487, MARCH 2000.

6 "BIMSTEC Leaders Sign and Adopt the BIMSTEC Charter during the Fifth Summit." *BIMSTEC,* March 30, 2022. https://bimstec.org/?event=bimstec-leaders-sign-and-adopt-

the-bimstec-charter-during-the-fifth-summit-on-30-march-2022.

7 Wong, Catherine. "China Can Extend Port Lease to 198 Years, Sri Lankan Minister Says." South China Morning Post, February 25, 2021. https://www.scmp.com/news/china/diplomacy/article/3122975/mistake-china-can-extend-hambantota-port-lease-198-years-sri.

8 "Myanmar Junta Pushing Ahead with China-Backed Kyaukphyu Sez and Port." *The Irrawaddy*, August 6, 2021. https://www.irrawaddy.com/news/burma/myanmar-junta-pushing-ahead-with-china-backed-kyaukphyu-sez-and-port.html.

9 Chowdhury, Kamran Reza. "China Can Use Bangladesh's Largest Seaports, PM Hasina Says." *Benar News*, November 13, 2019. https://www.benarnews.org/english/news/bengali/bangladesh-china-11132019171915.html.

10 Mishra, Rahul. "Indo-Pacific Oceans' Initiative: Providing Institutional Framework to the Indo-Pacific Region." *Asia-Europe Institute*, August 20, 2021. https://aei.um.edu.my/img/files/AIC commentary No 20 August 2021 final.pdf.

11 "Rohingya Crisis." UNICEF, n.d. https://www.unicef.org/emergencies/rohingya-crisis.

2

Region Building in BIMSTEC: Understanding the Geo-economics of Trade and Connectivity

Faisal Ahmed and Vinod Anand

The Bay of Bengal Initiative for Multi-Sectoral Technical and Economic Cooperation (BIMSTEC) is a regional grouping. Its members envision to commit in the littorals and the surmounted areas of the Bay of Bengal region constituting a contiguous regional unity.[1] It is imperative to understand that BIMSTEC's institutional evolvement has been gradual. It was during the Third BIMSTEC Summit in 2014, that its secretariat was established in Dhaka, Bangladesh. The key area of cooperation initially focussed on six sectors *viz.* trade, technology, energy, transport, tourism and fisheries, and then expanded to other sectors thereafter.[2] The Fourth BIMSTEC Summit was held in Kathmandu, Nepal, on August 30-31, 2018. It focussed on the need to review, restructure and rationalise existing areas of BIMSTEC cooperation and streamline operational modalities, besides activating mechanisms to bring out effective outcomes.[3]

Subsequently, based on recommendations set forth at the Fifth BIMSTEC Summit in Colombo, Sri Lanka, on March 30, 2022, the grouping agreed to include more sectors and sub-sectors for BIMSTEC cooperation. Besides trade, investment, and development, issues like environment and climate change; security; agriculture and food security; people-to-people contacts, and science and technology were flagged for discussion and cooperation. Further, the inclusion of the blue economy as a sub-sector under the broader domain of environment and climate change was approved for adoption in the 19th BIMSTEC Ministerial Meeting held virtually on March 9, 2023, ahead of the Sixth BIMSTEC Summit.[4]

It has been accepted and acknowledged within the BIMSTEC that in order to monitor and operate effectively, organisational reforms are needed.[5] The Sixth BIMSTEC Summit, which was held in Bangkok, Thailand, on April 4, 2025, focussed on the welfare of the region through shared growth.[5] During the summit, Prime Minister Narendra Modi presented a comprehensive 21-point agenda aimed fostering growth and collaboration across different sectors.[6] In the business sector, the Prime Minister proposed the establishment of a BIMSTEC Chamber of Commerce, and for organising an annual BIMSTEC business summit. He also proposed a feasibility study to explore local currency trade. The Digital Public Infrastructure (DPI), Unified Payment Interface (UPI), disaster management and mitigation, and other areas of cooperation, also came up for discussion.[7] Prime Minister Modi suggested the setting up of "BODHI"-BIMSTEC for the organised development of human resource infrastructure, besides calling for other technical and capacity-building measures.[8]

BIMSTEC, in fact, faces challenges of poor road and rail connectivity, and heavy customs and clearance procedures that hamper regional trade.[9] It was agreed that physical infrastructure is essential to facilitate smooth connectivity and improved trade practices in the region. Since trade and connectivity are among the priority areas of cooperation and given that, the region is one of the least integrated in the world, there is a lot of scope for region building. This article, therefore, discusses the region-building efforts within BIMSTEC in terms of geo-economic potential for trade and connectivity.

Region building through geo-economics of trade

The Bay of Bengal region has immense geo-economic potential. While on one hand, countries are pressing forward for bilateral trade arrangements, on the other, the real onus actually falls on the political will of the countries to engage in deeper cooperation. Of course, the objectives of this region align clearly with India's policies of "Neighbourhood First" and "Act East". This has been instrumental in enhancing physical connectivity by building new roads and upgrading existing road, rail and maritime linkages to boost cross-border trade and public diplomacy initiatives.[11] In order to ensure connectivity, the North-East states act as a prime source for land connect between both regions and can also serve as a prominent economic corridor. Reinvigorating and renewing these connect can leverage the much-needed socio-economic transformation within the BIMSTEC.

BIMSTEC's intra-regional trade has been increasing steadily since 2000. In recent years, it has shown an upward trend, despite the global downturn experienced during the Covid-19 pandemic. In this way, BIMSTEC has not only achieved better performance in intra-regional trade than that of the South Asian Association for Regional Cooperation (SAARC) but has also signalled better performance overall.[10] The BIMSTEC Vision 2030 envisages a roadmap for early completion of the BIMSTEC Free Trade Agreement (FTA) negotiations. There are six working groups negotiating constituent agreements for trade in goods, trade in services, investments, trade facilitation and disputes settlement.[11] A possible FTA can facilitate the integration of Micro, Small, and Medium Enterprises (MSMEs) into regional and global value chains, enhancing consumer choice.[12] A study on value chains in the BIMSTEC region has revealed that from 1995 to 2011, the engagement of BIMSTEC member nations in global value chains has risen consistently. For instance, while India's participation has predominantly been global, Thailand's involvement has been more regional. Thailand's backward linkage participation facilitated the production of relatively high value-added products and services. In contrast, India's focus was on relatively low value-added products and services.[13]

Region-building through Connectivity

Transportation and connectivity is an integral part of region building among the BIMSTEC member countries. However, there are several key challenges. These include: (a) Enhancing arterial road connections that facilitate substantial intra-BIMSTEC trade; (b) Upgrading border connections, particularly access to ports and (c) Synchronising Road initiatives to improve connectivity among member nations.[14] The requirement of trans-shipment of cargo at international borders incurs elevated transaction costs, particularly for importing countries. The establishment of well-coordinated transportation systems is, therefore, essential for enhancing transport efficiency and minimising trade costs. Consistent and sufficient funding is essential for the timely completion of these initiatives.[15]

The India-Myanmar-Thailand Trilateral Highway (IMT) project is arguably the most crucial road connectivity initiative in the BIMSTEC region, with Myanmar's strategic position being essential to it. Myanmar is the only nation apart from India whose involvement is essential for establishing a land connection between all BIMSTEC members. Upon completion, the trilateral framework will link Cambodia, Laos and Vietnam. The BIMSTEC transport infrastructure report designates six road initiatives in Myanmar as priority projects, five of which, are essential elements of the IMT. These include three projects linking Myanmar to Thailand, and two connecting Myanmar to India.[16]

The Railway network enhances economic development by enabling the efficient transportation of goods and people. In the BIMSTEC region, trains present a dependable and economical alternative for freight and passenger transit, as compared to road transportation.[17] The Master Plan emphasizes the necessity for enhancing railway connectivity between the member states, including targeting major ports, dry ports and land borders. This strategic initiative seeks to enhance intra-regional trade, while promoting economic and social advancement in inland areas.[18] Recognising the varied needs within the BIMSTEC community, the Plan adopts a customised strategy to meet distinct connectivity demands of landlocked member nations, facilitating the investigation of feasible modal alternatives. According to the Plan, port connectivity is far more complex than rail and road connectivity due to changes in physical infrastructure, layouts, cargo types, services offered and container handling efficiency among ports. It also considers the execution of regional coastal shipping.

Fifteen principal ports are located along the coastline arc of the Bay. India's eastern seaboard is serviced by six principal ports, four of which are particularly noteworthy. These are: (a) The Kolkata Port, which facilitates Indian trade and also provides transit services to neighbouring countries (Bangladesh, Bhutan and Nepal); (b) The Paradip Port in Odisha that has the highest traffic volume on the east coast; (c) The Visakhapatnam Port, seen as a reliable and potential trans-shipment hub and (d) The Chennai Port, which services a diverse range of cargo, particularly automobiles.

Besides Chittagong in Bangladesh, one more port, i.e. Mongla is of immense geo-economic significance. It is strategically located and important for Bangladesh, India and China. China is eyeing strategic control of the Mongla Port, while India too seeks operational control over it. In fact, Mongla will also help India secure trade routes and increase intra-regional trade. It also provides opportunities for developing resilient supply chains and improved trade competitiveness in the Bay of Bengal region.[19] India can control the trans-shipments by accessing both Chittagong and Mongla ports and would boost regional connectivity under India's "Act East Policy".

In Lieu of a Conclusion

BIMSTEC member states must use regional synergies and strive to utilise available resources optimally. This would contribute to the establishment of a more robust and dynamic congregation. To realise India's objective of strengthening trade and connectivity within the congregation, an FTA would be quite helpful. The development of coastal shipping and an integrated electrical grid along with the Master Plan for Transport Connectivity can also help in region building. To actualise its trade and economic potential, the revitalised coalition requires India to assume a leadership position in alleviating concerns regarding power imbalances among the smaller members and to enhance cross-border connectivity and investment flows by reducing barriers to the movement of people and goods.

BIMSTEC should prioritise future initiatives in sectors such as the blue economy, digital economy and cooperation within the MSMEs of the member countries. BIMSTEC must focus on overcoming the impeding challenges related to connectivity and trade facilitation. Region building requires a robust institutional framework that can upgrade domestic productive capacity among the member countries.

NOTES

1 History of BIMSTEC, Website of BIMSTEC
2 Ibid.
3 Sectors of Cooperation, BIMSTEC Website; https://bimstec.org/pages/sectors-of-cooperation
4 Bhatia. Rajiv, "Incorporating the Blue Economy into BIMSTEC Agenda." *India Foundation.* May 2, 2022. https://indiafoundation.in/articles-and-commentaries/incorporating-the-blue-economy-into-bimstec-agenda/
5 "Prime Minister Participates in the 6th BIMSTEC Summit, Thailand." Ministry of External Affairs, Government of India. April 4, 2025. https://www.mea.gov.in/press-releases.htm?dtl/39366/Prime_Minister_participates_in_the_6th_BIMSTEC_Summit_Thailand_April_ 04 _2025
6 "PM Modi Unveils 21-point action plan at 6th BIMSTEC Summit." *ET Government.* April 5, 2025. https://government.economictimes.indiatimes.com/news/policy/pm-modi-unveils-21-point-action-plan-at-6th-bimstec-summit/120000063
7 "List of Initiatives, Prime Minister's Participation in the 6th BIMSTEC Summit." Ministry of External Affairs, Government of India, April 4, 2025. https://www.mea.gov.in/bilateral-documents.htm?dtl/39367/List_of_Initiatives__Prime_Ministers_participation_ in _ the_6th_BIMSTEC_SUMMIT_April_04_2025
8 Ibid.
9 Basu, Pratnashree and Nilanjan Ghosh."Breathing New Life into BIMSTEC: Challenges and Imperatives." *Observer Research Foundation.* April 27, 2020.

10 "BIMSTEC- The Road Ahead." *BIMSTEC.* 2016. https://bimstec.org/images/publication_pdf_file/1696658122_BIMSTEC%20Report%20(3)%20(2).pdf

11 Pandey, Indra Mani. "BIMSTEC FTA Part of 'Bangkok Vision 2030." *BIMSTEC.* April 3, 2025. https://theprint.in/diplomacy/bimstec-fta-part-of-bangkok-vision-2030-roadmap-to-be-agreed-upon-at-summit-secretary-general-pandey/2576196/

12 Ghosh, Nilanjan."Regional Comprehensive Economic Partnership: Issues and Concerns for India." Prabir De and Ajitava Raychaudhury (eds), *25 Years of the WTO and India: A Retrospective.* Sage Publications, New Delhi, 2020.

13 Bari. Estiaque, "Value Chains in BIMSTEC Region: Current Status, Possibilities and Challenges." *Policy Brief No. 10. Centre for Policy Dialogue.* 2018.

14 Bose, Sohini, Banerjee, Sriparna and Anasua Basu. "The BIMSTEC Master Plan for Transport Connectivity: A Stocktaking." *Observer Research Foundation.* June 3, 2024. https://www.orfonline.org/research/the-bimstec-master-plan-for-transport-connectivity-a-stocktaking

15 Ibid.

16 "BIMSTEC Master Plan for Transport Connectivity. April 2022

17 Bose, Sohini, Banerjee, Sriparna and Anasua Basu. "The BIMSTEC Master Plan for Transport Connectivity: A Stocktaking." *Observer Research Foundation.* June 3, 2024. https://www.orfonline.org/research/the-bimstec-master-plan-for-transport-connectivity-a-stocktaking

18 Ibid.

19 "Beyond Chabahar: India's Port Power Play in Bangladesh to Boost Regional Trade, Counter China." The Economic Times, April 12, 2025. https://economictimes.indiatimes.com/small-biz/trade/exports/insights/beyond-chabahar-indias-port-power-play-in-bangladesh-to-boost-regional-trade-counter-china/articleshow/111825513.cms?from=mdr.

PART II

Economic Integration and Connectivity

3

Trade and Investment Cooperation in BIMSTEC: Unlocking Regional Potential

Sanjay Chadha

The Bay of Bengal Initiative for Multi-Sectoral Technical and Economic Cooperation (BIMSTEC) stands at a critical juncture.

Bridging South and Southeast Asia, this bloc of seven nations—Bangladesh, Bhutan, India, Myanmar, Nepal, Sri Lanka, and Thailand—represents a market of 1.8 billion people and a combined GDP surpassing USD 4.5 trillion.

Yet, despite its strategic location and economic heft, BIMSTEC is still seen as an underperforming grouping far from achieving its promised goal of regional integration.

Facts bear this out. Intra-regional trade languishes below seven percent. Geo-political tensions, infrastructure gaps and institutional inertia continue to stifle its progress.

As global supply chains pivot toward resilience and regionalism gains momentum, BIMSTEC's revival is a necessity, not just to be seen as an opportunity.

This article analyses the bloc's untapped potential, diagnoses its persistent challenges and proposes actionable strategies to transform it into a 21st-century economic powerhouse.

The Promise of BIMSTEC: A Regional Powerhouse in the Making

BIMSTEC's diversity is its defining strength. The bloc spans advanced economies like Thailand and India, resource-rich Myanmar, agile manufacturing hubs like Bangladesh and hydropower giants Nepal and Bhutan. This complementarity positions BIMSTEC to build a multi-tiered supply chain network, rivalling ASEAN's USD 3.3 trillion GDP.

Digital Transformation

1. Southeast Asia's digital economy is projected to reach USD 330 billion by 2025. BIMSTEC can replicate this growth by harmonising e-commerce regulations, cross-border data flows and fintech standards.
2. India's Unified Payments Interface (UPI) and Thailand's PromptPay can serve as blueprints for a regional digital payments platform.
3. Encouraging the adoption of Artificial Intelligence-driven logistics solutions can reduce cross-border transaction costs and improve trade efficiencies.
4. Establishing a BIMSTEC-wide digital marketplace could facilitate greater B2B and B2C trade within the region.

Green Energy Transition

1. Bhutan and Nepal possess over 100 GW of untapped hydropower potential—enough to meet 40 percent of India's peak power demand. A regional energy grid could accelerate decarbonisation while earning Bhutan and Nepal USD 5 billion annually in export revenues.
2. India and Thailand's investments in solar energy and smart grids could complement this effort, creating a more resilient and sustainable energy ecosystem.
3. Implementing regulatory frameworks for cross-border electricity trade would ensure a stable and profitable green energy transition.

Supply Chain Diversification

Post-pandemic, global firms are adopting a "China+1" strategy. A unified BIMSTEC market, with India's manufacturing scale and Thailand's logistics prowess, could attract USD 150 billion in FDI by 2030.

1. Establishing regional trade hubs with seamless customs processing can facilitate supply chain efficiency.
2. BIMSTEC could also become a leader in high-tech manufacturing by creating incentives for electronics and semiconductor production.
3. Strengthening cold-chain logistics could boost agricultural exports and food security.

Textiles and Pharmaceuticals

1. India and Bangladesh both have a USD 45 billion garment industry which can be synergised to dominate global markets, rather than competing with each other for glob al space.
2. Standardising labour laws and sustainability practices can enhance the bloc's competitiveness in international markets.
3. Creating a regional pharmaceutical supply chain can ensure medical security and reduce dependency on external producers.
4. Encouraging joint research and development initiatives can drive innovation in drug manufacturing.

Diagnosing BIMSTEC's Roadblocks

Political Inertia and Institutional Fragility

BIMSTEC lacks ASEAN's binding commitments, or SAARC's formal dispute mechanisms. Despite adopting a Charter in 2022 to formalise decision-making, progress remains glacial. Member states prioritise bilateral ties over bloc-wide initiatives:

- India focuses on ASEAN and the Indo-Pacific Economic Framework (IPEF).
- Thailand leans on the China's Belt and Road Initiative (BRI).
- Sri Lanka and Nepal grapple with debt crises, sidelining regional agendas.
- Bangladesh is grappling with political instability.

The absence of a permanent secretariat until 2021 and underfunded sectoral working groups reflect institutional apathy.

Trade Barriers and Regulatory Fragmentation

Non-tariff barriers (NTBs) inflate trade costs by 15–20 percent:

- India's Sanitary and Phytosanitary (SPS) standards are seen as barriers to Nepalese cardamom and ginger.
- Myanmar's import licensing deters Thai electronic firms.
- Sri Lanka's 30 percent customs processing time exceeds the ASEAN average.

The BIMSTEC Free Trade Agreement (FTA), proposed in 2004 remains in draft form despite revived talks in 2023. By contrast, ASEAN concluded its FTA in just seven years.

Infrastructure Deficits and Connectivity Gaps

Only 10 percent of regional trade uses BIMSTEC road networks due to:

- **Unratified Agreements**: The BBIN Motor Vehicle Agreement (2015) awaits Bhutan's ratification.
- **Project Delays**: Civil unrest has stalled the Kaladan Multi-Modal Project linking India to Myanmar.
- **Port Bottlenecks**: Sri Lanka's Colombo Port, a regional transshipment hub, faces a liquidity crisis post-default.

Geopolitical Tensions and Trust Deficits

- **China's Shadow**: Myanmar and Thailand host BRI projects, while India has countered it with the SAGAR Doctrine.
- **Internal Conflicts**: Myanmar's junta and Nepal's political instability have eroded investor confidence.
- **Resource Nationalism**: Nepal continues to resist foreign ownership of its hydropower projects.

Revitalising BIMSTEC: Five Point Action Plan

Accelerate BIMSTEC FTA with Sector-Specific Pacts

Finalise the FTA by 2025 through phased "early harvest" agreements:

- **Textiles**: Duty-free access for garments and fabrics, coupled with institutional support
- **Pharmaceuticals**: Mutual recognition of drug approvals (e.g., India's generics for Myanmar's healthcare needs).
- **Digital Services**: Streamline data laws to enable cross-border IT services (e.g., Sri Lankan fintech in Thailand).

  Case Study: The India-Sri Lanka FTA (2000) boosted bilateral trade from USD 658 million to USD 5.4 billion. A BIMSTEC-wide pact could replicate this at scale.

Build War Chests for Connectivity

- **Land Corridors**: Fast track Bangladesh, Bhutan, India, and Nepal (BBIN) Corridor using Japan's USD 1.5 billion ASEAN-Japan Connectivity Fund.
- **Maritime Modernisation**: Develop and Convert Thailand's Ranong Port and India's Vizag-Chennai Corridor into regional transshipment hubs.

- **Digital Highways**: Launch a BIMSTEC digital payments platform, integrating India's UPI and Thailand's PromptPay.
  Cost-Benefit: A 2023 Asian Development Bank study estimated that for every dollar invested in BIMSTEC connectivity yields three dollars in trade gains.

Forge BIMSTEC Investment Pact

- **Unified FDI Policy**: Offer tax holidays for Greenfield projects in renewables, logistics, and agri-processing.
- **Dispute Resolution Mechanism**: Establish a regional tribunal to address investor grievances.
- **Sovereign Wealth Fund**: Pool 0.5 percent of member states' FOREX reserves (USD12 billion) for infrastructure.
  Precedent: ASEAN's USD 1.3 billion Infrastructure Fund has financed 80+ projects since 2011.

Engage Private Sector Strategically

- **BIMSTEC Business Council**: Assign industry leaders (e.g., L&T/Tata Group, Thai Union, BRAC) to advice on policy.
- **Sector-Specific Corridors**:
  - **Bay of Bengal Pharma Corridor**: Integrate Indian Application Programming Interfaces (APIs), Bangladeshi formulations, and Myanmar's distribution networks.
  - **Renewable Energy Grid**: Link Bhutan-Nepal hydropower with India's national grid and Thailand's solar farms.

  Success Story: The Bangladesh-Myanmar-India gas pipeline, backed by Japanese firms, reduced regional LNG costs by 18 percent.

Mitigate Geopolitical Risks

- **Myanmar Engagement**: Nominate an envoy to ensure humanitarian aid and trade remain delinked from politics.
- **Climate Resilience**: Establish a BIMSTEC Disaster Response Fund, modelled on ASEAN's USD one million standby fund.

Recent Strides Demonstrate BIMSTEC's Latent Potential

Energy Integration

India-Nepal cross-border transmission lines now deliver 1,200 MW daily, with plans to triple capacity by 2026. Bhutan's hydropower exports to India hit USD 500 million in 2023.

Trade Facilitation

The BIMSTEC Single Window Initiative, piloted in Chennai and Colombo, slashed cargo clearance from seven days to 48 hours.

Crisis Response

The 2023 BIMSTEC Disaster Management Exercise improved cyclone preparedness, saving 5,000 lives during Cyclone Mocha.

Digital Leap

Thailand and India's UPI-PromptPay linkage (2023) enabled instant cross-border remittances, reducing fees from seven to one percent.

Conclusion: From Vision to Reality

BIMSTEC's moment is now. With global trade fragmenting and climate urgency rising, the bloc must move from rhetoric to action. India and Thailand, as the largest economies, must lead by ratifying pending agreements and funding joint infrastructure. A "BIMSTEC 2.0" strategy—prioritising FTA implementation, digital integration, and private-sector dynamism—could elevate intra-regional trade to 15 percent by 2030.

Call to Action: The next BIMSTEC Summit must deliver:

- A ratified FTA roadmap.
- A USD five billion Connectivity Fund.
- A Regional Investment Promotion Agency.

The Bay of Bengal need not remain a "zone of unfulfilled potential." With political will and pragmatic cooperation, BIMSTEC can emerge as the Indo-Pacific's next economic powerhouse.

4

Building Secure and Sustainable Connectivity for BIMSTEC

Constantino Xavier and Riya Sinha

Building on some of our earlier research on the potential, as well as continued obstacles to regional integration in the Bay of Bengal, this article unpacks "connectivity" from two different dimensions. We offer different policy recommendations for BIMSTEC and its member-states to foster more secure and sustainable forms of connectivity.

First, we identify the "hard" connectivity dimension of transportation infrastructure across the Bay of Bengal region. This type of connectivity, whether land or maritime, hinges on a favourable security environment. At the same time, better road, rail and shipping links between BIMSTEC member states may also help spur development, economic integration and reduce regional tensions.

Second, we also forward with suggestions for the "soft" connectivity dimension, i.e., of people-to-people exchanges in the region. BIMSTEC remains a largely state-driven initiative with political, top-level and bureaucratic channels. To sustain official initiatives, the organisation will also have to invest more in Track II engagements between different civil society stakeholders across academia, think tanks and other non-governmental organisations.

"Hard" Connectivity: Secure Transportation Infrastructure

Despite historical linkages, the Bay of Bengal region today faces significant gaps in transportation infrastructure, limiting economic integration. Addressing these deficits through robust hard connectivity initiatives like roads, railways, ports and energy corridors is critical to realising BIMSTEC's potential.

Since its inception in 1997, BIMSTEC has identified connectivity as a core priority. Initially termed "Transport and Communication," this focus was renamed "Connectivity" at the Fifth BIMSTEC Summit in 2022 to encompass a broader vision.[1] During this summit, India's Prime Minister, Narendra Modi, also emphasised on the early implementation of the 2018 BIMSTEC Master Plan for Transport Connectivity (BMPTC) and urged acceleration on other connectivity initiatives:

> "...we also have to move forward on the already ongoing initiatives in the field of connectivity. To set up a 'Coastal Shipping Eco-system' in Bay of Bengal, a legal framework should be developed soon. The time has come to take electricity grid interconnectivity beyond the discussions and take it to the implementation stage. Similarly, establishing legal framework for increasing road connectivity is also important."[2]

Several connectivity projects have been revived in the last decade, particularly with Indian investments. India has operationalised six out of seven historical railway links with Bangladesh, launched the first passenger railway to Nepal and constructed multiple land ports to enhance trade with Nepal, Bhutan and Bangladesh. Additionally, India has restarted a ferry service with Sri Lanka and facilitated sub-regional energy cooperation with Nepal and Bangladesh.[3]

However, connectivity between South Asia and Southeast Asia remains constrained. The India-Myanmar-Thailand Trilateral Highway, a flagship project meant to link the two sub-regions, has faced delays.[4] Similarly, the Bangladesh-Bhutan-India-Nepal Motor Vehicles Agreement (BBIN-MVA), even without Bhutan, is yet to be operationalised.[5] While coastal shipping agreements exist between India and Bangladesh, inefficiencies in port operations and regulatory mismatches limit their potential. Cross-border freight movement by rail remains underutilised, accounting for less than four percent of total trade, largely due to inconsistent standard operating procedures and customs inefficiencies.[6]

While connectivity is not a panacea for all regional challenges, it is a foundational pillar for deeper economic and security cooperation. To improve hard connectivity, BIMSTEC nations need to complement infrastructure creation with policy harmonisation and institutional strengthening. This section outlines four key enablers to enhance infrastructure-led connectivity in the region. Building hard connectivity requires a comprehensive, coordinated approach. By implementing these strategies, BIMSTEC can transform itself into a truly integrated economic bloc, enhancing trade, investment and regional stability.

Adopt a Transport Corridor Development Approach: A corridor-based strategy ensures infrastructure investments are integrated rather than fragmented. Transport corridors serve dual functions: they enhance physical connectivity and streamline border regulations. Scholars have proposed the concept of "Highly Facilitated Trade Corridors" in the Bay of Bengal region to close connectivity gaps and create efficient multimodal transport networks.[7] Currently, road and shipping linkages receive disproportionate attention, often at the expense of a comprehensive multimodal strategy. For instance, in the Building Materials and Technology Promotion Council (BMPTC), 46 percent of projects are focused on road development, 11 percent on ports and 11 percent on railway development. For railway development, the emphasis is on access to ports.[8] BIMSTEC must prioritise the development of strategic transport corridors linking economic hubs. A Nepal-India-Bangladesh-Myanmar Multimodal Connectivity Corridor could be one such initiative, integrating road, rail and air links. Feasibility studies should assess traffic demand and investment requirements for these corridors, while public-private partnerships (PPPs) can play a crucial role in financing and execution.

Address the softer challenges and invest in trade facilitation: Hard infrastructure alone cannot resolve connectivity bottlenecks. Non-physical barriers, such as regulatory misalignment, customs inefficiencies and logistical mismatches, must be addressed. According to a World Bank study, border procedures, harmonising vehicle standards and adopting digital customs clearance mechanisms can significantly reduce trade friction. Except for India, no other country in the region has met its World Trade Organization Trade Facilitation Agreement (TFA) commitments, hovering between 40 to 60 percent between countries in the region.[9] For instance, standardising railway gauges and implementing electronic cargo tracking across BIMSTEC countries could improve freight efficiency. Additionally, ensuring consistent application of trade facilitation agreements will lower transaction costs and expedite goods movement. Reducing bureaucratic hurdles and ensuring transparency in policy implementation will boost investor confidence and expedite project execution. BIMSTEC nations should also develop integrated logistics hubs near major border crossings to optimise cross-border trade. Towards this, it will be important to finalise the draft Agreement on Trade Facilitation for the BIMSTEC Free Trade Area.[10] These are low-hanging fruits for cross-border connectivity in the region.

India must leverage its development cooperation for infrastructure development: New Delhi's strategic advantage in its immediate neighbourhood lies in its capacity to undertake and execute infrastructure projects through robust development cooperation mechanisms, backed by financial tools such as grants and Lines of Credit (LoCs).[11] These financial mechanisms have been instrumental in funding connectivity projects in South Asia and beyond. However, India's development assistance should not be limited to financial support alone. A more comprehensive approach could include knowledge transfer, technical assistance and capacity-building initiatives. This could involve sharing best practices in railway management, project execution and operational efficiency. Additionally, as cross-border railway development remains challenging, India should facilitate training programs for railway staff, engineers and drivers, focusing not just on technical qualifications, but also on language skills and operational coordination to enhance cross-border cooperation. Such initiatives will strengthen connectivity and reinforce India's role as a key development partner in the Bay of Bengal region.

Strengthening institutional coordination: Successful cross-border connectivity projects require seamless coordination between multiple stakeholders. Governments, transport authorities and security agencies must collaborate closely to address policy bottlenecks, infrastructure development challenges and operational hurdles. Establishing dedicated coordination committees, or task forces can help streamline decision-making and ensure timely implementation of projects. In security-sensitive border areas, joint patrolling mechanisms and shared security protocols can build mutual trust and reduce risks associated with cross-border movements. Information-sharing frameworks between security agencies and transport authorities can further enhance the safety and reliability of railway and road networks. Additionally, diplomatic and security dialogues should incorporate infrastructure development discussions to prevent political and strategic considerations from impeding progress.

"Soft" Connectivity: Sustainable People-to-People Exchanges

Regional organisations are often built on top of existing cultural similarities but can also play a crucial role in fostering new identities. BIMSTEC's role today may be situated somewhere in-between, seeking to reactivate the Bay of Bengal's historical legacy of mobility and community. To do so more efficiently, given the abysmal levels of intra-regional connectivity since the mid-20th century, it is essential for BIMSTEC to foster people-to-people links that can help revive a sense of common belonging to the Bay of Bengal. This will also help to create sustainable links that enhance the "hard connectivity" dimension on economic and security parameters.

For Sumit Nakandala, BIMSTEC's first Secretary General, the organisation's main mission is, therefore, "to re-enable the environment of cooperation and community in the Bay of Bengal."[12] This requires an investment into less tangible forms of connectivity that increases flows of knowledge among scholars, experts and other key audiences in different countries.

Quality research and mutual exposure will accelerate the rediscovery of a common regional narrative for the Bay of Bengal as a distinct community with its own historical, cultural and geostrategic profile. Former Thai ambassador Kobsak Chutikul, thus, underlines that "when we imagine a bridge spanning the Bay of Bengal, it is not only physical infrastructure, a two-lane highway for trucks, but also a bridge of the mind, a bridge for imagination."[13]

BIMSTEC can play an important role as a facilitator to revive the collective attachment to the Bay of Bengal and restore the sense of community through greater people-to-people links. As a platform, the organisation could follow some of the following five recommendations.

Bolster the organisational brand: Despite celebrating its 25th anniversary in 2022, the organisation remains largely unknown to people beyond the official corridors of government. To change this, member states must shore up their budgets for promotional campaigns and activities, following India's lead, in 2017, with new funds to "enhance the visibility of 'Brand BIMSTEC.'"[14] As the leader of the working group on People-to-People exchanges, Thailand took enthusiastic initiatives between 2004 and 2007 in terms of sports, exhibitions, competitions and other public outreach, which it could not replicate during its recent chair. The organisation's annual foundation day, observed on June 6, can also be renamed as "Bay of Bengal Day" with a wider set of celebratory initiatives across the region. Finally, the eleven word, Bay of Bengal Initiative for Multi-Sectoral Technical and Economic Cooperation as a name (probably among the world's longest and most complex among regional organizations), can possibly be renamed as Bay of Bengal Community (BBC), or any other shorter option to facilitate easier mental recall.

Engage policy experts and entrepreneurs: Situated between the government and the wider public, expert groups play a crucial intermediary role to foster regional integration agendas. BIMSTEC must expand efforts to engage these communities and leverage their technical knowledge in specific areas as advocates for greater regional cooperation. Established in 2008, the BIMSTEC Network of Policy Think Tanks (BNPTT) should be divided into different sub-sectors and held on a more regular basis. Rather than a one-time affair to launch a vision for 2030, the BIMSTEC Eminent Persons' Group (EPG), should be formalised as an advisory council with senior representatives from government, business and other interest groups. Following the Thai government's announcement of a new BIMSTEC Centre, other member-states should be encouraged to designate more nodal research institutions for Track II and other Peer to Peer (P2P) initiatives. BIMSTEC could also re-institute its Young Ambassadors program, not held since 2006.

Refresh research regionally: No new Bay of Bengal narrative will emerge unless scholars are incentivised to dig into the past and recover the rich sense of community that animated the region until the 20th century. At their retreat in 2016, in Goa, BIMSTEC's leaders accordingly agreed "to expand linkages among educational and research institutions of member States." To do so, member-states need to commit dedicated resources for cross-country scholarship that identifies both past and present flows of people, capital and ideas across the region. This should also include specific BIMSTEC scholarships and grants for educational exchanges and collaborative research programs, visiting chairs and a network of universities focusing on the Bay of Bengal region.

Let tourism thrive: Tourism remains one of the most underdeveloped areas in the Bay of Bengal, particularly when it comes to intra-regional flows. Following up on the Kolkata Declaration of the BIMSTEC Tourism Ministers (2005), which committed to "providing a fresh impetus to further development of tourism within the region," the second summit, in 2008, agreed "to harness the region's natural, cultural and historical endowments in order to enhance intra-BIMSTEC tourism."[15] To facilitate visitor mobility, BIMSTEC should keep pushing for a special visa scheme for the region. Ideally, member states should aim to make BIMSTEC an area for free tourism mobility. Following up on the Outcome Document of 2016, the organisation should also develop a specialised Buddhist and Temple Tourist Circuit in the Bay of Bengal region based on common "civilizational, historical and cultural linkages."[16]

Cooperate on heritage conservation: Most of the region's monumental heritage have common historical and architectural origins and are in dire need of specialised conservation. BIMSTEC should facilitate cooperative exchanges and joint projects to pool expertise for such restoration and preservation operations. Such collaborative network must include member countries' apex public institutions like the Archaeological Survey of India, or the Department of Archaeological Survey in Sri Lanka, as well as private non-governmental bodies such as the Aga Khan Foundation, or the Yangon Heritage Trust (Myanmar). India's recent investments in conservation efforts in Nepal, Myanmar, Cambodia and Laos open up new possibilities and should lead to a focused effort on other BIMSTEC members.[17]

Conclusion

"Connectivity" has become a buzzword not only for BIMSTEC, but also for other regional integration initiatives across the Indo-Pacific. This often adds a burden on the decision-making capacity of smaller states, given the pressures from different extra-regional players, including China, the United States, Japan, the EU and other bilateral and multilateral actors in the race for connectivity amidst geo-political competition.

In some cases, unsustainable connectivity initiatives have weakened states, potentially undermining political stability and regional security. Recent crises in Bangladesh and Sri Lanka may be indicative of this trend.

BIMSTEC is placed well to nurture regional connectivity initiatives that are both secure and sustainable. Security here must be understood from a broader perspective, referring to the economic and developmental elements that regulate "hard" transportation infrastructure. With several low and middle-income countries marked by weak governance and state capacity, BIMSTEC member states need to make careful choices about financial and other terms that shape their decisions to upgrade their infrastructure, whether it is ports, roads, railways or power plants and electricity distribution systems.

Similarly, connectivity must also be understood from a human and cultural perspective. The Bay of Bengal is not an artificial political construct, but a space marked by centuries of deep linkages and mutually enriching flows. Here, again, states will benefit from investing in people-to-people exchanges that will serve as catalysts to revive this legacy of regional integration. Such human ties will serve as the foundation for more sustainable connectivity, beyond state-to-state relations or immediate economic or geopolitical interests.

On both accounts, the harder and softer dimensions of connectivity, BIMSTEC can play the role of an enabler for a more prosperous, resilient and open region, in line with its Bangkok Vision 2030.[18]

NOTES

1 Sohini Bose, Sreeparna Banerjee, and Anasua Basu Ray Chaudhury. The BIMSTEC Master Plan for Transport Connectivity: A Stocktaking. Observer Research Foundation, 2023. Accessed March 27, 2025. https://www.orfonline.org/research/the-bimstec-master-plan-for-transport-connectivity-a-stocktaking.

2 Ministry of External Affairs, Government of India. "English Translation of Remarks by Prime Minister Shri Narendra Modi at the 5th BIMSTEC Summit." March 30, 2022. Accessed March 28, 2025. https://www.mea.gov.in/Speeches-Statements.htm?dtl/35090/English_Translation_of_Remarks_by_Prime_Minister_Shri_Narendra_Modi_at_the_5th_BIMSTEC_Summit.

3 Sinha, Riya, and Constantino Xavier. "Beyond the Coastline: India's Land Connectivity Options around the Bay of Bengal." *Centre for Social and Economic Progress*, May 6, 2024. https://csep.org/working-paper/beyond-the-coastline-indias-land-connectivity-options-around-the-bay-of-bengal/. Sinha, Riya. "Express Routes India's Railway Connectivity with South Asia." *Centre for Social and Economic Progress*, December 2024. https://csep.org/wp-content/uploads/2024/12/Express-Routes_India-Railway-Connectivity.pdf.

4 Mattoo, Shashank. "Why One of India's Most Valuable Strategic Projects Is Stuck?" India Today, March 25, 2025. https://www.indiatoday.in/world/story/why-one-of-indias-most-valuable-strategic-projects-is-stuck-glbg-2698911-2025-03-25.

5 Taneja, Nisha, Biswajit Nag, Sanjana Joshi, Rashmi Rastogi, and Sanya Dua. "Bangladesh, Bhutan, India, Nepal Motor Vehicle Agreement." *Economic and Political Weekly*, November 16, 2024. https://www.epw.in/journal/2024/46/global-value-chains/bangladesh-bhutan-india-nepal-motor-vehicle.html.

6 Sinha, Riya. "Express Routes India's Railway Connectivity with South Asia." Centre for Social and Economic Progress, December 2024. https://csep.org/wp-content/uploads/2024/12/Express-Routes_India-Railway-Connectivity.pdf.

7 Banerjee, Pritam. "Conceptualising Highly Facilitated Trade Corridors in Southern Asia." ed. by Xavier, Constantino and Amitendu Palit. *Centre for Social and Economic Progress*, February 17, 2023. https://csep.org/reports/conceptualising-highly-facilitated-trade-corridors-in-southern-asia/.

8 "Bimstec Master Plan for Transport Connectivity." Asian Development Bank, April 2022. https://www.adb.org/documents/bimstec-master-plan-transport-connectivity.

9 World Trade Organization. "Trade Facilitation Agreement Database." https://www.tfadatabase.org/en.

10 "3rd Meeting of the BIMSTEC Working Group on Trade Facilitation." *BIMSTEC*, March 19, 2025. https://bimstec.org/event/240/3rd-meeting-of-the-bimstec-working-group-on-trade-facilitation.

11 "Overview of India's Development Partnership." Ministry of External Affairs, Government of India, August 29, 2023. https://www.mea.gov.in/Overview-of-India-Development-Partnership.htm.

12 Author interview with Sumith Nakandala, Former Secretary General, BIMSTEC, New Delhi, March 30, 2017.

13 Hassin, Shoumik. Building a Stronger BIMSTEC in Next 20 Years, May 29, 2017. https://bdnews24.com/neighbours/building-a-stronger-bimstec-in-next-20-years.

14 "Statement by External Affairs Minister Dr S. Jaishankar at the BIMSTEC Ministerial Meeting." Ministry of External Affairs, Government of India, August 11, 2017. https://mea.gov.in/Speeches-statements.htm?dtl%2F35088%2FStatement_ by_External_ Affairs_ Minister_Dr_S_Jaishankar_at_the_BIMSTEC_Ministerial_Meeting=.

15 "Second BIMSTEC Summit Declaration." Ministry of External Affairs, Government of India, November 13, 2008. https://mea.gov.in/bilateral-documents.htm?dtl%2F5418%2F Second +BIMSTEC+Summit+Declaration=.

16 "BIMSTEC Leaders' Retreat 2016 Outcome Document." live.narendramodi.in, October 17, 2016. https://live.narendramodi.in/mar/bimstec-leaders-retreat-2016-outcome-document-532768.

17 Kuzmenchuk, Aleksandr, and Constantino Xavier. "India's Heritage Diplomacy: The Case of Archaeology and Conservation." *Centre for Social and Economic Progress*, March 13, 2025. https://csep.org/blog/indias-heritage-diplomacy-the-case-of-archaeology-and-conservation/

18 "6th BIMSTEC Summit to Focus on Trade, Security and Regional Cooperation." The *Indian Awaaz*, April 4, 2025. https://theindianawaaz.com/6th-bimstec-summit-to-focus-on-trade-security-and-regional-cooperation/.

5

Building Ports Cooperation in BIMSTEC: A Gateway to Regional Prosperity and Stability

Shitesh Ranjan

The Bay of Bengal Initiative for Multi-Sectoral Technical and Economic Cooperation (BIMSTEC) represents a unique convergence of South and Southeast Asia, encompassing seven nations with shared aspirations for economic growth and regional stability. Among many avenues for cooperation, maritime connectivity stands out as a cornerstone for fostering trade, security and integration. India, as the largest and most economically advanced member of BIMSTEC, is poised to lead the charge in developing maritime cooperation between the region's ports. This essay explores India's pivotal role and the strategic initiatives it has been taking to enhance port connectivity within BIMSTEC, focusing on its potential to drive regional prosperity.

Importance of BIMSTEC Port Cooperation

Ports act as critical nodes of trade, economic activity and cultural exchange. In BIMSTEC, efficient port cooperation can substantially lower logistics costs, enhance intra-regional trade and support economic growth. Despite shared maritime interests, BIMSTEC currently experiences limited port collaboration due to infrastructural disparities and regulatory inconsistencies. Addressing these challenges through effective collaboration can transform ports into regional economic engines.

India's Strategic Role and Initiatives

India has taken many steps towards advancing BIMSTEC maritime cooperation through infrastructure development, maritime connectivity and security enhancements.

Enhancing Maritime Connectivity

India has been instrumental in promoting initiatives that improve maritime linkages across the Bay of Bengal. The anticipated signing of the Maritime Transport Cooperation Agreement will simplify logistics, reduce trade costs and enable transshipment through member countries' ports. This agreement reflects India's commitment to addressing the current intra-regional trade deficit, which stands at a mere seven percent despite significant maritime trade potential.

Infrastructure Development

India has pioneered several large-scale regional port and connectivity projects, not necessarily within the BIMSTEC framework, but still very vital for setting the right intent and capacity. These are:

- **Kaladan Multi-Modal Transit Transport Project:** This critical initiative connects Kolkata in India with Myanmar's Sittwe Port and further links to Mizoram in Northeast India. This alternative trade route significantly reduces dependency on the congested Siliguri Corridor, boosting economic integration and prosperity, particularly benefiting landlocked regions.
- **Chattogram and Mongla Port (Bangladesh):** India's investments and support in upgrading Bangladesh's ports, including the Ashuganj River Port infrastructure under the Indo-Bangladesh Protocol, facilitates improved cross-border trade. This enhances economic cooperation, supporting Bangladesh's maritime infrastructure and promoting mutual prosperity.
- **Trincomalee Port (Sri Lanka):** India has played a pivotal role in developing Sri Lanka's Trincomalee Port and aligning it with its broader strategic objectives in the Indian Ocean. The port's transformation into an energy hub, with India's involvement in oil storage tank farms, underscores its economic and geo-political potential. This initiative has helped in counterbalancing China's influence in Sri Lanka, particularly at Hambantota Port. By investing in Trincomalee, India has enhanced its maritime security and trade routes, reinforcing its Indo-Pacific strategy. The project also supports Sri Lanka's economic growth and regional stability, ensuring that India remains a key player in regional maritime dynamics.

Maritime Security and Stability

Recognising the importance of secure sea lanes, India can actively contribute to maritime security within BIMSTEC. For example, initiatives such as the Trilateral Maritime Security Cooperation with Sri Lanka and Maldives enhance regional capacity against piracy, trafficking and other maritime threats, reinforcing stability and safe navigation across the Bay of Bengal. Similarly, the port security-related knowledge sharing workshops like the ones being held through The ASEAN Regional Forum (ARF) sets the right template.

Opportunities for India-Led Cooperation

India's proactive leadership can provide multiple opportunities to position BIMSTEC as a significant regional maritime group of country:

Economic Integration and Regional Trade

Notably, the GDP of member countries are primarily driven by exports. That share of merchandise has a good proportion and to facilitate that, shipping and ports, play a vital part. Cooperation for efficient port operation can significantly reduce costs of trade, improve export competitiveness and attract foreign direct investment, and thus, foster closer economic ties and interdependence between member states.

Countering External Influence

India's proactive development of BIMSTEC ports can provide a strategic counterweight to external influences, notably China's Belt and Road Initiative. Through regional connectivity and infrastructure investments, India can strengthen its geo-political position while fostering a spirit of self-reliance among BIMSTEC nations.

Promoting Sustainability and Green Ports

India can spearhead efforts within BIMSTEC to adopt environmentally sustainable port practices by leveraging initiatives such as the Green Tug Transition Scheme and other ESG frameworks. Among others, India's voluntary "Green Port Index" may serve as a benchmark, encouraging port operators to upgrade their environmental performance. Expanding this index across the region would foster a widespread adoption of uniform sustainability standards, significantly reducing marine pollution and ecological damage, while equitably motivating all regional ports to pursue greater environmental responsibility and sustainable maritime practices.

Challenges to BIMSTEC Port Cooperation

Several challenges remain significant barriers to effective cooperation:

(i) **Infrastructure Gaps:** There exists substantial differences in port capabilities and infrastructure standards among BIMSTEC countries. Without significant investments and collaborative projects, regional integration will remain hindered.

(ii) **Regulatory Barriers:** Varied customs procedures and policies create inefficiencies, delays and higher operational costs, hampering smooth trade flows.

(iii) **Funding Constraints:** Limited financial resources of some member states restricts the capacity to undertake necessary infrastructural expansions and modernisations.

Leveraging India's Institutional Strengths for Regional Development

India possesses specialised maritime institutions and public-sector enterprises uniquely suited to addressing BIMSTEC's port development needs.

Specific to seaport and connectivity through rail transport, Indian entities like the India Ports Global Limited (IPGL) and Indian Port Rail & Ropeway Corporation Limited (IPRCL) can play transformative roles in enhancing regional port cooperation:

India Ports Global Limited (IPGL)

(i) **Strategic Operations:** IPGL can extend its operational expertise in international port management—demonstrated through its work at Chabahar Port, Iran—to BIMSTEC ports. This could facilitate smoother trade routes both within the region and with external partners.

(ii) **Infrastructure Development:** IPGL can collaborate with BIMSTEC nations to develop port infrastructure by sharing its experience in handling large-scale port operations and modernisation projects. This would elevate the efficiency of regional ports while promoting sustainable practices.

Indian Port Rail & Ropeway Corporation Limited (IPRCL)

(i) **Enhanced Connectivity:** IPRCL can contribute to developing railway systems that connect BIMSTEC ports to their hinterlands more effectively. Improved connectivity would reduce logistical costs, enhance supply chain efficiency and integrate maritime transport with land-based networks.

(ii) **Project Implementation:** Leveraging its expertise in infrastructure projects, IPRCL can assist BIMSTEC countries in planning and executing rail links that support port activities. This would ensure better integration between maritime hubs and inland trade routes.

Leveraging IWAI Expertise for Hinterland Connectivity

The Inland Waterways Authority of India (IWAI) has demonstrated remarkable success in developing inland waterways to connect ports with hinterlands. In the BIMSTEC context, IWAI's expertise could be leveraged to enhance connectivity between member states:

(i) **Cross-Border Waterways Projects:** IWAI's experience with projects like the Indo-Bangladesh Protocol Route highlights its ability to facilitate seamless waterway connectivity between nations. For instance, dredging initiatives on rivers such as Jamuna and Kushiyara, have improved navigability between Bangladesh and India's northeastern states. Such efforts can be replicated across other BIMSTEC nations to develop inland water routes that complement port operations.

(ii) **Hinterland Integration:** IWAI's work on National Waterways (NW-1, NW-2, NW-16) demonstrates how inland waterways can reduce logistical costs while boosting trade efficiency. By extending this model to other BIMSTEC countries like Myanmar or Thailand, IWAI can help establish multimodal transport corridors that integrate ports with their hinterlands.

(iii) **Economic Corridors:** IWAI's vision for an Eastern Waterways Connectivity Transport Grid offers a blueprint for creating a network of navigable waterways connecting Northeastern India with Bangladesh, Bhutan, Nepal and Myanmar. This initiative could transform inland waterways into vital economic corridors for regional integration.

Strategic Recommendations for Strengthening Ports Cooperation

India can further deepen BIMSTEC port cooperation by adopting a multifaceted strategy:

Policy Harmonisation and Institutional Coordination

India should promote the harmonisation of customs policies, tariffs and operational standards, facilitating seamless cross-border movements. Establishing a regional body for port coordination within BIMSTEC, potentially the envisaged Joint Shipping Committee (JSC), could streamline decision-making, enhance policy coherence and improve overall maritime governance.

Joint Infrastructure Investments

India should initiate collaborative infrastructure projects, leveraging its financial and technical resources. Engaging regional and global financial institutions (e.g., ADB, World Bank) for funding can mitigate resource constraints, allowing for equitable distribution of developmental responsibilities. India's leading ports may also participate or even lead such joint infrastructure projects, depending on the agreement signed.

Capacity-Building Initiatives

India should lead training and capacity-building programs in areas such as port operations, port security, sustainable practices and disaster management. India's premier maritime institutes can provide targeted technical training, skill development and knowledge-sharing workshops for regional stakeholders.

Strengthening Multilateral Engagement

India can foster continuous dialogue through forums such as the BIMSTEC Conclave of Ports, encouraging regular exchanges on best practices, operational challenges, innovations and future collaborations. Such initiatives will ensure consistent stakeholder engagement, enhancing trust and mutual understanding.

Facilitating Regional Shipping Promotion

Pursuing the equitable treatment of BIMSTEC member states vessels within regional ports, will promote competitive shipping services. This approach would significantly reduce shipping costs, streamline operational efficiencies and incentivise regional maritime trade. Another approach is to recognise each other's domestic certification regime of vessels, which are in line with, or equivalent to the 'Indian Coastal Vessel' and 'Indian River Sea Vessel-IV', which may potentially reduce building and operational costs without compromising on a vessel's safety aspects.

Conclusion

India's leadership in building ports cooperation within BIMSTEC presents a transformative opportunity for regional prosperity, stability and sustainable economic growth. By leveraging its extensive maritime experience, geopolitical influence and institutional strengths, India can play a decisive role in addressing regional disparities, reducing logistical inefficiencies and promoting economic integration. Through strategic partnerships, collaborative investments, capacity building and sustainable development initiatives, India can effectively transform BIMSTEC ports into vibrant economic gateways, significantly enhancing regional trade, connectivity and stability across the Bay of Bengal.

Ultimately, India's visionary leadership and collaborative approach on port development can redefine BIMSTEC's maritime landscape, turning shared challenges into collective strengths and creating enduring prosperity and stability for the region.

NOTES

1 Prajapati, Harshit. "Why BIMSTEC's Maritime Transport Agreement Is Essential for India." *Stimson Centre*, August 23, 2024. https://www.stimson.org/2024/why-bimstecs-maritime-transport-agreement-is-essential-for-india/#:~:text=By%20offering%20concessional% 20port% 20fees,integrate%20with%20each%20others'%20economies.

2 "Greening in India Gets a Boost with Green Tug Transition Program SOP Launched by Sarbananda Sonowal." Press Information Bureau, October 2024. https://pib.gov.in/PressReleasePage.aspx?PRID=2045946.

3 "Eastern Waterways Grid to Benefit Bangladesh, Bhutan, India and Nepal." *World Bank*, August 2021. https://documents1.worldbank.org/curated/en/114771631170648686/txt/The-World-Bank-in-India-Newsletter-Vol-24-No-1.txt.

4 "First BIMSTEC Conclave of Ports, Vishakhapatnam." Ministry of External Affairs, Government of India. November 7-8, 2019. https://www.mea.gov.in/press-releases.htm?dtl/32010/First+BIMSTEC+Conclave+of+Ports+Vishakhapatnam+November+78+2019#:~:text= The% 20first%20 ever%20BIM STEC%20Conclave,best %20practices%20 among %20Member%20Countries.

5 "India and Bangladesh Sign Agreements for Enhancing Inland and Coastal Waterways Connectivity." Press Information Bureau, October 25, 2018. https://pib.gov.in/Pressreleaseshare.aspx?PRID=1550795.

6 Trincomalee Oil Tank Farm Venture Moves Forward Despite Past Opposition." *Tamil Guardian.* January 17, 2025. https://x.com/tamilguardian.

7 "Centre Notifies SOP for Green Tug Transition Program, Investment of over 1000 CR." *BWSustainability.* August 18, 2024. https://bwsustainabilityworld.com/centre-notifies-sop-for-green-tug-transition-program-investment-of-over-1000-cr/.

8 "BIMSTEC Ports Conclave Held in Visakhapatnam." *IndBiz*, November 7-8, 2019. https://indbiz.gov.in/bimstec-ports-conclave-held-in-visakhapatnam/.

9 "Maritime India Vision 2030." Press Information Bureau, March 28, 2025. https://pib.gov.in/PressReleaseIframePage.aspx?PRID=2116164#:~:text=A%20total%20of%2075%20port,Port%20 modernization %20projects%20worth%20Rs.

PART III

Maritime Cooperation and Regional Security

6

The Bay of Bengal: A Case for Enhanced Maritime Security Cooperation

Anurag Bisen

The Bay of Bengal (BoB), the largest bay in the world and part of the northeastern Indian Ocean, spans approximately 2.6 million square kilometres.[1] India, Bangladesh, Myanmar, Sri Lanka, Thailand and Indonesia are on its border and almost a quarter of the world's population calls it home.[2]

With critical shipping lanes, rich natural resources and growing geopolitical interests, the BoB plays a crucial role in terms of regional security, economic development and environmental sustainability.

While its strategic position—linking the consumption hubs of the Indian Ocean with the production centres of the Pacific—enhances its geopolitical significance, it continues to face persistent developmental and environmental challenges.[3]

Bay of Bengal littoral states have an average Human Development Index (HDI) ranking of 110.[4] As one of the world's most disaster-prone areas, changes in climate pose a serious threat, particularly to the coastal communities. Climate change impacts have led to the marine environment becoming increasingly fragile, characterised by rising sea levels, ocean acidification, shifting weather patterns and prevalence of illegal, unreported, and unregulated (IUU) fishing, among other concerns.[5]

Further, increasing security threats, unresolved territorial disputes and the need for regional cooperation make the Bay of Bengal a complex maritime domain requiring enhanced governance and collaborative mechanisms.

Geopolitical and Economic Significance of Bay of Bengal

The BoB is located at the heart of the Indo-Pacific and is India's geostrategic gateway to wider waters.[6] It serves as a crucial trade and energy corridor. Major sea routes traverse this maritime space, effectively linking South Asia with Southeast Asia, the dynamic economies of East Asia and the energy-rich Middle East. Around 50 percent of global container traffic and 80 percent of oil shipments transit through the Indian Ocean, with the Bay of Bengal being a critical part of these movements.[7] The region also plays a vital role in India's SAGAR (Security and Growth for All in the Region) Initiative, which aims to ensure both maritime security and economic cooperation.

The Bay of Bengal is abundant in oil, natural gas and other valuable resources. Bangladesh, Myanmar and India have significant offshore oil and gas reserves, contributing to their national energy strategies. Myanmar alone has around 23 trillion cubic feet of natural gas reserves in its offshore waters.[8] Additionally, the region holds potential for renewable energy development, including offshore wind farms and tidal energy projects, which could contribute to sustainable economic growth.[9] The BoB is also rich in fisheries, being home to 31 percent of the world's fishermen and contributing six million tons of fish catch annually, making up seven percent of global production.[10] The fisheries sector supports over four million livelihoods in Bangladesh alone.[11]

However, the region is highly disaster-prone, occupying just 0.6 percent of the world's ocean area, yet accounting for nearly 80 percent of global cyclone-related deaths.[12] Additionally, it remains highly vulnerable to maritime security threats.

Maritime Security Challenges in Bay of Bengal

Despite its economic and strategic potential, the Bay of Bengal faces numerous security threats, ranging from territorial disputes and piracy to transnational crimes and environmental challenges.

Territorial Disputes and Maritime Boundary Conflicts

A primary security concern in the Bay of Bengal are maritime boundary disputes between littoral states. While India and Bangladesh successfully resolved their dispute through the Permanent Court of Arbitration in 2014,[13] Myanmar and Bangladesh continue to have disagreements over maritime boundaries and offshore resource exploitation.[14] Unresolved disputes can lead to regional tensions and potential conflicts over access to marine resources.

Piracy, Illegal Fishing, and Smuggling

Though not as severe as in the Gulf of Aden, or the Strait of Malacca, piracy remains a security concern in the Bay of Bengal. Armed robberies targeting small fishing vessels and cargo ships have been reported, particularly near the coasts of Bangladesh and Myanmar.[15]

Illegal, Unreported, and Unregulated (IUU) Fishing

Another pressing issue is IUU fishing. Foreign trawlers, particularly from China, have been accused of overfishing in the exclusive economic zones (EEZs) of coastal areas of various countries, depleting fish stocks and threatening local fishing communities.[16] Human trafficking and drug smuggling is prevalent, with criminal networks using the BoB as a transit route for narcotics, particularly methamphetamine from Myanmar's Shan State, and for trafficking Rohingya refugees.[17] The increasing use of advanced surveillance technologies, including satellite tracking and UAV patrols, has been proposed to counteract these illegal activities.[18]

Environmental and Climate-Related Threats

The BoB is one of the world's most climate-vulnerable regions. Rising sea levels, coastal erosion and extreme weather events such as cyclones (Cyclone Amphan in 2020 and Cyclone Mocha in 2023) have had a devastating impact on coastal communities.[19] These environmental threats also increase security risks as climate-induced displacement raises the potential for humanitarian crises and resource conflicts.[20] Addressing these issues requires enhanced disaster preparedness, coordinated response mechanisms and investments in climate adaptation strategies.[21]

Extra-Regional Maritime Presence

The BoB is now increasingly becoming a strategic arena for contest between extra-regional powers due to its critical maritime trade routes, abundant natural resources and proximity to key chokepoints like the Strait of Malacca. China's Belt and Road Initiative (BRI) has increased its investments in regional ports like Kyaukpyu (Myanmar) and Hambantota (Sri Lanka),[22] heightening India's concerns. The United States, through its Indo-Pacific strategy, has also increased its engagement in the region, emphasising freedom of navigation and regional security. The growing US-China rivalry reflects broader geopolitical rivalries, where maritime security, resource access, and regional influence drive strategic manoeuvring in the Bay of Bengal. India, in response, has also strengthened its naval presence in the Andaman and Nicobar Islands and enhanced maritime collaborations under its Act East Policy.[23]

Cooperative Mechanisms for Maritime Security in the Bay of Bengal

Recognising these challenges, countries along the Bay of Bengal have developed various cooperative mechanisms to enhance maritime security, economic collaboration and environmental sustainability.

Bay of Bengal Initiative for Multi-Sectoral Technical and Economic Cooperation (BIMSTEC)

BIMSTEC (established 1997), comprising India, Bangladesh, Myanmar, Sri Lanka, Thailand, Nepal, and Bhutan, is a key regional organisation aimed at fostering economic and security cooperation. It focuses on trade and investment, transport and communication, energy, technology, tourism, and fisheries connectivity, poverty alleviation, agriculture, cultural cooperation, counter-terrorism and transnational crimes, environment and disaster management, public health and people-to-people contacts.[24]

Some of the aims of BIMSTEC include creation of an enabling environment for rapid economic development, acceleration of economic growth and social progress in the Bay of Bengal, promotion of collaboration on matters of common interest in the economic, social, technical and scientific fields, maintenance of peace and stability in the Bay of Bengal region, eradication of poverty, establishment of multidimensional connectivity for shared prosperity and promotion of trade and investment.[25]

Indian Ocean Rim Association (IORA)

The IORA is a broader regional mechanism that includes BoB nations. It facilitates cooperation on security, trade and disaster response. The association has played a role in maritime domain awareness and collaborative efforts against piracy and transnational crimes.[26]

Indian Ocean Naval Symposium (IONS)

The IONS serves as a platform for naval collaboration between Indian Ocean littoral states. It promotes inter-operability and information-sharing between navies, helping to address maritime threats collectively.[27]

Bilateral and Multilateral Naval Exercises

Several joint naval exercises have strengthened maritime security cooperation in the region:

- **MILAN Exercises**: Led by the Indian Navy, involving multiple regional and extra-regional navies.[28]
- **Malabar Exercise** (India, US, Japan, Australia): While not Bay of Bengal specific, these exercises contribute to broader regional maritime security.[29]
- **India-Bangladesh Maritime Cooperation**: Includes joint patrols and intelligence-sharing efforts to combat piracy and illegal activities.[30]

Maritime Security Cooperation under BIMSTEC

Apart from being a founding member, India is an active participant in all BIMSTEC cooperation programs.[31] "*Neighbourhood First*" and "*Act East*"—both of which are relevant for BIMSTEC—are the cornerstones of India's foreign policy.[32]

Cooperation in the security domain is considered of special relevance under BIMSTEC. This is reflected in the meetings of **BIMSTEC National Security Advisors.** They have met four times, in 2017 in New Delhi, 2018 in Dhaka, 2019 in Bangkok and 2024 in Nay Pyi Taw, and have underscored the importance of recognising the Bay of Bengal as common security space. They have agreed to work collectively in dealing with regional challenges, including maritime security cooperation.[33]

To enhance coastal security and connectivity in the Bay of Bengal, India took the lead and organised the first **BIMSTEC Ports Conclave** at Visakhapatnam on November 7 and 8, 2019,[34] as well as the first **Coastal Security Workshop** for BIMSTEC Countries at the Information Fusion Centre-Indian Ocean Region (IFC-IOR), Gurugram, between November 20 and 22, 2019.[35] However, these pioneering initiatives have not been repeated.

Key BIMSTEC ongoing efforts in maritime security cooperation include:

Expert Group on Maritime Security Cooperation:[36] Established to strengthen collaboration between member states, this group has identified five primary focus areas:

- Maritime Domain Awareness (MDA)
- Humanitarian Assistance and Disaster Relief (HADR)
- Oil Pollution Response
- Blue Economy
- Maritime Security Cooperation

In its meetings, the group has developed and refined several key documents:[37]

- Concept Paper on Maritime Cooperation in the Bay of Bengal
- BIMSTEC Guidelines for Maritime Component of Humanitarian Assistance and Disaster Relief (HADR)
- BIMSTEC Guiding Principles: Conduct of Maritime Law Enforcement Agencies during Interaction at Sea
- BIMSTEC Guidelines for Coordinated Marine Oil Spill Response

These documents aim to establish frameworks for coordinated responses to maritime security challenges.

Maritime Transport Agreement (MTA):[38] An agreement designed to enhance maritime connectivity between BIMSTEC countries. The MTA aims to:

- Provide concessional port dues for various types of cargo
- Allow trans-shipment of cargo using member countries' ports
- Simplify logistics to facilitate regional trade

This initiative is likely to boost trade by improving maritime connectivity across the Bay of Bengal.

The likely signing of the **BIMSTEC Maritime Transport Agreement** during the upcoming summit in Thailand, will substantially enhance connectivity in the region.[39] India has vital stakes in the India Myanmar-Thailand Trilateral Highway and the Kaladan Multi-Modal Transit Transport Project, both of which are a part of the BIMSTEC Master Plan for Transport Connectivity, for the development of its Northeastern Region.[40]

Information Fusion Centre – Indian Ocean Region (IFC-IOR):[41] Hosted by the Indian Navy, the IFC-IOR collaborates with BIMSTEC member states to enhance maritime domain awareness. The centre focuses on:

- Fusing, analysing, and disseminating information on maritime activities.

- Collaborating with national and regional agencies to promote maritime safety and security.

By sharing critical information, the IFC-IOR contributes to a comprehensive understanding of maritime activities in the region.

Counter-Terrorism and Transnational Crime (CTTC) Sub-Sector:[42] The 8th BIMSTEC Ministerial Meeting, held in Dhaka, Bangladesh, on December 18-19, 2005, designated CTTC as a key priority sector for BIMSTEC. To strengthen collaboration at both policy and operational levels in addressing terrorism and transnational crime, the meeting also approved the establishment of the BIMSTEC Joint Working Group on Counter Terrorism and Transnational Crime (JWG-CTTC). This active sub-sector within BIMSTEC addresses various security challenges, including:

- Human trafficking
- Combating financing of terrorism
- Countering radicalisation
- Legal and law enforcement cooperation
- Prevention of illicit trafficking

These initiatives reflect BIMSTEC's commitment to fostering a secure and cooperative maritime environment in the Bay of Bengal region.

Despite various initiatives, maritime security in the Bay of Bengal remains precarious. This is evident from the tragic loss of 569 Rohingya refugees at sea in 2023—the highest toll in nine years,[43]—underscoring the persistent risks of human trafficking and irregular migration. Similarly, the Indian Coast Guard's record-breaking seizure of 5,500 kilograms of banned methamphetamine from a fishing trawler in the Andaman Sea in November 2024[44] highlights the scale of ongoing drug smuggling operations in the region. These incidents illustrate the enduring security vulnerabilities that demand stronger regional cooperation and enforcement mechanisms.

Recommendations for Enhancing Maritime Security in the Bay of Bengal

Develop a BIMSTEC Maritime Strategy: BIMSTEC should formulate a comprehensive maritime strategy using India's *Security and Growth for All in the Region* (SAGAR) initiative as a guiding framework. This strategy should align regional maritime policies, ensuring a collective approach to security, governance and economic development in the Bay of Bengal.

Strengthen Maritime Domain Awareness (MDA): A regional *Maritime Domain Awareness (MDA)* network should be established to enhance surveillance, intelligence-sharing and coordination among BIMSTEC nations. This network should integrate existing mechanisms such as IFC-IOR and facilitate real-time communication on maritime security threats.

Enhance Coordination Among Maritime Mechanisms: Existing maritime interaction mechanisms—such as the *Western Pacific Naval Symposium (WPNS)*, *Indian Ocean Rim Association (IORA)*, *Indian Ocean Naval Symposium (IONS)*, and *Indian Ocean Commission (IOC)*—should be streamlined to avoid duplication and enhance cooperation. A dedicated intra-BIMSTEC consultative mechanism on maritime issues could convene on the sidelines of IORA and IONS meetings to improve policy coordination.

Establish Norms to Prevent External Naval Base Development: BIMSTEC members should collectively develop regional norms to prevent extra-regional powers from establishing permanent military bases in the Bay of Bengal. This would help maintain regional stability and sovereignty while preventing the militarisation of strategic maritime zones.

Improve Legal and Regulatory Frameworks

- Establish a *legal expert group* to standardise interpretations of UNCLOS and other relevant maritime laws.
- Develop common *Standard Operating Procedures (SOPs)* for enforcing the *International Ship and Port Facility Security (ISPS) Code*, port security measures, and legal frameworks.
- Harmonise fishing regulations among Bay of Bengal littoral states to prevent illegal fishing activities.

Strengthen Regional Coordination on Maritime Crimes: BIMSTEC nations should enhance coordination in combating transnational maritime crimes such as drug trafficking, arms smuggling, and human trafficking. This requires improved intelligence sharing, joint maritime patrols, and strict enforcement of international maritime security laws.

Integrate Transport Connectivity Plans: The *BIMSTEC Master Plan for Transport Connectivity* should be aligned with the *ASEAN Master Plan on Connectivity* to facilitate seamless trade, improve port security and boost regional economic growth.

Enhance Search and Rescue (SAR) and Disaster Response: A Memorandum of Understanding (MoU) between BIMSTEC countries should be signed for joint search and rescue (SAR) operations, coordinated responses to maritime accidents and addressing irregular migration. A unified *Humanitarian Assistance and Disaster Response (HADR)* strategy is also essential for better preparedness and response to natural disasters.

Protect Submarine Cables and Critical Infrastructure: A common framework should be developed to safeguard submarine communication cables, which are vital for regional connectivity and economic stability. BIMSTEC nations should collaborate on setting security protocols and rapid response mechanisms in case of disruptions.

Deployment of BOB Ship *Sindhu:* The Indian Navy, in a pioneering initiative, recently announced the deployment of an Offshore Patrol Vessel (OPV) designated as **Indian Ocean Ship** (IOS) *Sagar*, towards continued cooperation with Indian Ocean Region (IOR) nations. The warship is being deployed to the Southwest IOR, for over a month, in April 2025, with a combined crew of India and nine "Friendly Foreign Countries" (Comoros, Kenya, Madagascar, Maldives, Mauritius, Mozambique, Seychelles, Sri Lanka and South Africa). This initiative can be replicated in the Bay of Bengal with an Indian warship and a combined crew of BIMSTEC countries.

Conclusion

The Bay of Bengal is a region of immense economic potential and geo-political importance, offering opportunities for trade, investment and sustainable development. However, it faces significant maritime security challenges that threaten its stability and prosperity. While existing cooperative mechanisms have made valuable contributions to regional stability, a more robust collaboration will effectively address the complex and interconnected threats of piracy, illegal fishing, smuggling and environmental degradation.

Strengthening maritime domain awareness through enhanced surveillance and information sharing, enhancing joint security initiatives to deter and respond to maritime threats and fostering diplomatic engagement to resolve disputes and build trust will be essential for ensuring a secure and prosperous Bay of Bengal for all stakeholders. The future of the region depends on the collective commitment of its nations to work together to overcome these challenges and realise the Bay's full potential.

BIMSTEC member states are committed to strengthening maritime security in the Bay of Bengal and enhancing regional capacity to address traditional and non-traditional security threats. As the lead of BIMSTEC's Security Pillar, India must encourage member states to enhance maritime capacity building. By implementing these recommendations, BIMSTEC can enhance maritime security, ensure sustainable development and foster greater regional stability in the Bay of Bengal.

NOTES

1 Misachi, John. "Bay of Bengal." *World Atlas*, February 4, 2021. https://www.worldatlas.com/bays/bay-of-bengal.html.

2 Dutta, Sabyasachi. "Forging a Bay of Bengal Community is the Need of the Hour," *ASIA PACIFIC BULLETIN,* May 12, 2021

3 Mohan, C. Raja. "The Bay of Bengal in the Emerging Indo-Pacific." *Observer Research Foundation.* May 12, 2023. https://www.orfonline.org/research/the-bay-of-bengal-in-the-emerging-indo-pacific.

4 "Country Insights." Human Development Reports, United Nations Development Programme n.d. https://hdr.undp.org/data-center/country-insights#/ranks.

5 Chaturvedi, Sanjay. "Climate Change and the Bay of Bengal." books.google.co.in, 2015. https://books.google.co.in/books?hl=en&lr=&id=PaxgCwAAQBAJ&oi=fnd&pg=PR5&dq= Climate+ change+ impact+on+ Bay+of+Bengal&ots= 6jYvw75h4P&sig=o FIl4 Xn25s 2hdpP__O1zXBhWHiI&redir_esc=y#v=onepage&q=Climate%20change %20impact %20on%20Bay%20of%20Bengal&f=false.

6 "Exploring Connectivity in the Bay of Bengal Region: Importance of India's Northeast." *Observer Research Foundation*, March 5-6, 2021. https://www.orfonline.org/event/exploring-connectivity-bay-bengal-region-importance-india-northeast.

7 "Connecting South Asia and Southeast Asia." *Asian Development Bank and Asian Development Bank Institute,* April 2015. https://www.adb.org/publications/connecting-south-asia-and-southeast-asia.

8 "Myanmar Energy Sector Update: Energy Poverty amid Plenty." World Bank, June 2024. https://openknowledge.worldbank.org/server/api/core/bitstreams/2b24c33e-d399-5304-ac7c-8f1ea9f95fd7/content.

9 "The Blue Economy and Fisheries Management." *Indian Ocean Rim Association (IORA),* 2024. https://www.iora.int/sites/default/files/2024-03/e-magazine-blue-economy.pdf.

10 "Interesting Facts About Bay Of Bengal." *Centre for Coastal Zone Management and Coastal Shelter Belt,*

11 "The State of World Fisheries and Aquaculture 2024: Blue Transformation in Action." *FAO,* October 14, 2024. https://openknowledge.fao.org/items/06690fd0-d133-424c-9673-1849e414543d.

12 "Foreign Secretary's Address at the International Symposium on 'BIMSTEC: A Vehicle for Growth and Development' Organized by ISCS Kolkata." Ministry of External Affairs, Government of India, October 25, 2021. https://www.mea.gov.in/Speeches-Statements.htm

13 "Bay of Bengal Maritime Boundary Arbitration between Bangladesh and India." Permanent

Court of Arbitration, July 8, 2014. https://www.pcacases.com/web/sendAttach/410.

14 "Dispute Concerning Delimitation of the Maritime Boundary between Bangladesh and Myanmar in the Bay of Bengal." *International Tribunal for the Law of the Sea* (ITLOS), March 14, 2012. https://www.itlos.org/fileadmin/itlos/documents/cases/case_no_16/published/C16-J-14_mar_12.pdf.

15 "Indian Navy Annual Report 2023." *IFC-IOR*, 2023. https://ifcior.indiannavy.gov.in/themes/custom/ifc_ior/static/data/reports/annual/IFC-IOR_ANNUAL_REPORT_2023.pdf.

16 "Human Trafficking." *United Nations: UNODC Regional Office for Southeast Asia and the Pacific*. https://www.unodc.org/roseap/en/what-we-do/toc/human-trafficking.html.

17 "Climate Change Report 2024." *Intergovernmental Panel on Climate Change (IPCC)*, November 12, 2024. https://www.ipcc.ch/2024/.

18 Choudhury, Angshuman, Siddharth Anil Nair, Ashutosh Nagda, and Garima Maheshwari. "Climate Security in the Bay of Bengal." *Institute of Peace and Conflict Studies*, January 2012. https://ipcs.org/issue_briefs/issue_brief_pdf/ipcssr%20212_climate%20 security%20in%20the%20bay%20ofbengal_jan%202022.pdf.

19 Samuel, Jency. "Why the Bay of Bengal Is More Prone to Cyclones than the Arabian Sea." *IPE Global*, January 7, 2025. https://www.ipeglobal.com/why-the-bay-of-bengal-is-more-prone-to-cyclones-than-the-arabian-sea/.

20 Bose, Sohini, and Anasua Basu Ray Chaudhury. "India and a sStable Indo-Pacific: Managing Maritime Security Challenges in the Bay of Bengal." Observer ResearchFoundation (ORF), March 27, 2024. https://www.orfonline.org/research/india-and-a-stable-indo-pacific-managing-maritime-security-challenges-in-the-bay-of-bengal.

21 "Iora Priority Areas: Maritime Security and Safety." *Indian Ocean Rim Association (IORA)*, n.d. https://www.iora.int/maritime-safety-security.

22 Anwar, Anu. "South Asia and China's Belt and Road Initiative: Security Implications and Ways Forward." *Daniel K. Inouye Asia-Pacific Center for Security Studies*, n.d. https://dkiapcss.edu/wp-content/uploads/2020/09/10-Anwar-25thA.pdf.

23 Wadhwa, Anil. "India's Act East Policy." Ministry of External Affairs, Government of India, August 9, 2019. https://www.mea.gov.in/distinguished-lectures.htm.

24 Ibid.

25 "History – Home-The Bay of Bengal Initiative for Multi-Sectoral Technical and Economic Cooperation (BIMSTEC)."

26 Indian Ocean Rim Association

27 Indian Ocean Naval Symposium

28 "Milan 2024 Press Release." Indian Navy, February 20, 2024. https://indiannavy.nic.in/content/milan-2024-press-release-20-feb-2024.

29 MALABAR- 2024

30 "India, Bangladesh Conduct Naval Exercise in Bay of Bengal to Enhance Interoperability." *The Economic Times,* March 13, 2025. https://economictimes.indiatimes.com/news/defence/india-bangladesh-conduct-naval-exercise-in-bay-of-bengal-to-enhance-interoperability/articleshow/118983731.cms.

31 Kumar, Sujeet. "Participation with BIMSTEC Alliance." Rajya Sabha, August 5, 2021. https://rsdebate.nic.in/bitstream/123456789/720842/2/IQ_254_05082021_ U2016_p298_p298.pdf.

32 "Foreign Secretary's Address at the International Symposium on 'BIMSTEC: A Vehicle for

Growth and Development' Organized by ISCS Kolkata." Ministry of External Affairs, Government of India, October 25, 2021. https://www.mea.gov.in/Speeches-Statements.htm

33 "Fourth Meeting of the BIMSTEC National Security Chiefs." *BIMSTEC*, July 26, 2024. https://bimstec.org/event/205/fourth-meeting-of-the-bimstec-national-security-chiefs.

34 "First BIMSTEC Conclave of Ports, Vishakhapatnam (November 7-8, 2019)." Ministry of External Affairs, Government of India, November 7, 2019. https://www.mea.gov.in/press-releases.htm?dtl%2F32010%2FFirst+BIMSTEC+Conclave+of+Ports+Vishakhapatnam+November+78+2019

35 Home-The Bay of Bengal Initiative for Multi-Sectoral Technical and Economic. "Coastal Security Workshop for BIMSTEC Countries." *BIMSTEC*, November 20, 2019. https://bimstec.org/event/18/coastal-security-workshop-for-bimstec-countries#:~:text= 20%20 Nov %202019%2 D%2020%20Nov%202019&text=The%20Workshop%20aimed%20at%20 provi ding,the%20seven%20BIMSTEC%20Member%20States.

36 "Expert Group on Maritime Security Cooperation in the Bay of Bengal." *BIMSTEC*, October 12, 2023. https://bimstec.org/expert-group-on-maritime-security-cooperation-in-the-bay-of-bengal.

37 Ibid.

38 Prajapati, Harshit. "Why BIMSTEC's Maritime Transport Agreement Is Essential for India." Stimson Center, August 23, 2024. https://www.stimson.org/2024/why-bimstecs-maritime-transport-agreement-is-essential-for-india/.

39 "India to Sign Maritime Transport Agreement with BIMSTEC during PM Modi's Thailand Visit." *Sarkaritel.com*, March 29, 2025. https://www.sarkaritel.com/india-to-sign-maritime-transport-agreement-with-bimstec-during-pm-modis-thailand-visit/.

40 "BIMSTEC Master Plan for Transport Connectivity Asian Development Bank." *Asian Development Bank*, April 2022. https://www.adb.org/documents/bimstec-master-plan-transport-connectivity.

41 "Maritime Security: Memorandum of Understanding (MOU) Between the Information Fusion Centre - Indian Ocean Region and Regional Coordination Operations Centre." Press Information Bureau, February 22, 2023. https://pib.gov.in/PressRelease Page.aspx?PRID=190 1371.

42 "Joint Working Group on Counter-Terrorism and Transnational Crime." *BIMSTEC,* January 2023. https://bimstec.org/joint-working-group-on-counter-terrorism-and-transnational-crime.

43 "UNHCR: 569 Rohingya Died at Sea in 2023, Highest in Nine Years." *Al Jazeera*, January 24, 2024. https://www.aljazeera.com/news/2024/1/24/unhcr-569-rohingya-died-at-sea-in-2023-highest-in-nine-years. Al Jazeera,

44 "5,500 Kg of Methamphetamine Seized from Trawler near Andamans Is Biggest Drug Haul by ICG: Official." *The Hindu*, November 26, 2024. https://www.thehindu.com/news/national/5500-kg-of-methamphetamine-seized-from-trawler-near-andamans-is-biggest-drug-haul-by-icg-official/article68914711.ece.

7

Maritime Security in BIMSTEC: Navigating Complexities for Stability and Resilience in the Region

Soumya Tiwari and Faisal Ahmed

The BIMSTEC region is culturally vibrant, economically competitive and geo-politically significant. Countries, including India, Bangladesh, Myanmar, Thailand and Sri Lanka are dependent on fishing, maritime trade and other resources such as oil and gas.[1] This region has a complex and ambiguous landscape because of uncertain and rising geo-political risks. It is dominated by the strategic competition between India and China, as it allows access to vital sea lanes and is a gateway to the Indian Ocean Rim (IOR).[2] Thus, this dual competition has broader geo-political and security concerns. In a way, it highlights several implications for maritime security, coastal infrastructure development and diplomatic engagement for BIMSTEC nations.[3]

It is, therefore, imperative to understand the impact of geo-political factors like the Indo-Pacific strategy and China's Belt and Road Initiative (BRI) on the region.[3] The region's geo-political gravity is characterised by the inter-connectedness between marine security, geo-economic competitiveness and political stability. The foremost strategy to promote collaborative growth has been to reconcile economic interests with the management of geo-political issues and promotion of peaceful coexistence.[4] Countries in the region plan to reach a consensus by placing emphasis on non-traditional objectives, which includes protection of vital trade routes, improving connectivity and promoting economic cooperation. Policymakers and economists see this region as a unified maritime area promoting connectivity, expansion and economic advancement.[5]

Maritime Security

There are several perspectives on understanding this region. First and foremost is to see the region as an autonomous strategic system characterised by discrete dynamics and interrelationships. Another is to understand that maritime security in the Bay of Bengal requires recognising the region's intricacies with its broader framework and mechanisms. Several researchers have asserted that the Bay of Bengal (BoB) is at the centre of the Indian Ocean Region (IOR). This is primarily because interactions between nations in this region promote the objective of safeguarding the Sea Lines of Communication (SLOCs) through vigorous security alliances.[6] If seen from this perspective, it suggests that regional interactions must not be examined in isolation because multifarious actors are involved. Bay of Bengal analysts and experts perceive China as having a huge influence over the region because countries here rely entirely on Chinese assistance and investments for infrastructure development.[7] Lastly, this perspective sees the Bay region as a strategic buffer between the eastern IOR and the Western Pacific. Its advocates assert that Bay security dynamics might fuel a more complex rivalry between China and the United States.[9]

Analysts contend that the Bay's strategic position in South and Southeast Asia intensifies competition for strategic rivalry between Asia's dominant navies. In this way, the Bay, is central to its Pacific counterpart—the South China Sea, and is a crucial theme of maritime security in Asia.[8] While another set of economists and analysts view this region as being positioned between two significant geo-economic blocs, viz. the Association of Southeast Asian Nations (ASEAN) and the Bay of Bengal Initiative for Multi-Sectoral Technical and Economic Cooperation (BIMSTEC), thereby emerging as a potential hotspot for military exercises. Unlike the initial perspective, which focuses primarily on progress and prosperity in the Bay, the second viewpoint emphasises on the steadiness of economic power. The third interpretation centres on geo-politics and power competition as being fundamental to marine security.[9] This is not linked to the shared aim of the region and, therefore, we must understand that Bay states reveal more diverse forms of policies and procedures to ensure cohesive maritime security collaboration. Hence, India in this sense, tries to accentuate by gaining an edge of supremacy over the regions, protecting Sea Lines of Communication (SLOCs) and coastal interests.

It is, therefore, imperative to gauge on several fronts as to how BIMSTEC countries address these issues. Bangladesh, in this sense, has emphasised the need to resolve and address non-traditional security threats, including illegal fishing, human trafficking, etc. Myanmar, on the other hand, has called for addressing problems pertaining to maritime security. Sri Lanka wants to exploit its geo-economic and strategic position to expand its economic horizons and cater to the interests of significant regional stakeholders.[12] For instance, the approval for Chinese research at the Port of Hambantota despite India's protests often reveals the very inconsistent image on security. Thailand and other ASEAN members like Indonesia are engaged in economic and collaborative interests to ensure security in the Bay region and consensus-based decision-making.[10] Moreover, it is important to understand that enhancing maritime security in the Bay of Bengal requires a multi-faceted approach between BIMSTEC member states.

Although there are variances in their perceptions of maritime security, the viewpoints of Bay states appear to converge around Maritime Domain Awareness (MDA). Bay countries concur that comprehending the global marine domain necessitates an understanding of probable implications of issues related to national security, safety, economics and ecology. They agree that MDA should extend beyond detection and tracking of vessels to include identification and attribution of specific maritime activities.[11] In this regard, the initiative that could be taken in collaboration with other countries is to establish a BIMSTEC maritime information centre for real-time intelligence sharing. It is also important that public-private partnerships be encouraged for data sharing and technological advancement in maritime monitoring.

It is also imperative for the government to conduct joint naval exercises to counter piracy, illegal fishing and trafficking. It is also the need of the hour to strengthen legal frameworks and harmonise maritime laws across BIMSTEC nations to prosecute transnational maritime crises effectively. It is thus essential to implement strict port security measures under the International Ship and Port Facility Security (ISPS) Code. On the contrary, not all Bay navies possess interoperable tactical data connection systems to integrate naval communications between manned and unmanned units. Numerous militaries are just commencing the acquisition of tactical communications systems utilised by more sophisticated navies like the Indian Navy. The lack of pre-emptive data connectivity obstructs uninterrupted data exchange between the coastguards during maritime operations.[12]

In order to enhance maritime security in the region, it is necessary to develop a regional framework for sustainable fisheries management to overcome such issues and to counter Illegal, Unreported and Unregulated (IUU) fishing in particular. On the other hand, enforcing environmental security policies can also help to eradicate marine pollution and protect biodiversity. This will ensure smoother facilitation of maritime trade security protocols for safe passage of commercial vessels. Further, modernising coastal infrastructure can also guarantee better maritime surveillance and disaster resilience. It is the need of the hour to promote cooperation in climate adaptation strategies for coastal and maritime communities.

In fact, it is also important to ensure strong institutional frameworks and diplomacy dialogues. A strong and effective BIMSTEC Maritime Security Forum (BMSF) could serve as a platform for regular dialogue between maritime agencies of member countries. This will facilitate information sharing on maritime threats and on emerging security challenges. Additionally, it is imperative to conduct much stronger joint maritime exercises to improve coordination. It is also important for members to exchange bilateral and multilateral agreements, specifically on intelligence sharing, search and rescue operations and joint patrols to beef up regional security. By establishing a BIMSTEC Maritime Security Forum, intensifying diplomatic interactions and conforming to international maritime frameworks, BIMSTEC member states can improve maritime security. Such actions would enhance security of trade routes, safeguard marine resources and promote overall regional stability in the Bay of Bengal. By adopting a collaborative and organised strategy, BIMSTEC may become a pivotal entity in advancing marine security and economic development in the region. The above-mentioned policy measures are of utmost priority. However, we must be aware of micro-level challenges lying ahead, including developing regional protocols and guidelines on pollution. There is also a need for more scientific research on the impact of climate change and on fisheries in particular.[13] The legislation and regulations in coastal states must be synchronised and the humane treatment of fishermen must be guaranteed based on interactions with marine law enforcement organisations.[14]

The difficulties facing the Bay of Bengal region must not be postponed. BIMSTEC must take action before it is too late. The summit must initiate regular meetings of officials, with the cooperation of scientists and experts, to address illegal and unsustainable fishing and to avert future environmental degradation of the Bay of Bengal. Further, to have critical port infrastructure, BIMSTEC must implement a thorough and multifaceted approach to strengthen resilience of its essential port infrastructure. This includes disaster preparedness, security improvements, regional collaboration and policy-oriented strategies to address both natural and anthropogenic threats like terrorism, smuggling and cyberattacks. A robust, safe and technologically secured port network is essential for BIMSTEC's economic and maritime security. By incorporating disaster preparedness, advanced security technology, regional intelligence cooperation and policy-driven enforcement, BIMSTEC can prevent growing threats to its ports and guarantee sustainable, secure trade and maritime operations.

Conclusion

We can say that a collective understanding of the maritime area serves as the foundation for enhancing trust. An enhanced networked and enduring domain awareness capability can foster a greater feeling of community in the Bay region. A detailed, real-time overview of activity could serve as a foundation for enhanced coordination in the maritime commons. Maritime security agencies must address deficiencies in current arrangements, especially the absence of operational coherence in key sectors. The establishment of capabilities is equally essential. Bilateral and multilateral information security agreements should focus on enhancing collective capabilities to refuel, restock and repair maritime assets promptly. Regional security agencies must implement a network of local data connections to enhance communication.[15] A standardised operational framework and consensus on regulations would facilitate enhanced collaboration throughout the region. A cohesive strategy will allow partner states to exert significant influence over behaviour in the maritime domain.

We are yet to see how the world transitions itself in the face of rising geo-political risks, because at the micro level, both policies and the institutional framework need to be strengthened to yield better outcomes for the region and its member countries. As far as issues like climate change, enhancing security and illegal fishing are concerned, a mechanism of regular meetings and cooperation is needed. This must encompass planned summits to address emerging concerns, a humanitarian response contingency fund and the recognition of shared security risks, including terrorism, piracy and natural catastrophes.[16] To ensure the continued relevance and efficiency of BIMSTEC, resilience must be integrated. For India, this entails steering the organisation towards adopting a more holistic approach to regionalism to be of advantage all members. Furthermore, it must navigate the delicate balance between exerting its leadership and respecting the sovereignty and independence of its partner nations.

Interestingly, exhibiting a sincere commitment to regional stability and collaboration may facilitate inclusive growth and development. This may exemplify collaboration between South and Southeast Asian nations, potentially regarded as beneficiaries of improved peace, stability and development.

NOTES

1 Singh, Abhijit. "Maritime Security in the Bay of Bengal: Obstacles and Opportunities." *Observer Research Foundation.* May 14, 2024. https://www.orfonline.org/research/maritime-security-in-the-bay-of-bengal-obstacles-and-opportunities.

2 Prakash, Arun. "A Strategic Encirclement." *Indian Express.* April 25, 2017. https://indianexpress.com/article/opinion/columns/indias-political-and-security-establishment-needs-a-strategy-in-light-of-chinas-naval-expansion-4626796/.

3 Samaranayake, Nilanthi. "Special Report: China's Engagement with Smaller South Asian Countries." *US Institute of Peace.* April 2019. http://www.jstor.com/stable/resrep20220.

4 Xavier, Constantino, and Amitendu Palit. "Fostering Cooperation to Connect the Bay of Bengal Region." *Centre for Social and Economic Progress.* April 14, 2023. https://csep.org/reports/introduction-fostering-cooperation-to-connect-the-bay-of-bengal-region/.

5 Bhandari, Amit. "Unfinished Connectivity in the Bay of Bengal." *Gateway House.* October 21, 2021. https://www.gatewayhouse.in/unfinished-connectivity-bay-bengal/.

6 Naha, Alik. "Geostrategic Significance of the Bay of Bengal in India's Maritime Security Discourse." *The Journal of Territorial and Maritime Studies,* Vol.9, No.2, 2022. pp. 47-64.

7 Das, Udayan. "What Stagnates Regionalism in the Bay of Bengal?" *Hindustan Times.* https://www.hindustantimes.com/author/udayan-das-101650980874695.

8 Anwar, Anu. "Positioning the Bay of Bengal in the Great Game of the Indo-Pacific Fulcrum." *Journal of Indo-Pacific Affairs.* April 1, 2022. https://www.airuniversity.af.edu/JIPA/Display/Article/2980896/positioning-the-bay-of-bengal-in-the-great-game-of-the-indo-pacific-fulcrum/.

9 Ibid.

10 Gopal, Prakash. "Maritime Security Cooperation between India and Indonesia: Imperatives, Status and Prospects." *Sage Journals,* Vol.77, Issue 2. May 4, 2021. https://www.researchgate.net/publication/328039672_httpjournalssagepubcomdoiabs 10117 70887302X0730362

11 Bell, Curtis. "Stable Seas: Bay of Bengal." *One Earth Future,* March 16, 2020. https://www.stableseas.org/post/stable-seas-bay-of-bengal.

12 "Coast Guard to Get Modern Ships and Communication System Soon, PM Says." *The Financial Express,* February 21, 2022. https://thefinancialexpress.com.bd/national/coast-guard-to-get-modern-ships-and-communication-system-soon-pm-says-1644922239#google_vignette.

13 Rajamony, Venu. "A Sub-Regional Grouping That Must Get Back on Course." *The Hindu,* March 29, 2022. https://www.thehindu.com/opinion/op-ed/a-subregional-grouping-that-must-get-back-on-course/article65268299.ece.

14 Ibid.

15 Singh, Abhijit. "Maritime Security in the Bay of Bengal: Obstacles and Opportunities." *Observer Research Foundation*, May 14, 2024. https://www.orfonline.org/research/maritime-security-in-the-bay-of-bengal-obstacles-and-opportunities.

16 Deka, Bidisha."A Test of Resilience: Ensuring BIMSTEC's Cohesion during Political Turmoil in Bangladesh." *Asian Confluence*, September 16, 2024. https://www.asianconfluence.org/publication-details-full/a-test-of-resilience-ensuring-bimstec-s-cohesion-during-political-turmoil-in-bangladesh.

8

Netting Cooperation: A Framework for Fisheries-Centric Collaborative Action among BIMSTEC Countries

Pandian Krishnan, Murugesan SriHari and Rajdeep Mukherjee

The Bay of Bengal Initiative for Multi-Sectoral Technical and Economic Cooperation (BIMSTEC) brings together seven nations in different stages of development, but facing common challenges of poverty, inequality and climate vulnerability. Across the region, nearly 300 million people still live in poverty, with coastal communities particularly vulnerable to the twin threats of ecological degradation and economic instability. The Bay of Bengal, shared by five BIMSTEC members (Bangladesh, India, Myanmar, Sri Lanka, and Thailand), represents both a problem and a potential solution. This biodiverse marine ecosystem supports over 40 million livelihoods through fisheries, yet faces severe threats from overexploitation, climate change and illegal fishing. Across the region, where rice forms the bedrock of daily sustenance for millions, fish plays an indispensable complementary role, not just as a protein source, but also as an essential accompaniment that makes rice-based meals palatable and nutritious.

This reality makes fisheries cooperation an urgent priority and unique opportunity for BIMSTEC. A collaborative framework could simultaneously address multiple challenges like lifting fishing communities out of poverty, ensuring regional food security, protecting shared marine resources and building climate resilience. By moving from competition to cooperation, BIMSTEC can transform the Bay of Bengal from a potential flashpoint into an engine of sustainable development, benefiting not just coastal states, but also landlocked members Bhutan and Nepal through improved regional trade and food systems.

The following analysis proposes a fisheries-centric approach to regional cooperation, outlining how BIMSTEC can harness this vital sector to reduce poverty, enhance food security and promote climate-resilient development across the Bay of Bengal region, with a focus on the marine fisheries sector, the area of competence of the Bay of Bengal Programme Inter-Governmental Organisation (BOBP-IGO).

Importance of Fisheries in BIMSTEC Countries

Marine and inland riverine capture fisheries are traditional activities in the region. Fish rearing was usually a homestead activity. However, over the years, inland capture fisheries has declined largely due to diverse usage of river waters and degradation of river health. Marine capture fisheries and aquaculture, on the other hand, has boomed and now constitutes major sources of fish in these countries (except Nepal and Bhutan) (Table 1).

Coastal and island BIMSTEC countries have adopted a planned approach towards development of the marine fisheries sector since 1950s, investing heavily on infrastructure and fishing technology and, thus, transforming the sector from a largely artisanal dispersed activity to a commercial centralised activity.

Table 1: State of Fisheries in the BIMSTEC Countries in 2022

Country	*Sources of production (tonnes)*			*Marine fisheries (%)*	*Per capita fish availability (kg)*
	Capture	*Culture*	*Total*		
Bangladesh	20,27,661	27,31,070	47,58,731	15	27.08
Bhutan	9	191	200	-	0.25
India	55,39,025	1,02,35,300	1,57,74,325	23	10.78
Myanmar	18,64,730	11,97,078	30,61,808	33	55.77
Nepal	21,000	87,385	1,08,385	-	3.55
Sri Lanka	3,32,623	59,080	3,91,703	70	17.64
Thailand	14,06,934	10,01,181	24,08,115	53	33.63

Source: FAO. 2024. FishStat: Global production by production source 1950-2022. [Accessed on 29 March 2024]. In: FishStatJ. Available at www.fao.org/fishery/en/statistics/software/fishstatj. Licence: CC-BY-4.0.

On the socio-economic front, this has led to three distinct advantages:

Increase in food availability: While BIMSTEC countries have achieved self-sufficiency in food production; they are still exposed to the vagaries of nature.

Until recently, countries had to import food, but now the increase in fish production has helped ease the situation. An important aspect of fish as a product is that it is available at all price points and while the commercially "low value" species such as sardines, lag in taste and usability, they pack a nearly equal nutritional value as a commercially high value species and, thus, remain a vehicle of protein security to the lower income groups.

Inclusive employment generator: Fisheries generate 20-44 full-time equivalent employment per 100 tonnes of fish (depending on the type of production and the level of technology), which translates into about seven to eight million jobs in the region, the bulk of which is in coastal areas, thus giving shape to the coastal economy. However, another key characteristic of fisheries is that women are traditionally involved as activities are largely carried out by family units. That is, fisheries also facilitate the participation of women in economic activities and ensure their empowerment.

Generating surplus: Coastal BIMSTEC countries are major exporters of fish. While Sri Lanka imports a large volume of fish, it still maintains a positive balance of trade. India and Bangladesh are largely exporters, earning sufficient foreign exchange to lessen trade deficit, while Thailand has emerged as the fish factory of the world, importing fish for re-exporting to different parts of the world.

Need for Cooperation: The Case of Marine Fisheries in the Bay of Bengal

The Bay of Bengal (BOB) is a complex and dynamic marine ecosystem shared by all BIMSTEC countries and is one of the 66 Large Marine Ecosystems (LME) in the world. In the Eastern Indian Ocean, nearly 80 percent of the catch comes from states bordering the Bay of Bengal Large Marine Ecosystem (BOBLME). It has many fish stocks, which are shared between states through the transboundary migration of fish (or) larvae.[1]

As marine fisheries in the region (BIMSTEC and non-BIMSTEC countries) transformed, so also is the intensity of marine fisheries production from the BOB. Between 1950 and 2019, marine production increased by 700 percent, (Figure 1) exerting pressure on fish stocks and the fisheries ecosystem accentuated by intensive trawling and pollution. While the BOB is exploited historically by multiple countries, including distant water fishing nations such as China, BIMSTEC coastal countries, have taken about 73 percent of the cumulated catch from 1950 to 2019 and have the largest stake in its sustainability. Taking into account fish stocks for which analytical data is available (n=286) by the SeaAroundUs Project, it shows that 24 percent of stocks are either collapsed or over-exploited, while only about 13 percent of stocks are still developing, indicating a strong need for management.

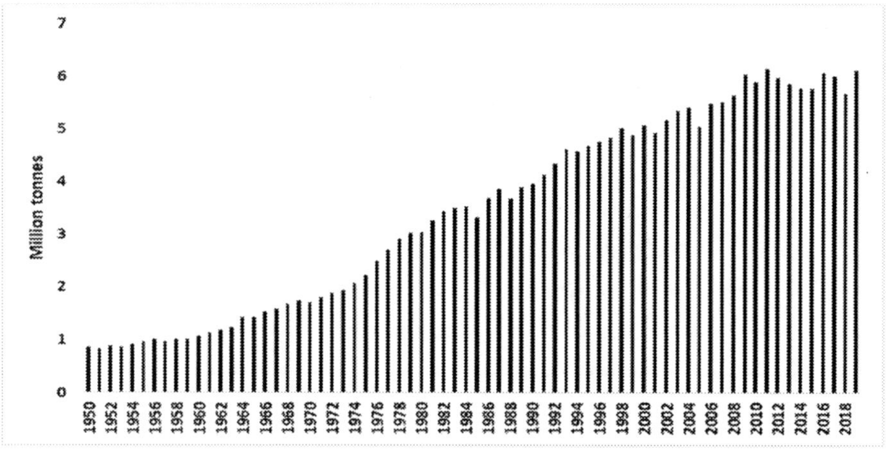

Figure 1: Growth of Marine Fisheries Production in the BOB

Source: SeaAroundUs

Despite geographical and ecological proximity, regional collaboration in fisheries management has remained limited. The need for cooperation is now crucial with severe depletion status of the stocks, standing at an unsustainable level of 36.5 percent.[2] Illegal, Unreported and Unregulated fishing (IUU) remains one of the primary challenges, significantly impacting fisheries in the area. A recent study revealed that out of 33 IUU hotspots identified in the Asia-Pacific region, eight hotspots were in the Bay of Bengal.[3] It is to be noted that illegal fishing costs around the Bay of Bengal as much as USD 10 billion per year.[4]

In addition to these significant threats, climate change vulnerability poses a looming challenge, affecting blue economy-related growth in these countries. The BOB is particularly vulnerable to climate shocks due to its high reliance on the blue economy. The sea surface temperature warming trend in the Indian Ocean was the strongest over the last seven decades (1950–2020), at a rate of 0.12°C per decade. Moreover, the maximum intensity of marine heatwaves is projected to increase. A reduction in surface chlorophyll concentrations is also anticipated.[5]

Since the Second BIMSTEC Ministerial Meeting (1998), the fisheries sector has been a priority sector for BIMSTEC cooperation. Given the critical role of fisheries in the region, BIMSTEC leaders reiterated the urgency for enhanced regional cooperation in fisheries/marine sciences, with a reaffirmed commitment to conservation, management and sustainable utilisation of marine resources. The leaders have also called on respective national agencies to actively explore avenues for collaboration, policy harmonisation and data sharing to strengthen sustainable marine fisheries across the BOB region.[5]

Framework of Cooperation

Exchange of Knowledge: Joint Research and Harmonisation

One of the issues in BOB fisheries management, which has been flagged by the SeaAroundUs analysis, is the widening gap between estimated catch and reported catch (Figure 2). While it does not per se indicate IUU fishing, it does indicate that fisheries information is not being properly captured, creating uncertainty about the impact of fishing in the Bay and over the flow of resources within the economy.

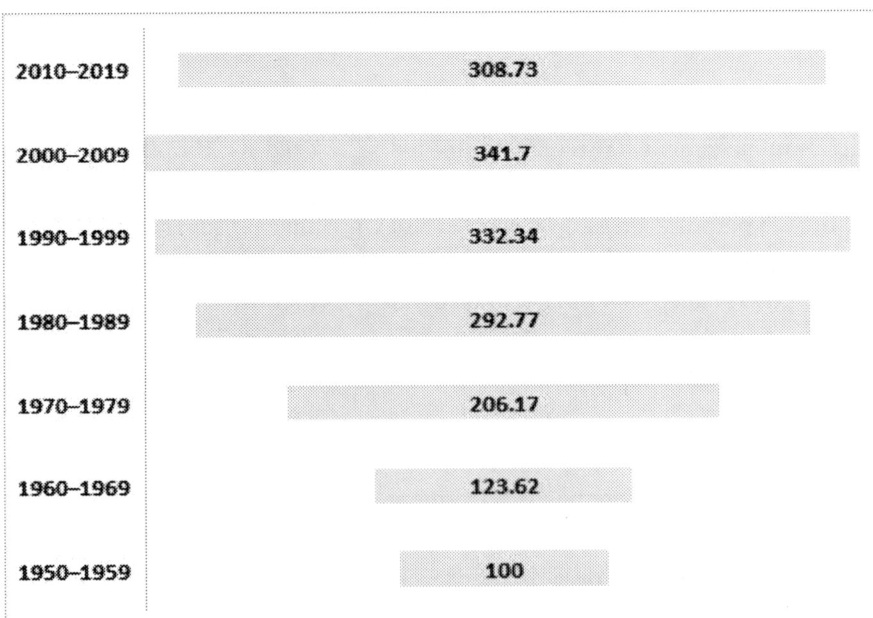

Figure 2: Gap between Total and Reported Catch (Index of unreported catch with 1950-59 as base)

Sharing scientific research and technological advancements can significantly improve understanding of marine ecosystems and facilitate better fisheries management. However, research institutions across BIMSTEC countries often operate in silos, hindering the exchange of knowledge despite the shared ecosystem and everyday challenges.

Considering the importance of fisheries, it is imperative for Bay of Bengal countries to work together in fisheries for mutual benefit. Establishing a robust communication and knowledge-sharing platform that facilitates exchange of ideas, best practices and lessons learned will ultimately promote a more robust and integrated regional community.[6]

India's commitment to this collaborative vision is reflected in the establishment of the **BIMSTEC-India Marine Research Network (BIMReN)** programme, being implemented by BOBP-IGO and the Ministry of External Affairs, Government of India, which offers twinning research grants and split-site fellowships for academic and research institutes in BIMSTEC countries to conduct collaborative fisheries research benefitting the region. BIMReN aligns with the core objectives of BIMSTEC, enhancing people-to-people contact and cultural cooperation, besides promoting key sectors such as fisheries, aquaculture, trade, and energy. Inspired by the *"Kochi Declaration for Cooperation in Marine Sciences among Bay of Bengal Littoral Countries,"*[7] *this initiative has yielded good results.* While this network is limited to academic exercises, there is strong need for extending such collaborative platforms to policy-level actions.

For this, a valuable parallel can be taken from multilateral naval exercises such as MILAN (a biennial multilateral naval exercise hosted by the Indian Navy), which brings together friendly navies for coordinated exercises, professional seminars and personnel exchanges. These activities enhance regional trust, interoperability and strategic cooperation. A similar model can be adopted in the fisheries sector, which can strengthen regional capacities, foster trust in the exchange of data and ensure sustainable management of shared marine resources. As MILAN reinforces maritime security cooperation, a united approach in fisheries science and governance could conserve and sustain marine ecosystems.

Curbing IUU Fishing: BIMSTEC-Coast Guard Consortium

As mentioned above, IUU fishing and its associated transnational organised crimes significantly undermine national and regional efforts to manage marine resources. Despite initiatives by individual littoral states, the trans-boundary nature of these activities demands a collective response. Regional groupings such as QUAD (Quadrilateral Security Dialogue) also reinforce the need for collaborative approaches to address challenges like IUU fishing in the Asia–Pacific.[8] Joint inspections are seen as one of the potential solutions for strengthening compliance and cooperation in regional fisheries management.[9]

In this context, a **BIMSTEC-Coast Guard/Navy Consortium** could bring together fisheries scientists, enforcement agencies, and naval/coast guard authorities to strengthen surveillance, intelligence sharing and enforcement across maritime boundaries. The Information Fusion Centre – Indian Ocean Region (IFC-IOR), which the Indian Navy hosts, can support this consortium. By integrating vessel-monitoring data into the IFC-IOR framework, BIMSTEC countries can improve maritime domain awareness specific to IUU fishing. Given that many regional fishery bodies rely on external agencies for at-sea patrols, joint patrols among BIMSTEC member states emerges as a practical solution. The platform has to be designed to evolve as a "joint fisheries management exercise" and not as a "military exercise."

A relevant example of practical regional cooperation comes from the Pacific Islands Forum nations, where the Forum Fisheries Agency (FFA) has demonstrated the capacity of shared surveillance in curbing IUU fishing. The Niue Treaty on Cooperation in Fisheries Surveillance and Law Enforcement, signed in 1992, provides a robust legal framework for data sharing and coordinated action. It states:

> "Each Party shall, to the extent permitted by its national laws and regulations, provide to the South Pacific Forum Fisheries Agency, or to any other Party directly, information relevant to the purposes of this Treaty, including but not limited to information about:
>
> (a) the location and movement of foreign fishing vessels;
>
> (b) foreign fishing vessel licensing; and
>
> (c) fisheries surveillance and law enforcement activities."

While MILAN and RIMPAC (Rim of the Pacific, the world's largest international maritime exercise) are regular maritime exercises, "Operation Kurukuru" is an annual joint exercise of Pacific Islands Forum nations and one of the most significant fisheries surveillance operations in the world. Starting in 2005, this operation has played a significant role in enhancing surveillance and enforcement and strengthened regional cooperation and capacity building. The recent two-week Operation Kurukuru-2024 covered approximately 21.3 million km^2,[10] which is nearly three times the size of the Bay of Bengal's Large Marine Ecosystem, which is over 6.2 million km^2.

Available data indicates that such cooperative measures have significantly reduced IUU fishing in the region.[11] Drawing lessons from these successful models, BIMSTEC can establish a similar mechanism (BIMSTEC-Coast Guard / Navy Consortium) and have fisheries-specific surveillance operations/exercises, including the coast guards and navies of member countries, in collaboration with international organisations to ensure sustainable and secure use of Bay of Bengal marine resources.

Harmonisation of Scientific Methodologies

A significant challenge in regional fisheries management within the Bay of Bengal is the lack of standardised scientific methodologies, particularly in stock assessment,[12] which serves as the cornerstone of sustainable fisheries management. Without harmonised approaches, countries risk mismanaging shared fish stocks. To address this, there is a need for developing and adopting regionally harmonised stock assessment methodologies. A standardised approach would ensure more accurate assessments of shared fish stocks and lead to coordinated management measures.

In response to this gap, the **Bay of Bengal Stock Assessment Network** (BOB-SAN) of practicing stock assessment professionals perform their tasks under the Bay of Bengal Programme Inter-Governmental Organisation (BOBP-IGO), which is the key nodal agency. BOB-SAN seeks to leverage the collective experience and technical expertise of its members to strengthen stock assessment practices and contribute toward coordinated regional fisheries management. The formalisation and recognition of BOB-SAN and the integration of its outputs into national and regional policy-making frameworks would ensure that harmonised stock assessment becomes a foundational element of the fisheries cooperation agenda of BIMSTEC.

Climate Resilience and Disaster Management

Regional cooperation is crucial for enhancing climate resilience and disaster management, which involves strengthening early warning systems, promoting inclusive risk governance and increasing financing for resilience. Coastal and marine fisheries are particularly climate-sensitive, with small-scale fishers being highly vulnerable due to limited capacity, inadequate infrastructure and poor access to technology and insurance.

Recognising the importance of addressing climate change, the BIMSTEC Secretariat has established the BIMSTEC Centre for Weather and Climate with the objective of promoting and encouraging fundamental and applied scientific research, capacity building and regional cooperation in weather and climate science. As an extension to this initiative, BIMSTEC nations can consider developing Standard Operating Procedures (SOPs) specifically focused on joint emergency response, rescue operations and post-disaster rehabilitation in the fisheries sector.

In addition, BIMSTEC can play a pivotal role in promoting region-wide investment in climate-resilient fishery infrastructure, including climate-proof harbours, climate-smart villages, storm shelters, and early warning dissemination systems. To support these efforts, BIMSTEC countries may jointly explore the establishment of a dedicated funding mechanism—the **BIMSTEC Fisheries Climate Resilience Fund (BIMSTEC-FCRF).** This fund can be used to support projects that build climate resilience in fisheries and coastal communities, including innovation in adaptive technologies, community-based risk management and ecosystem restoration.

Way Forward

The Bay of Bengal contributes to a significant portion of fish catch within the Indian Ocean. Marine capture fisheries in the Bay of Bengal Rim countries, knowingly or unknowingly, target the same stock leading to overfishing and stock decline or collapse. Global experience in fisheries management indicates that cooperation and coordinated action are vital to ensure long-term sustainability in fisheries management.

To address the multifaceted challenges facing Bay of Bengal fisheries and to harness the full potential of regional cooperation, BOB countries may consider preparing a coordinated, inclusive roadmap for the sustainable management of fisheries resources in the region.

Currently, BIMSTEC has established or planned various centres across different sectors, including the Energy Centre (Bangalore, India), Centre for Weather and Climate (Noida, India), Cultural Industries Observatory (to be established in Thimphu, Bhutan) and Technology Transfer Facility (Colombo, Sri Lanka). However, in the field of fisheries, there is currently only an Expert Group on Fisheries and Livestock under the Sector of Agricultural Cooperation.

Considering this pressing need, it is considered that a BIMSTEC Centre for Fisheries, on the lines of similar thematic centres, be established, to serve as a regional knowledge and coordination hub focused on marine fisheries governance, research, capacity building and innovation. Since the existing Regional Fisheries Management Organisation in the Indian Ocean has a species/group-specific focus, it often lacks a sub-regional pivot for ecological connectivity, small-scale fisheries and the political will of the countries. Further, the centre of excellence will be acting as a facilitator, not as a regulating body, in managing fishing and enforcing compliance. The Centre of Excellence will focus on all three dimensions of fisheries' governance: research, policy and innovation.

Furthermore, a Fisheries Action Plan might be developed under the framework, taking regional good practices from the Association of Southeast Asian Nations (ASEAN), such as the Strategic Plan of Action for ASEAN Cooperation on Fisheries 2021-2025. The action plan for fisheries could include evidence-based fisheries management, combating IUU fishing, increasing the climate resilience of fishers, facilitating trade among BIMSTEC countries and reducing the carbon footprint from fisheries. The Action Plan may align with Sustainable Development Goal 14, the FAO Code of Conduct for Responsible Fisheries, and, most importantly, the FAO's Voluntary Guidelines for Securing Sustainable Small-Scale Fisheries.

NOTES

1 Bay of Bengal Large Marine Ecosystem Project (BOBLME). *Transboundary Diagnostic Analysis. Volume 1: Issues, Proximate, and Root Causes*. 2012. https://www.boblme.org/documentRepository/BOBLME-2012-TDA-Volume_1.pdf

2 "The State of World Fisheries and Aquaculture 2024". *FAO*. p. 45.

3 Wilcox, C., Mann, V., Cannard, T., Ford, J., Hoshino, E. and Pascoe, S. "A Review of Illegal, Unreported and Unregulated Fishing Issues and Progress in the Asia-Pacific Fishery Commission Region. Bangkok". *FAO and Hobart: CSIRO*, 2021. https://doi.org/10.4060/cb2640en.

4 Benson, Jay. "Stable Seas: Bay of Bengal". Curtis Bell et.al, *One Earth Future Foundation*, January 2020. https://dx.doi.org/10.18289/OEF.2020.044.

5 "Fourth BIMSTEC Summit Declaration: Towards a Peaceful, Prosperous and Sustainable Bay of Bengal Region." *BIMSTEC*. Kathmandu, Nepal, August 30–31, 2018.

6 "HD-BOBP Dialogue on Development of a Marine Fisheries Research Network for the Bay of Bengal Region: Event Report." *Centre for Humanitarian Dialogue and Bay of Bengal Programme (BOBP)*. February 14, 2023. https://www.bobpigo.org/publications/HD-BOBP%20 Dialogue% 20on%20Development%20of%20a%20Marine%20Fisheries%20 Research%20Netwo rk%20for%20the %20Bay%20of%20Bengal%20Region.pdf

7 Ibid.

8 "Quad Leaders' Joint Statement." Ministry of External Affairs, Government of India. May

20, 2023. https://www.mea.gov.in/bilateral-documents.htm?dtl/37065/Quad_Leaders_ Joint _Statement.

9 "Review Conference on the Agreement for the Implementation of the Provisions of the United Nations Convention on the Law of the Sea relating to Conservation and Management of Straddling Fish Stocks and Highly Migratory Fish Stocks." December 10, 1982. A/ CONF.210/2016/5.

10 "Operation Kurukuru 2024 Successfully Concludes". *Pacific Islands Forum Fisheries Agency (FFA).* November 1, 2024. https://www.ffa.int/blog/operation-kurukuru-2024-successfully-concludes.

11 Yildiz, Auld. Okafor-Yarwood, K.G., Geymonat, I., Han, S.J., Blaha, D.P., Baumler, F., and Neat, F., "Regional Coordination and Cooperation in the Fight Against Illegal, Unreported, and Unregulated Fishing: Contrasting Experiences from Four Developing Regions".

12 "Bay of Bengal Programme Inter-Governmental Organisation (BOBP-IGO). Compendium of Stock Assessment Practices in South Asia." BOBP-IGO, Chennai, 2023.

PART IV

Climate, Environment, and Water Governance

9

BIMSTEC's Climate Future: Independent, Adaptive and Just

Sukrit Joshi and JR Bhatt

The Bay of Bengal Initiative for Multi-Sectoral Technical and Economic Cooperation (BIMSTEC) seeks to promote regional cooperation in South Asia. It has emerged as an alternative to the South Asian Association for Regional Cooperation (SAARC) due to geo-political challenges bridging South Asia and Southeast Asia.[1] Comprising seven member states—Bangladesh, Bhutan, India, Myanmar, Nepal, Sri Lanka, and Thailand—it represents an approximately 1.77 billion people, accounting for 22 percent of the world's population and 4.4 percent of the world's GDP.[2] The region, bound by deep cultural affinity, shared histories, religions, languages, trade practices and a reverence for nature, is connected via the Bay of Bengal. At the Sixth BIMSTEC Summit in Bangkok, Thailand, India's Prime Minister, Narendra Modi, proposed a 21-point action plan, which would act as a comprehensive regional blueprint, recognising the shared vulnerabilities, cultural context and opportunities of BIMSTEC nations.

The Bay of Bengal is s one of the world's 61 Large Marine Ecosystems (LMEs) and contains high marine biodiversity, including endangered and endemic species of plants and animals. The region hosts the Sundarbans, shared by India and Bangladesh, which has the world's largest mangroves. Serving as a vital source of livelihood for millions of people through fisheries and marine trade, the region features diverse economic structures, energy profiles and climate vulnerabilities.

The United Nations Framework Convention on Climate Change (UNFCCC) has urged developed countries, which contribute the most too historical and current global greenhouse gas emissions, to take responsibility for mitigation efforts. The per capita annual and historical cumulative emissions of BIMSTEC countries remains relatively low and their share of global emissions will rise as they work to address their social and developmental needs in order to improve the standard of living of their people. Given these complexities, a one-size-fits-all global climate policy is neither practical nor just. Instead, BIMSTEC nations must pursue sustainable growth and climate action on their own terms.

Economic and Development Priorities

BIMSTEC countries have experienced significant economic growth over the past decade. The region's total GDP was an estimated USD 4.5 trillion in 2022, up from USD 2.5 trillion in 2011.[2] It accounted for 4.1 percent of global trade. However, all BIMSTEC nations have a trade deficit, with variations in export-import ratios across different economies. Countries like India and Thailand exhibit relatively balanced trade flows, whereas Bangladesh, Nepal and Bhutan struggle with low export percentages relative to imports.

Table One summarises the National Circumstances of the countries in the BIMSTEC region.

Economic development remains a pressing priority in BIMSTEC, with large segments of the population still dependent on agriculture. Figure one (1) shows the share of agriculture in GDP is substantial in Myanmar, Nepal and Bhutan, whereas India and Thailand exhibit a more diversified economic structure, with strong industrial and service sectors. Rapid industrialisation and urbanisation, particularly in India and Bangladesh, demand significant energy resources to sustain growth.

Table 1: National Circumstances (2022)

Indicator	*Bangladesh*	*Bhutan*	*India*	*Myanmar*	*Nepal*	*Sri Lanka*	*Thailand*	*BIMSTEC*	*World*
Population, total (million)[3]	169.38	0.78	1,425.42	53.76	29.72	22.83	71.74	1,701.90	8,021.41
Total area (sq. km)[2]	1,30,170	38,140	29,73,190	6,52,700	1,43,350	61,864	5,10,890	45,10,304	12,99,48,830
Land area used for agricultural purposes (sq. km of gross cropped area)[4]	96,273	5,130	17,91,156	1,30,713	41,210	28,116	2,28,457	23,21,055	4,77,39,252
Forest and tree cover (sq. km)[4]	18,834	27,290	7,26,928	2,79,645	59,620	21,067	1,98,010	13,33,814	4,05,99,554
Urban population (percentage of total population)[4]	39.71	43.69	35.87	31.77	21.45	19.03	52.89	34.92	56.81
Life expectancy at birth, total (years)[4]	74	72	68	67	70	77	80	73	72
GDP (current million USD)[2]	4,32,906	2,898	34,28,512	65,163	39,749	74,586	4,95,646	45,39,460	10,16,29,391
GDP real growth rate in % (in constant 2015 USD)[2]	7.1	4.1	6.6	0.5	5.7	-6.9	3.3	2.9	3.1
Agriculture, forestry, and fishing, value added (current Million USD)[4]	51,615.74	425.20	5,57,998.00	13,903.81	8,613.15	6,300.16	43,243.25	6,82,099.32	43,26,680
Industry (including construction), value added (current million USD)[4]	1,56,077.00	922.36	8,47,894.00	23,810.01	5,016.59	22,101.61	1,74,230.00	12,30,051.56	2,77,03,700
Services, value added (current million USD)[4]	2,34,842.00	1,483.80	16,62,550.00	24,539.23	21,590.18	42,273.44	2,78,172.00	22,65,450.65	6,28,56,000
Exports of goods and services (current million USD)[4]	59,275.21	739.01	7,78,022.00	..	2,760.24	15,984.91	3,23,968.00	11,80,749.37	3,15,42,600
Imports of goods and services (current million USD)[4]	96,157.13	1,741.03	8,97,551.00	..	17,408.44	18,626.98	3,34,528.00	13,66,012.59	3,07,79,400
Trade (percentage of GDP)[2,4]	35.90	85.58	48.87	..	50.74	46.41	132.86	56.10	61.32
Access to electricity (percentage of population)[4]	99.4	100.0	99.2	73.7	91.3	100.0	99.9	94.8	91.3

Sources: UNCTAD, 2025[2]; UN Population Division, 2024[3]; World Bank, 2025[4].

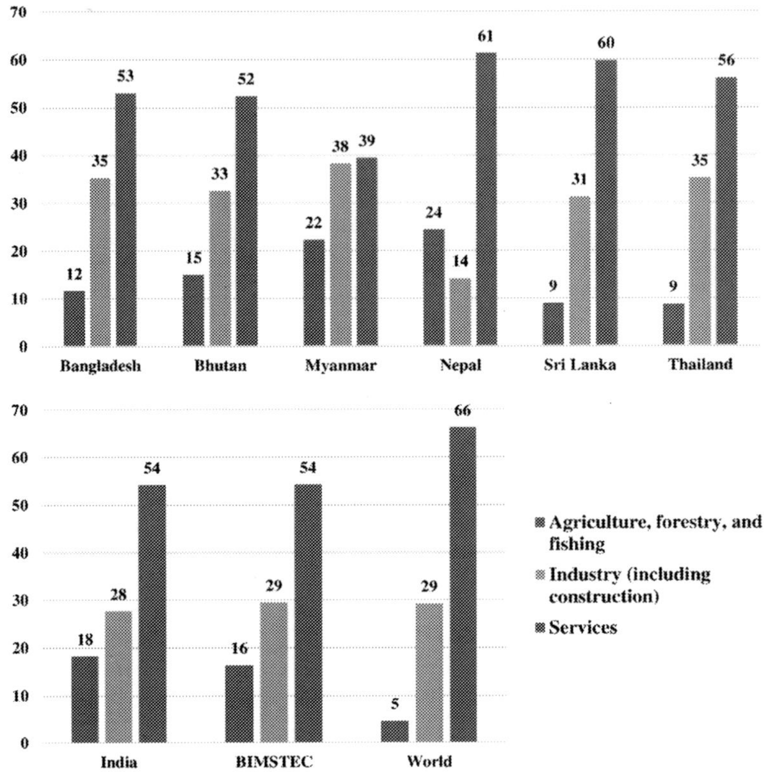

Figure 1: Percentage of Value Added to GDP from Economic Sectors

Source: World Bank, 2025.[4]

The BIMSTEC region faces a range of development issues that are deeply intertwined with the basic needs of its people, such as access to clean water, healthcare, education and sustainable livelihood. Agriculture is a vital for the region, especially for Bangladesh, Myanmar and Nepal, where the majority of the population depends on it for survival. These countries are also highly vulnerable to climate change, facing the threat of floods, droughts and rising sea levels, all three of which, hinder development.

The region has a diverse developmental landscape. The United Nations currently classifies Bangladesh, Myanmar and Nepal as Least Developed Countries (LDCs). Bangladesh, Bhutan and Nepal are expected to be declared developing countries by 2026.[5] These development disparities pose a challenge for BIMSTEC member nations to either individually or collectively address the impacts of climate change, especially when they have little or no role to play in precipitating the problem.

Vulnerability and Impacts

The BIMSTEC region as a whole, houses 22 percent of the population and faces almost all types of climate risks, especially heatwaves and water stress, besides urban-rural disparities. Table Two shows Myanmar and India being in the list of the top ten most climate-impacted countries due to their exposure to heatwaves, droughts, tropical cyclones and sea-level rise. Bhutan and Nepal, which are landlocked while emitting little greenhouse gases, face high risk from glacier retreat, Glacial Lake Outburst Flood (GLOF) events and landslides, affecting all sectors of the economy, including hydropower and agriculture.

Table 2: Key Vulnerabilities, Impacts and Risks due to Climate Change in BIMSTEC Nations

Country	*Key Climate Vulnerabilities*	*Major Impacts*	*Climate Risk Index Rank (1993-2022)*
Bangladesh	Sea-level rise, cyclones, floods	Coastal erosion, displacement, food insecurity	31
Bhutan	Glacial lake outburst floods (GLOF), Glacier retreat, landslides	Hydropower disruption, biodiversity loss	88
India	Heatwaves, droughts, floods	Urban stress, water scarcity, crop failures	6
Myanmar	Cyclones, deforestation, floods	Coastal damage, food insecurity, migration	4
Nepal	GLOF events, landslides, erratic rainfall	Hydropower risk, agriculture disruption	69
Sri Lanka	Droughts, floods, rising seas	Water scarcity, crop loss, economic shocks	59
Thailand	Urban floods, sea-level rise, droughts	Infrastructure damage, tourism loss	30

Source: Climate Risk Index, 2025.[6]

Energy Resources and Consumption Patterns

The BIMSTEC region is endowed with natural resources comprising 331 billion tonnes of coal, 718 million tonnes of oil, 76 trillion cubic feet (TCF) of natural gas, 386 GW of large hydropower and renewable energy of 1359 GW potential.[7] India, Myanmar and Thailand possess coal reserves, while Bhutan and Nepal have hydropower capacity. Primary energy consumption within BIMSTEC is largely dependent on coal and oil products, with hydro, solar and wind energy share also increasing gradually. Coal (50 percent) and oil (29 percent) together contributed to 79 percent of the region's primary energy supply in 2023.[8] The bulk of hydropower potential is in India, Myanmar, Nepal and Bhutan. India also has the highest coal reserves and large renewable energy (solar and wind) potential. Myanmar, Thailand and Bangladesh also have gas reserves. There is also Sri Lanka, where exploration activities are underway for oil and gas. Therefore, there could be discoveries of proven reserves in the near future.

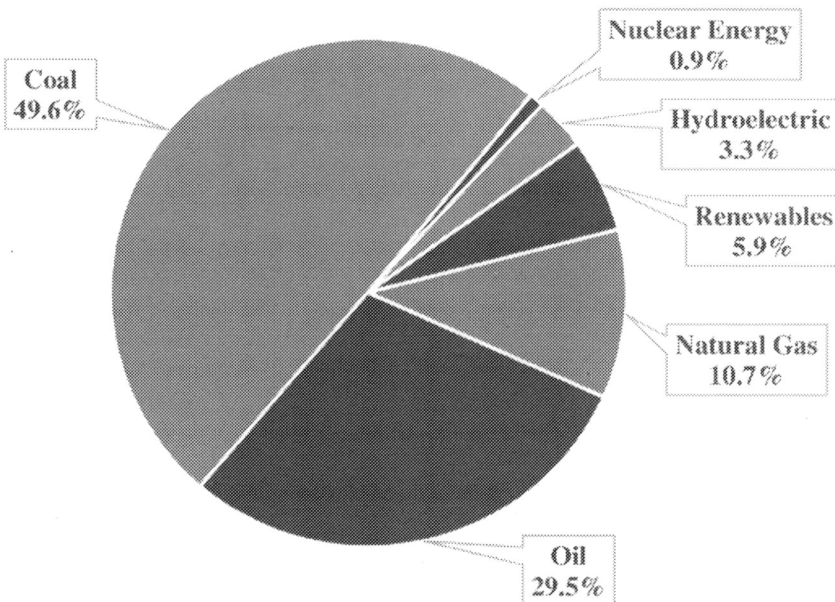

Figure 2: Primary Energy Consumption by Fuel (2023) in BIMSTEC Region in GWh
Source: EI, 2025.[8]

The installed capacity of electricity in the BIMSTEC region increased by 47 percent between 2014 and 2019, from 297 GW in 2014 to 438 GW in 2019.[7] The Compound Annual Growth Rate (CAGR) of installed capacity during this period was eight percent. The steepest growth rate was in renewables, which increased at a CAGR of 23 percent. In absolute terms, the highest capacity addition was for coal power plants, where 60.5 GW was added between 2014 and 2019.[7]

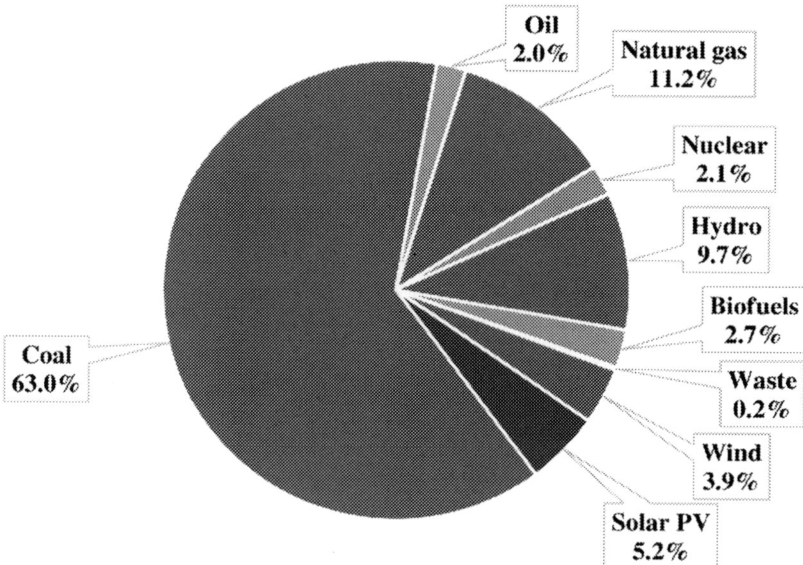

Figure 3: Electricity Generation (2022) in GWh in BIMSTEC Region

Source: IEA, 2022.[9]

Regional Energy Cooperation

BIMSTEC nations possess diverse and complementary energy resources, making regional power trade highly strategic and a mutually beneficial area of cooperation. These have a long history of bilateral cooperation in the electricity sector. Table Three details the various cross-border transmission interconnections and power trades between many BIMSTEC member states. This includes the export of power from hydropower plants in Bhutan and Nepal to India and the import of power from India by Bangladesh, Nepal, and to a very small extent, Myanmar. The renewable energy potential, especially solar and wind, in Sri Lanka and Thailand, is seen as part of the interconnected grid. An MoU for the BIMSTEC Grid Interconnection framework[10] has been signed by member states and the establishment of the BIMSTEC Energy Centre has already been proposed and discussed in meetings of the BIMSTEC Energy Ministers. Regional energy cooperation among BIMSTEC nations is crucial not only for energy security but also for accelerating the transition to net zero in line with the Paris Agreement goals.

Table 3: Interconnection of Electricity Grids between India and BIMSTEC Countries

Country	*Descriptor*	*Initiatives*
Bangladesh	Overview	• Bangladesh India Friendship Power Company Limited (BIFPCL), a 50:50 Joint Venture company of NTPC and Bangladesh Power Development Board (BPDB) is setting up a coal-based power plant of 1320 MW capacity in Khulna and has been christened as 'Maitree Super Thermal Power Plant' financed by Indian EXIM Bank for USD 1.6 Billion and implemented by BHEL.
	Existing transmission lines	• Bangladesh has been connected with India with transfer capacity of 1160 MW through three existing interconnections (CEA, 2021)[11]
		1. 1000 MW through Bahrampur (India) to Bheramara (Bangladesh) 400 kV 2x D/c line with 2x500 MW HVDC back-to-back station at Bheramara
		2. 160 MW through Surajmaninagar (India) to North Comilla (Bangladesh) – South Comilla (Bangladesh) 400 kV D/c link (presently operated at 132 kV)
		3. Implementation of the 765kV D/C Katihar (India) – Parbotipur (Bangladesh) – Bornagar (India) cross border link has been agreed, and modalities of its implementation are being finalised
	Support for future projects	• Assisting Bangladesh in construction of transmission lines as well as power evacuation facilities from the upcoming Rooppur Nuclear Plant in Bangladesh using concessional credits (MEA, 2021).[12]
		• Constructing 1320 MW Maitree Super Thermal Power Project at Rampal in Bangladesh, with Unit 1 commissioned in November 2021 and Unit-2 in March 2022.[10]
	Private partnership	• Adani Power Ltd signed an MoU with Bangladesh Power Development Board in November 2017 for supply of power to Bangladesh from a 1600 MW coal-based plant which is being constructed in Godda, Jharkhand.
		• L&T have commissioned 225 MW at Sikalbaha (near Chittagong), and the 360 MW project at Bheramara (Kushtia District, Khulna Division), reiterating the growth and potential of this area.
Bhutan	Overview	• Out of the present hydro-capacity of 2326 MW, 2136 MW has been developed with Indian technical and financial assistance. Further, 2820 MW is under construction and 7285 MW is under various stages of development with Indian technical and financial assistance. (Ministry of Power, Government of India, 2022)[13]
	Existing transmission lines	• Presently, about 2070 MW power from the existing hydro projects in Bhutan is being imported to India from Bhutan. The associated cross-border transmission system for evacuation and transfer of power from these HEPs is being operated in synchronism with the Indian Grid.[9]

Country	*Descriptor*	*Initiatives*
		• Bulk power generated at Hydro Electric Projects (HEP) at Tala HEP (1020 MW), Chukha HEP (336 MW), Kurichu HEP (60 MW) and Mangdechu HEP (720 MW), inaugurated in 2019, is being exported to India through 400kV, 220kV and 132kV lines.[9]
	Support for future projects	• Punatsangchu-I (1200MW), Punatsangchu-II (1020MW) and Kholongchhu (600 MW) HEPs are under construction and expected to be commissioned in 2024-25.[9]
Nepal	Overview	• Agreement on 'Electric Power Trade, Cross-border Transmission Interconnection and Grid Connectivity' between India and Nepal was signed in 2014.
		• NTPC Vidyut Vyapar Nigam (NVVN) has been designated as the nodal agency for cross border trading of electricity with Nepal's nodal agency Nepal Electricity Authority (NEA).
	Existing transmission lines	• Total of 1000 MW of power is being exported to Nepal: – 350 MW through 11kV, 33kV, 132 kV voltage level transmission lines and
		– 650 MW between Dhalkebar (Nepal) – Muzaffarpur (India) 1st high capacity 400 kV D/C line.[9]
	Support for future projects	• Second High Capacity 400 kV Gorakhpur – New Butwal D/c (Quad) line is being taken up for implementation to facilitate increased transfer of power between the two countries.[9]
		• For evacuating power from Arun-3 (900MW) HEP in Nepal and other hydro projects in vicinity in future, Arun-3 HEP (Nepal) – Dhalkebar (Nepal) – Sitamarhi (India) 400 kV D/c (Quad) line is under consideration.[9]
		• Second circuit of Kataiya-Kusaha and Raxaul-Parwanipur 132kV lines.[9]
		• New 132kV radial lines from Uttar Pradesh to Nepal.[11]
		• India–Nepal Interconnection Master Plan.[11]
	Private partnership	• Lower Arun project was awarded to SJVNL. A consortium led by GMR is developing the 900 MW Upper Karnali hydroelectric projects in western Nepal. Upper Karnali is an export-oriented project, where power is to be supplied to India and Bangladesh. Private sector participation in the hydropower sector holds enormous promise.[9]
Myanmar	Overview	• Hydro-potential in Myanmar is about 108GW with exploitable capacity of about 43GW. However, presently only 3-4GW has been tapped.[11]
	Existing transmission lines	• India is providing about 2-3 MW of power since 2016 from Manipur (India) to Myanmar through 11 kV transmission line from Moreh in Manipur (India) to Tamu town in Myanmar.[9]
	Support for future projects	• Further, a 500 MW HVDC interconnection between India (Imphal) and Myanmar (Tamu) is under discussion. Additionally,

Country	*Descriptor*	*Initiatives*
		low voltage radial interconnection between India and Myanmar from Indian states (Arunachal Pradesh, Manipur, Mizoram and Nagaland) are under consideration.[10] • Discussions on high-capacity voltage grid interconnection between India and Myanmar have taken place. REC Transmission Projects Company Limited offered a proposal for rural electrification of Myanmar.[10]
Sri Lanka	Overview	• Trincomalee Power Company Ltd. (TPCL) is a joint venture Company between NTPC Ltd. and Ceylon Electricity Board, Sri Lanka (CEB) incorporated in 2011. NTPC and CEB each hold 50% equity share capital of the Company.[11]
		• Joint Venture & Shareholders' Agreement (JVSHA) for incorporating a new JV company in Sri Lanka has been signed between NTPC and CEB.[11]
	Support for future projects	• Phase-1: 1000MW Madurai-New (India) to New Habarana (Sri Lanka) HVDC (overhead) line (about 397km) along with 500MW VSC based HVDC terminals at both ends by 2025.[11]
		• Phase-2: 2nd 500MW VSC based HVDC terminals at Madurai-New and New Habarana: by 2030.[11]
		• Development of 50MW solar power project at Sampur by TPCL.[11]
		• Development of 300 MW LNG Power Project at Kerawalapitiya by the proposed JVSHA incorporated joint venture company.[11]

Source: Authors' compilation from annual reports and bilaterally signed MoUs.

Contribution of BIMSTEC Countries to Global GHG Emissions

BIMSTEC countries have contributed only about 6 percent of historical cumulative GHG emissions, despite housing 22 percent of the world's population. These countries should not be held to the same emissions reduction commitments as historically high-emitting developed countries and petrostates. The countries in BIMSTEC together contributed to a mere 9 percent of global GHG emissions for the year 2023. The BIMSTEC region should together advocate for fairer emission targets adhering to the foundational principles of the UNFCCC and their fair share of carbon budgets. The per capita emissions of BIMSTEC nations, namely, Bangladesh (1277.21 kgCO_2eq per capita), Bhutan (3268.12 kgCO_2eq per capita), India (2565.94 kgCO_2eq per capita), Myanmar (1717.48 kgCO_2eq per capita), Nepal (1453.97 kgCO_2eq per capita), Sri Lanka (1232.13 kgCO_2eq per capita) and Thailand (5132.32 kgCO_2eq per capita), were less than the global per capita emissions (6216.22 kgCO_2eq per capita) in 2024. BIMSTEC nations continue to address GHG emissions, particularly those of methane, in line with their national contexts and UNFCCC principles, prioritizing poverty alleviation and sustainable development. The developed countries, who are yet to agree on the definition of climate finance, need to honour their commitments under UNFCCC to provide the means of implementation to developing countries, including both climate-specific finance and technology transfer that is adequate in terms of scale, scope and speed. The developed countries have prescribed that developing countries should decarbonise, while the fact of the matter is that they haven't even carbonised. "Just transitions" should be "global just transitions" and not focus on "intra-country transitions within BIMSTEC countries". Developed countries must take the lead in mitigating climate change, while developing countries balance mitigation with their pressing domestic developmental needs in the near term.

Table 4: Total GHG Emissions of BIMSTEC Countries for the Year 2023

Country	*Population (in mn)*	*Cumulative (1750-2019) in $GgCO_2eq$*	*Annual Emission (2023) in $GgCO_2eq$*	*Per Capita Emissions ($kgCO_2$ per person)*
Bangladesh	171	10115900	219000	1277.21
Bhutan	1	159083	2570	3268.12
India	1438	127116000	3690000	2565.94
Sri Lanka	54	1615538	33400	1232.13
Myanmar	30	4080890	66700	1717.48
Nepal	23	2805460	51000	1453.97
Thailand	72	13240930	368000	5132.32
BIMSTEC	1774	159133801	4430670	2498.08
World	8092	2565334000	50300000	6216.22

Sources: Gütschow, J. et.al.;[14] UN Population Division, 2024.[3]

Cooperation among BIMSTEC Countries

Cooperation within BIMSTEC focuses on various sectors and sub-sectors led by different member countries. Countries are already strengthening cooperation on maritime connectivity, trade, currency cooperation, counterterrorism, trans-national crime and payment mechanisms such as UPI bilaterally, trilaterally and through extant BIMSTEC institutions.

In addition to this, BIMSTEC nations are strengthening cooperation in weather prediction, climate modelling and scientific capacity building. The Bay of Bengal Initiative for Multi-Sectoral Technical and Economic Cooperation Centre for Weather and Climate (BCWC) was established after the signing of a

Memorandum of Association in March 2014 at the National Centre for Medium Range Weather Forecasting, India.[15] It plays a key role in regional disaster risk reduction through annual workshops, training, real-time forecast sharing and regular virtual discussions with member country scientists to strengthen joint research and forecasting efforts.

Countries of BIMSTEC, as well as BIMSTEC as a grouping, should be encouraged to ratify some key international initiatives. Thailand may be requested to ratify the International Solar Alliance (ISA), and both Thailand and Myanmar may also like to be part of the Coalition for Disaster Resilient Infrastructure (CDRI). The BIMSTEC nations possess substantial biomass and biogas potential and may be integrated into the Global Biofuels Alliance. This will boost regional synergy in renewable energy and sustainable biofuel development. Given the challenge of Climate Change looming large, there is need among BIMSTEC nations to support real-time data exchange and sharing of best practices in early warning systems, disaster resilience and risk-informed development. In the wake of the recent earthquake in Myanmar (March 2025) also affecting Thailand, it becomes even more urgent to synergise efforts in the area of disaster risk reduction and become part of the CDRI. This is all the more important because as per IPCC Sixth Assessment Report (AR6) Working Group II, several categories of extreme events are likely to increase in frequency, intensity and duration with rising temperatures.[16]

Each BIMSTEC member may like to identify its endogenous energy reserve(s) bestowed by Mother Nature. This should be the workhorse for its economic development, as it only can provide the requisite energy security. The evaluation of its needs and deployment of the resources need to be irrespective of technology availability. The required technology, if not already harnessed (transferred and being domestically manufactured), needs to be transferred from other countries. In the rare case that technology has not been established anywhere, it should be developed locally. In both cases, i.e., technology development as well as transfer, India can play a central role. Technology activities, even internal capacity building specifically, as part of development, can take decades. In such an intervening period, India must build coal-fired power plants in its eastern part, which is also coal-rich, to supply electricity to these member states. The contract needs to be on commercial terms for sustained viability and for investment in transmission networks outside Indian territory and on a sharing basis for capital expenditure of the power plant.

Imposing uniform decarbonisation targets without considering national circumstances could stifle economic growth and poverty alleviation efforts in the BIMSTEC. With the US and several EU nations showing signs of retreat or delay in fulfilling their climate commitments, the burden of addressing climate change should not be unfairly shifted onto BIMSTEC nations which are already contending with pressing developmental challenges. Strengthening BIMSTEC institutions and enhancing their efficiency must continue. Structuring connectivity projects securely and effectively, alongside business integration and stronger trade links, will be key to making BIMSTEC a pivotal force in the Bay of Bengal. BIMSTEC nations may like to present a united front against geoengineering technologies like Solar Radiation Modification (SRM) and continue strengthening their collaboration on climate change adaptation efforts.[17] Adaptation is and will continue to remain a challenge for BIMSTEC countries. Development remains the foremost priority in the fight against climate change-related adaptation issues. The rich biodiversity in the BIMSTEC region could be harnessed appropriately for providing the necessary bulwark against the impacts of climate change.

The BIMSTEC countries collectively experience the vagaries of weather unique to the Bay of Bengal region, share a rich cultural heritage, and face similar developmental challenges. For the Bay of Bengal region to progress cohesively and reduce the developmental deficit, these nations must pursue regional cooperation while aligning with their individual national interests. They must also simultaneously address the global challenge of climate change based on the foundational principles of the UNFCCC, including equity and the principle of common but differentiated responsibilities and respective capabilities.

NOTES

1 "BIMSTEC: An Idea Whose Time Has Come?," *Observer Research Foundation.* New Delhi. 2023. https://www.orfonline.org/english/research/bimstec-an-idea-whose-time-has-come

2 "UNCTAD Handbook of Statistics 2023." *United Nations Conference on Trade and Development.* 2025. https://unctad.org/system/files/official-document/tdstat48_en.pdf

3 "World Population Prospects". Population Division. *United Nations.* 2024 https://population.un.org/wpp/

4 "World Development Indicator." *World Bank.* 2025. https://databank.worldbank.org/source/worlddevelopment-indicators

5 Chaudhary, Arbind, and Ramesh C. Paudel. "Navigating Economic Growth Challenges in Developing Countries: A Case Study of BIMSTEC." *Cogent Social Sciences* 10, no. 1, November 26, 2024. https://doi.org/10.1080/23311886.2024.2431591

6 "Climate Risk Index 2025." *Germanwatch e.V.* 2025 https://www.germanwatch.org/en/cri

7 "BIMSTEC Energy Outlook 2035." *South Asia Regional Initiative for Energy Integration. Integrated Research and Action for Development (IRADe).* 2021 https://irade.org/Bimstec%20Final%20Report%20Energy%20Outlook-2035.pdf

8 "Statistical Review of World Energy." *Energy Institute.* 2024. https://www.energyinst.org/__data/assets/pdf_file/0004/1055542/EI_Stat_Review_PDF_single_3.pdf

9 "Energy Statistics Data Browser." *International Energy Agency.* 2023 https://www.iea.org/data-and-statistics/data-tools/energy-statistics-data-browser?country=WORLD&fuel= Energy %20supply&indicator=TESbySource

10 BIMSTEC. (2018). Memorandum of Understanding for the Establishment of BIMSTEC Grid Interconnection. Bay of Bengal Initiative for Multi-Sectoral Technical and Economic Cooperation. https://bimstec.org/images/content_page_pdf/1696679515_Signed%20 Copy% 20of%20Memorandum%20of%20Understanding%20for%20the%20Establish ment%20 of%20 BIMSTEC% 20Grid%20Interconnection%20(1).pdf

11 "CEA Annual Report 2021-22." *Central Electricity Authority.*2021. https://cea.nic.in/wp-content/uploads/annual_reports/2022/AR_2021_22_dated_03.11.2022.pdf

12 "Foreign Secretary's Remarks at the Inauguration of the South Asia Group on Energy at the Research and Information System for Developing Countries." Ministry of External Affairs, Government of India. 2021.. https://www.mea.gov.in/Speeches-Statements.htm?dtl/33611/Foreign+Secretarys+Remarks+at+the+Inauguration+of+the+South+Asia+Group+on+Energy+at+the+ Research+ and+Inform ation+System+for+Developing+Countries

13 "Annual Report 2021-22." Ministry of Power, Government of India. 2022. https://powermin.gov.in/sites/default/files/uploads/MOP_Annual_Report_Eng_2021-22.pdf

14 Gütschow, J. et al. "The PRIMAP-Hist National Historical Emissions Time Series (1750-2023) v2.6.1. Zenodo." *Earth System Science Data.* 2025 https://doi.org/10.5281/zenodo.15016289

15 "BIMSTEC Centre for Weather and Climate (BCWC)." *Bay of Bengal Initiative for Multi-Sectoral Technical and Economic Cooperation.* 2025 https://bimstec.org/governing-board-of-bimstec-centre-for-weather-and-climate-bcwc-

16 IPCC. (2022). Climate change 2022: Impacts, adaptation and vulnerability. Contribution of Working Group II to the Sixth Assessment Report of the Intergovernmental Panel on Climate Change Cambridge University Press. https://doi.org/10.1017/9781009325844

17 Bhatt, J. R. (2024). Managing the sun to manage global warming? National Security, 67–72. https://doi.org/10.32381/NS

10

Enhancing Cooperation and Collaboration of India with BIMSTEC Countries for Climate Smart Agriculture

Suhas P. Wani

The Bay of Bengal, extending to 2090 kilometres, is the lifeline connecting BIMSTEC, an international organisation of seven South Asian and Southeast Asian countries, dependent on the Bay of Bengal. It was formed in 1997. BIMSTEC has identified fourteen sectors, including fisheries, agriculture, poverty alleviation, environment and climate change, cultural change, etc., for collaboration.

Need for Strengthening Collaboration in Agriculture amongst BIMSTEC Countries

All BIMSTEC countries are dependent on agriculture and the fisheries sector, which contributed 8.5 percent to 23.4 percent of GDP of these countries in 2021. Each country has its unique products for export[4] and the increased collaboration between these countries will strengthen the economy of member countries and enable them to tackle challenges of poverty, malnutrition, climate change, water scarcity, land degradation and enhance productivity and exports globally. Agriculture is acquiring a renewed importance for gainful employment to keep pace with a growing workforce in countries like India.[1] The greatest challenge in the twenty-first century for humankind is to have food, nutrition and income security, as more than 690 million people or 8.9 percent of the world population were still hungry in 2019. This was expected to go up by a further 60 million in five years, i.e., 2024, providing a huge challenge for achieving the "Zero Hunger" target by 2030.[2]

Increasing Population and Increasing Land Degradation with Growing Water Scarcity

The increasing population in BIMSTEC member countries (1.8 billion in 2020) is a cause of worry in terms of ensuring food and nutritional security. India alone contributes 1.4 billion people at present and as agriculture employs a large population (26 percent to 62 percent) in BIMSTEC countries,[3] it has a huge potential to transform economies and ensure sustainability in the region. Increased urbanisation and land degradation is limiting agricultural productivity and sustainability. Although, BIMSTEC countries contribute 10.67 percent to global trade and ten percent fish is exported globally, climate change is affecting sustainability. Increasing population and the mismanagement of water resources have reduced water availability as the present generation considers water God's gift. India, Bangladesh, Nepal, Sri Lanka and northern Thailand face severe water scarcity, while countries like Myanmar and Bhutan have relatively abundant water resources. India as the most populated nation in the region (1.36 billion), has been a water-deficient nation since 2013, with decreased, water availability of 977 m^3 capita.[1] Water scarcity could be physical, economic, or institutional. Globally about four billion people face severe physical water scarcity.

India with 1150 mm of annual rainfall, but the mismanagement of water resources, particularly in agriculture, creates scarcity. Water stress is primarily a blue water issue and large opportunities in managing rain-fed areas, (green water), as only 0.27 billion people will face water scarcity, as against 6.5 billion facing blue water stress by 2050 if both green and blue water are considered. Growing population impacts water availability for food production, as 80 percent of water withdrawals in India are for agriculture. Several Indian cities like Mumbai, Aurangabad, Bengaluru, Chennai, Coimbatore, Hyderabad, etc., face drinking water scarcity. India, with the largest arable agricultural land, has ensured food security for 1.4 billion people, with 332.3 million tonnes production in 2023-2024 by transforming the "ship-to-mouth" situation of the 1960s to "overflowing grain godowns." The challenges for India[4] and other BIMSTEC countries in the 21st century are:

- Water scarcity
- Growing population and increasing incomes
- Poverty elimination
- Minimising land degradation
- Large yield gaps with low crop yields

- Climate variability and impacts of climate change
- Integrated watershed management emphasising efficient use of green water (soil moisture)
- Rainwater harvesting, and its efficient use through drip, sprinklers
- Need-based irrigation scheduling using IT-Apps
- The new paradigm of "Fork to Farm" overcoming the minimum support price (MSP) culture to agro-eco region (AER) and market-based crop planning.

Low Crop Yields and Large Yield Gaps

Crop yields are low in developing countries in Asia, Africa, WANA and Latin America, with large yield gaps (0.5 to 5 t ha^{-1}) based on the agro-eco region and the technologies used by farmers.[5,6,7] The absence of a holistic approach to target system-level productivity, value-chains and market linkages along with climate change could widen these yield gaps further, unless technological innovations are taken to the farmer's doorstep urgently.[8]

Lack of extension support and timely availability of agriculture-related information to farmers

In India, 59 percent of farmers do not get any extension support and government machinery supports only eleven percent of farmers, while 30 percent get support from other sources,[9] which severely hampers their ability to increase productivity and income and reduce vulnerability.[10] Over a six-year period (2012 to 2018) government support declined from 6.2 to 3.1 percent.[11]

Impact of Climate Change

Climatic variability, climate change, population growth, health pandemics (AIDS, malaria), a degrading natural resource base, poor infrastructure, and changing patterns of demand and production[12,13] threatens sustainability in BIMSTEC countries that experience a disproportionate share of global cyclone-related deaths (over 80 percent).[14] Himalayan glaciers are melting at an accelerated pace due to the increased incidence of floods and landslides in the hills, sea levels rising and tropical storms in coastal regions becoming more intense.

Planetary Boundaries: Safe Operating Space for Humanity

The safe operating space for humanity[15] must not be transgressed to facilitate unacceptable environmental change. By 2009, three out of nine changes, i.e., climate change, loss of biodiversity and atmospheric nitrogen fixation, have already been exceeded. Richardson et al.[16] reported that six of the nine boundaries have been breached and suggested that if action is taken promptly, the Earth's life support system can be rejuvenated and rebalanced.

Sustainable Water Management Strategy

In place of a business as usual (BAU) approach, innovative, implementable and scalable strategy and policies for water management must be developed and implemented earnestly. Agriculture in BIMSTEC countries is an untransformed sector, plagued with a lack of rainwater, surface water, groundwater and wastewater policies, causing inefficient use and overexploitation of finite resource. Water sector is plagued with regulations and policies, a low level of scientific agriculture, etc. The COVID lockdown has aggravated the woes of our "Annadatas" further in addition to climate change.[17]

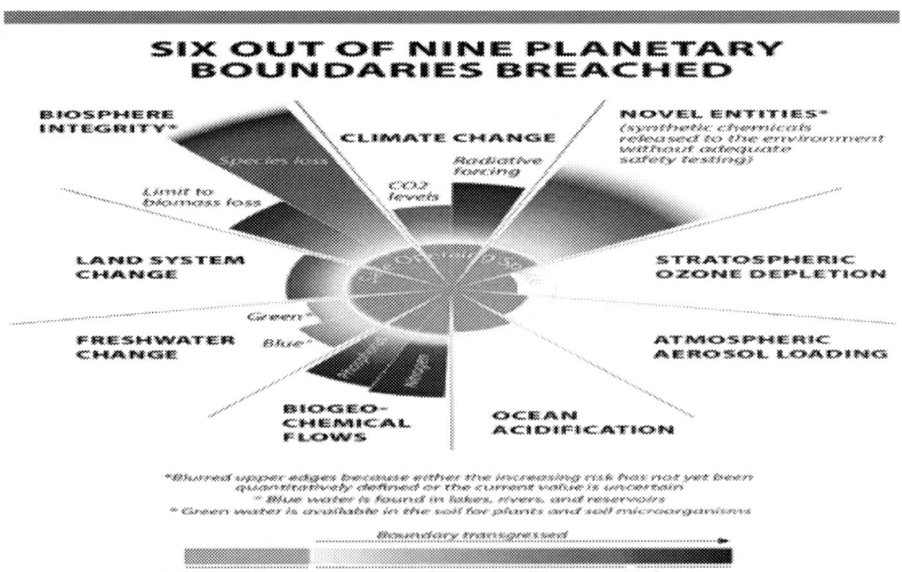

Figure 1: Six Out of Nine Planetary Boundaries Crossed by 2022

Urgent Need to Cross the "Death Valley of Impacts" in India

Because of the Death Valley of impacts,[18] in spite of game-changing technologies available, large yield gaps for all crops are observed. Science needs to change its focus for achieving impact.[19] and scientists, research managers, extension staff, policymakers, donor agencies, publishers of the research journals and farmers, must change their mindset to provide demand-based solutions, rather than supply-driven solutions. A good example of a national initiative, "Swacch Bharat" with community participation, building public-private-people centric-partnerships (PPPP), as well as monitoring evaluation and learning (MEL), made 98 percent of rural areas open defecation free.

Water Management should be the Business of Everyone

From childhood, water is considered God's gift and has no value, which is reflected in local proverbs such as "*Pani Jaisa Paisa Baha Rahe Ho*", meaning "You are spending money like water." Awareness building and enabling policies need to be implemented earnestly. Water supply must be metered and charged suitably for all users, without adopting the strategy of freebies for short term political gain and sacrificing the national agenda of sustainable water development.

Strengthen the Science of Delivery for One-stop Integrated Holistic Solutions to Farmers

The science of delivery must be strengthened to benefit small farm-holders for providing holistic solutions, as farmers' livelihoods are dependent on multifarious activities like livestock rearing, poultry, working as labour in addition to farming rain-fed and irrigated fields.[12]

Integrated Watershed for Managing Water Resources

A holistic and integrated consortium approach for developing rain-fed and irrigated areas sustainably through watershed development is recommended,[20,21] as it is a continuum from rain-fed to partially irrigated to fully irrigated crops during the year. World Bank-aided projects like the National Agriculture Technology Project (NATP) and the National Agriculture Innovation Project (NAIP) as well as several researchers and governments have also adopted the consortium approach.[22]

Agro-eco region and market-led diversified (Fork to Farm Approach) integrated value-chain agriculture using big data

At present farmers' have adopted a "farm to fork") approach, using the minimum support price (MSP) to produce and then seek markets to sell. Such an approach of growing water-guzzling paddy in Punjab with groundwater irrigation and sugarcane in Maharashtra's drought-prone districts causes substantial degradation of finite and scarce water resources. We need to adopt a "fork to farm" approach and produce what the market needs. Agro Economic Researched (AER)-based farming would diversify agricultural production in the country, using the power of big data, artificial intelligence (AI), machine learning (ML), remote sensing (RS), modelling, geographic information systems (GISs), etc., to guide farmers based on the needs of the market, the weather, and associated infrastructure for processing. The approach of "One district one product" (ODOP) proposed by the Government of India (GoI) needs to be adopted at the state level, like in Uttar Pradesh, considering market availability, promotion of skill development, value addition and linking up with markets to ensure a good livelihood for people in the district.

Integrated water resources management is a must

Water is the main driver for agriculture and integrated and sustainable rural development,[23] and, therefore, integrated water resource management (IWRM) is recommended. The consumptive use of green water is four times larger than that of blue water[24] dominates food production.

Figure 2: Strategy to Transform Agriculture in India[25]

Efficient green water (soil moisture) use is neglected, and farmers rarely consider it as a source of water. Farmers and policymakers always see providing irrigation (blue water) as the first and easy option. Conserving rainwater in the soil, reducing run-off and associated soil loss and avoiding unproductive losses due to evaporation are critical. The opportunity for green water productivity improvement, shifting non-productive evaporation to productive transpiration, with no downstream water trade-off in arid, semi-arid and dry sub-humid regions exists. IWRM adoption is a challenging task, as it calls for convergence of several departments related to agriculture, irrigation, drinking water, sanitation, rural development, etc. The government has initiated the convergence through the Jal Shakti Ministry, which must be taken forward vigorously. India's emphasis on integrated watershed development is commendable, but it needs further strengthening. We must emphasise on conserving rainwater in the soil (green water). This is to be, followed by the harvesting rainwater (blue water), recharging groundwater and ensuring its efficient use for crop growth. This can be achieved by minimising wasteful evaporation losses recycling and safe reuse of wastewater and other ecosystem services.[26,27,28,29] Reducing unproductive losses from water ponds and tanks is a priority. Using technologies like floating solar panels to harness solar energy and reduce evaporation losses is the need of the hour. (Figure 3).

Figure 3: Floating Solar Panels to Reduce Evaporation Losses and Harness Solar Power from Farm Ponds and Water Tanks

Integrated Soil Fertility Management for Producing More with Minimal Resources

Along with Water Use Efficiency (WUE), Nutrient Use Efficiency (NUE), particularly for nitrogen (25-30 percent) is of utmost importance.[30,31] Subsidised fertilisers, particularly nitrogenous in India, result in the overuse of nitrogen-based fertiliser and the ultimate distortion of nutrient (NPK) ratios resulting in a low NUE. Since 2016, India required all agricultural urea to be coated with neem seeds extract produced from Neem trees (*Azadrichta indica*) compulsorily to stop its diversion for industrial use. This was demanded to overcome shortages for agricultural use. reducing the subsidy burden and inhibiting denitrification, besides enhancing NUE by five to seven percent.[32] According to industry estimates, it saves about Rs.10, 000 crores on account of lower use[33] annually. Soil-test-based nutrient management does increase N use efficiency and India's efforts on soil health card as well as reducing the size of urea bag by five kilograms is useful in enhancing NUE. The use of nanotechnology for the controlled release of fertilisers can go a long way in doubling NUE.

Integrated Platform can Provide One-stop Advisories on Sale of Produce using Innovations

For overcoming challenges of millions of small-holders, new technologies such as Information and Communication Technology (ICT), Remote Sensing (RS), Internet of Things (IoT), Artificial Intelligence (AI), Machine Learning (ML), cloud computing, drones, robots and nanotechnologies need to be harnessed.[34] Farmers need information about best practices, technologies and post-harvest tasks, including processing, marketing, storage and handling as well as on allied sectors supporting farmers' livelihoods.

Fortunately, India has needed talent, technologies, and resources to undertake application of IT for big data, ML, AI, etc. However, the silos, which are created with watertight boundaries; need to be blasted through urgent reforms to enable the country to harness the power of the IT revolution. India is moving in the right direction of transforming agriculture, as is evident from the number of initiatives and concept papers like the Indian Digital Ecosystem for Agriculture (IDEA) by government departments. The Ministry of Statistics and Project Implementation needs to be strengthened and should work along with the IT Ministry to collect, sanitise, organise, and develop protocols for data security, sharing and use.

There is an urgent need to promote Public–Private–People–centric Partnerships (4Ps) for the implementation of holistic and integrated platforms for transforming rural areas. The challenge of an integrated platform for knowledge delivery to the farmers and the number of actors involved in complex agri-food systems can be overcome by promoting MSMEs in rural areas through farmer producer organisations (FPOs) to overcome the problem of fragmented agriculture and to reach a large number of small and marginal through value-chain approach, enhancing rural employment.[35]

The FPOs need to be empowered by creating an ecosystem ensuring finance as well as professional experts to strengthen knowledge delivery systems, value chains and marketing in the country. The FPOs must be run as business models to do the extension, processing, packaging and marketing, besides providing credit and empowerment through training and capacity-building through support organisation.[42]

Novel Approach to Reward Farmers Adopting Efficient Water Management Practices

Valuing water is critical for raising awareness and communicating the value put behind the product or process involving the use of water and providing incentives to farmers to use it sustainably. These values are often social and cultural in nature. The water expert group set-up by the Solidaridad to develop water standards and mechanisms for certification by an independent body.[36] The value for water should be fair, resource-efficient, should have relevance in currency and has value for all interest groups. The expert group of Solidaridad made a presentation during the G-20 meeting with recommendations. The group is pursuing water standards for sugarcane and cotton and as pilot to benefit farmers growing sugarcane and cotton by adopting water conservation and its efficient use for increasing productivity.

Summary

BIMSTEC countries face the challenge of feeding their growing population largely due to growing land degradation, water scarcity, large yield gaps and climate change impacts. There are member countries who have unique agricultural products and exports and can capitalise on the strengths of other member countries through collaboration. India has turned the tables from a "ship to mouth" situation to "overflowing godowns", and exports food grains in spite of challenges. Water and agricultural land is limited, and, on the other hand, the population is growing, climate change is affecting food production, food and nutrition security. There is an urgent need to provide integrated holistic solutions to small farmers using new technologies such as RS, ICT, IoT, cloud computing, GIS, modelling, etc. The science of delivery needs to be enhanced along with the science of discovery through collaboration between the BIMSTEC countries. Technologies trained human power in agriculture and allied sectors in India can benefit member countries. They can meet the goal of sustainable food and nutrition security in spite of the challenges of climate change, water and land scarcity by enhancing agricultural productivity.

NOTES

1 Chand, Ramesh. "Transforming Agriculture for Challenges of 21st Century." Niti Aayog, December 27, 2019. https://www.niti.gov.in/sites/default/files/2020-01/Presidential_Address.pdf. 15 (4) 1–23

2 "Hunger Hotspots: FAO-WFP Early Warnings on Acute Food Insecurity." *UN World Food Programme,* June 5, 2024. https://www.wfp.org/publications/hunger-hotspots-fao-wfp-early-warnings-acute-food-insecurity.

3 BIMSTEC Secretariat, "Priority Sectors of Cooperation," Bay of Bengal Initiative for Multi-Sectoral Technical and Economic Cooperation, accessed March 2025, https://bimstec.org.

4 Wani, Suhas P., Girish Chander, and Kaushal K Garg (eds). "A Holistic Approach for Achieving Impact through CSR." ICRISAT, 2018. https://oar.icrisat.org:443/10953/1/Chapter%2012_CSR-Book-Published-2018.pdf.
Wani, Suhas P., K.V. Raju (eds). Corporate Social Responsibility: Win-win Propositions for Communities, Corporates and Agriculture. *Centre for Agriculture and Biosciences International.* October 24, 2018. Pp.21-34. https://www.amazon.in/Corporate-Social-Responsibility-Propositions-Communities-ebook/dp/B07KXYNRSF/ref=sr_1_7?dib=eyJ2IjoiMSJ9.5XVXq_dBQ7Wja2yMC41J8BvuR.

5 Rockström, J., & Falkenmark, M. (2000). Semiarid Crop Production from a Hydrological Perspective: Gap between Potential and Actual Yields. Critical Reviews in Plant Sciences, 19(4), 319–346. https://doi.org/10.1080/07352680091139259

6 Wani, Suhas P., B. Venkateswarlu, and V.N. Sharda. "Integrated Watershed Management in Rainfed Agriculture." Wani, SP, Rockstrom, Johan and KL Sahrawat (eds) ICRISAT, July 8, 2011. Pp.52-86. CRC Press Taylor and Francis Group, Boca Raton London New York Leiden. https://oar.icrisat.org/3567/1/Chapter_3.pdf.

7 Anderson, Walter, Chris Johansen, and Kadambot H. M. Siddique. "Addressing the Yield Gap in Rainfed Crops: A Review." *Agronomy for Sustainable Development*, 2016. https://hal.science/hal-01532413/.

8 Wani, Suhas P. "Integrated and Holistic Approach is Must for Climate Resilient Agriculture." *Agriculture Observer*, Vol 1(3): 10–22. 2020. http://www.agricultureobserver.com/currentissue. aspx/

9 "Situation Assessment Survey of Agriculture Households in India". *NSSO* July 2012-June 2013. Ministry of Statistics and Program Implementation, New Delhi.

10 Reddy, A.A. "Reform Agri Extension to BoostRyotsIincome." *The Hans India,* July 24, 2018. https://www.thehansindia.com/posts/index/News-Analysis/2018-07-24/Reform-agri-extension-to-boost-ryots-income/400625

11 Patra, Subhajit. "Access to Information and Agriculture Extension Services for Farmer Households: Evidence from the Situation Assessment Surveys." *Foundation for Agrarian Studies,* August 10, 2021. https://fas.org.in/access-to-information-and-agriculture-extension-services-for-farmer-households-evidence-from-the-situation-assessment-surveys/.

12 Wani, S.P, Sreedevi T.K., Rockström J and Y.S. Ramakrishna. "Rainfed AgriculturePast Trends and Future Prospects in Rainfed Agriculture: Unlocking the Potential.". Wani, SP, Rockström., J. and T. Oweis. Pp.1–35. *Comprehensive Assessment of Water Management in Agriculture Series.* Wallingford, UK: CAB International. 2009

13 Walker, T. "Challenges and Opportunities for Agricultural R & D in the Semi-Arid Tropics: Internal Document for Strategic Planning. *ICRISAT* Patancheru, Andhra Pradesh, India.

14 Krishnan, R et al., "Assessment of Climate Change over the Indian Region." Springer, 2020, Singapore. https://link.springer.com/book/10.1007%2F978-981-15-4327-2.

15 Rockström, J, Steffen W, Noone K, Persson Å, Chapin FS. Lambin III, Lenton E T M, Scheffer M., C. Folke, H. Schellnhuber, B. Nykvist, C. A. De Wit, T. Hughes, S. van der Leeuw, H. Rodhe, S. Sörlin, P K, Snyder, R. Costanza, U. Svedin, Falkenmark M. Karlberg L, Corell W R, Fabry V. J., J. Hansen, B. Walker, D. Liverman, K. Richardson, P. Crutzen, and J. Foley. "Planetary Boundaries: Exploring the Safe Operating Space for Humanity." *Ecology and Society,* Vol. 14(2), Art.32. http://www.ecologyandsociety.org/vol14/iss2/art32/

16 Richardson, K., Will, S., Wolfgang, L., Bendtsen, J., Cornell, Sarah E., Jonathan, F., Markus, D,, Ingo Fetzer, D., Govindasamy, B., Werner, B von., Feulner, G., Fiedler, Stephanie., Gerten, D., Gleeson, T., Hofmann, M., Huiskamp, W., Kummu, M,, Mohan, C., NoguésBravo, D.H.,

17 Singh, D., Wani, Suhas P. "How to Transform Indian Agriculture during Covid-19 Lockdown." *Vivekananda International Foundation.* June 20, 2020. https://www.vifindia.org/article/2020/ june/01/how-to-transform Indian agriculture during covid-19 lockdown.

18 Wani, Suhas P..and K.V. "Corporate Social Responsibility: Win-Win Propositions for Communities, Corporates and Agriculture." *CABI.* Pp: 1-246, CABI, Nosworthway Oxfordshire, UK.

19 "Ending Hunger: Science Must Stop Neglecting Smallholder Farmers." *Nature News,* p.336. October 12, 2020. https://www.nature.com/articles/d41586-020-02849-6.

20 Singh, A K, Kumar A and K D Singh. "Impact of Rainwater Harvesting and Recycling on Crop Productivity in Semi-Arid Areas: A Review. *Agriculture Review* 19(1):6–10. 1998.

21 Wani, Suhas P., Maglinao, A.R, Ramakrishna. A, and Rego. T J. Integrated Watershed Management for Land and Water Conservation and Sustainable Agricultural Production in Asia. Proceedings of the ADB-ICRISAT-IWMI Annual Project Review and Planning Meeting, Hanoi, Vietnam. *ICRISAT,* December 10–14, 2001. Patancheru, Andhra Pradesh, India.

22 Wani, Suhas P. "Death Valley of Impacts in Agriculture: Why and How to Cross It with Scaling-up Strategy?" SpringerLink, November 18, 2021. Wani, Suhas P., Raju., K.V and Tapas Bhattacharyya (eds.). Pp.1–54. https://link.springer.com/chapter/10.1007/978-3-030-77935-1_1.

23 Wani, Suhas P, Raju KV, Bhattacharyya T (eds) "Scaling-up Solutions for Farmers: Technology,

Partnerships and Convergence." ISBN 978-3-030-77934-4 Springer Nature, Switzerland, 2021

24 Rockström, J, Falkenmark M, Karlberg L *et al.* (2009). Future water availability for global food production: the potential of green water for increasing resilience to global change. *Water Resources Research* 45, W00A12, doi:10.1029/2007WR006767

25 Dalwai, Ashok. "Secondary Agriculture Is of Primary Importance." The Financial Express, August 10, 2020. https://www.financialexpress.com/opinion/secondary-agriculture-is-of-primary-importance/2049891/lite/.

26 Reddy, K. R., K. L. Campbell, D. A. Graetz, and K. M. Portier. "Use of Biological Filters for Treating Agricultural Drainage Effluents." Journal of Environment Quality, October 1, 1982. https://acsess.onlinelibrary.wiley.com/doi/abs/10.2134/appliedstatistics.2015.0080.c6/.

27 Datta, A and Wani, S P and Patil, M D and Tilak, A S. "Field Scale Evaluation of Seasonal Wastewater Treatment Efficiencies of Free Surface-Constructed Wetlands." *ICRISAT*, May 2016. https://oar.icrisat.org/9499/

28 Garg, KK, Wani SP, Chander G, Anantha KH. Pardhasardhi G. "Water Productivity and Income. in Harnessing Dividends from Drylands: Innovative Scaling up with Soil Nutrients." Raju KV and Suhas P Wani (eds.), Pp. 236-258. *CABI*, Wallingford, Oxfordshire, UK. 2016.

29 Sawargaonkar, G, Sudi R, Wani SP. "An Integrated Approach for Productivity Enhancement in Harnessing Dividends from Drylands: Innovative Scaling up with Soil Nutrients." Raju KV and Suhas P Wani (eds.). pp. 201–235. CABI, Wallingford, Oxfordshire, UK. 2016

30 Rego, T.J., Sahrawat, K. L, Wani, S. P., Pardhasaradhi, G. and KVS Murthy. "Widespread Deficiencies of Sulfur, Boron, and Zinc in Indian Semi-Arid Tropical Soils: On-Farm Crop Responses." *Journal of Plant Nutrition*, 2007. Pp. 1428-1432.

31 Chander G, Wani SP, Sahrawat KL and Rajesh C "Enhanced Nutrient and Rainwater Use Efficiency in Maize and Soybean with Secondary and Micro-nutrient Amendments in the Rainfed Semi-Arid Tropics. Archives of Agronomy and Soil Science. 2014. DOI: 10.1080/03650340.2014.928928

32 Mangat GS and Narang GK. "Agronomical Trial for Efficiency of NFL Neem Coated Urea." Fertiliser. Marketing News. 35 (11) 1–7. 2004.

33 Gupta, Uttam. "Neem-Coated Urea: Why Is Narendra Modi Govt. Waiting for 5 Years to Make India Self-Sufficient in Fertilisers?" *Opinion News | The Financial Express*, November 24, 2016. https://www.financialexpress.com/opinion/neem-coated-urea-why-is-narendra-modi-govt-waiting-for-5-years-to-make-india-self-sufficient-in-fertilisers/454215/.

34 Wani, SP, G Chander and Kaushal K Garg. "A Holistic Approach for Achieving Impact through CSR." Corporate Social Responsibility: Win-Win Propositions. Wani, SP and KV Raju (eds.). pp 21–34. Wallingford, Oxfordshire: CAB International

35 Raju KV, Kumar R, Vikraman S, Moses D, S, Srikanth R, Kumara DC, Wani SP (2017) Farmer Producer Organisation in Andhra Pradesh: A Scoping Study. Rythu Kosam Project. Research Report IDC-16. Patancheru 502 324. Telangana, India: *International Crops Research Institute for the Semi-Arid Tropics.* p. 160.

36 Pastore Prashant, Wani Suhas, Tyagi Ashray and Banerjee Krtika. (2023. "Valuing Water in Agriculture to Reward Actions in Conservation." T 20 Policy Brief, Task Force 6: "Accelerating SDGs, Exploring New Pathways to the 2030 Agenda

11

Enhancing BIMSTEC's Role in Transboundary Water Governance

P.K. Khup Hangzo

A Global Commission on the Economics of Water (GCEW) report, published last October, had warned that by 2030, global freshwater demand could exceed supply by 40 percent due to mounting pressures from population growth, industrial expansion, climate change and inefficient water management.[1] It further highlighted that nearly three billion people and over half of global food production are concentrated in regions where water storage is likely to decline, making water security an urgent global concern. For BIMSTEC nations, this challenge is further intensified by China's unilateral control over key transboundary rivers, including the Brahmaputra and the Mekong. China's large-scale dam construction and water diversion projects on the upper reaches of these rivers have raised serious concerns regarding diminished downstream flows, erratic flooding, and significant ecological disruptions. A coordinated BIMSTEC strategy is thus critical for engaging China in meaningful dialogue on transboundary river governance and addressing the risks posed by its upstream interventions.

Transboundary Rivers: A Vital Lifeline for BIMSTEC

BIMSTEC depends heavily on transboundary rivers for freshwater. The Ganges, Brahmaputra and Meghna Rivers sustain vast populations across India, Bangladesh, Bhutan and Nepal, while the Salween and Mekong Rivers are vital lifelines for Myanmar and Thailand. These rivers, however, originate in China, giving that country a dominant position as Asia's hydro-hegemon, with significant influence over regional water flows. The extent of BIMSTEC nations' reliance on transboundary rivers originating from China varies across the region. One way to assess this is through the water dependency ratio, which quantifies the share of a country's total renewable water resources that originate beyond its borders. This ratio ranges from zero percent, where a country is entirely self-sufficient in its water resources, to 100 percent, indicating complete reliance on inflows from neighbouring countries. The water dependency ratios of BIMSTEC nations are as follows: Bangladesh (91.44 percent), Thailand (48.81 percent), India (30.52 percent), Myanmar (14.13 percent), Nepal (5.70 percent), Bhutan (0 percent) and Sri Lanka (0 percent).[2]

The water dependency ratios of BIMSTEC nations reveal varying degrees of reliance on transboundary water flows, with some countries significantly dependent on inflows from upstream neighbours. Bangladesh has the highest dependency ratio, with nearly all of its freshwater resources originating beyond its borders, primarily from India and China. Thailand similarly relies heavily on rivers originating beyond its territory, particularly from neighbours and China. India, despite its extensive river network, depends on upstream flows from China, Nepal and Bhutan. Myanmar, too, receives a portion of its freshwater from transboundary sources, particularly from China. Nepal, while an important upper riparian state, has a relatively low dependency ratio, whereas Bhutan and Sri Lanka are entirely self-sufficient in freshwater resources. These disparities underscore the critical need for regional cooperation in managing transboundary water resources effectively.

BIMSTEC nations have established several water management regimes to govern their shared rivers, aiming to promote cooperation and equitable water distribution. India, for instance, has signed multiple water treaties and agreements with Bangladesh, Bhutan, Nepal, and Pakistan—to regulate transboundary rivers. Notable agreements include the Indus Waters Treaty with Pakistan, the Ganges Water Sharing Treaty with Bangladesh, and various hydropower and water-sharing agreements with Nepal and Bhutan. In Southeast Asia, Cambodia, Laos, Thailand and Vietnam established the Mekong River Commission in 1995 to foster sustainable management and cooperative governance of the Mekong River. Despite these regional frameworks, a critical gap remains, i.e., none of the BIMSTEC nations have binding water-sharing or management agreements with China, the upper riparian state for several major rivers. China views transboundary rivers as sovereign assets and has consistently rejected international water conventions and legally binding water treaties.[3] While China has shared hydrological data with India since 2006 and Bangladesh since 2008, these measures remain limited in scope and effectiveness. Furthermore, China's Lancang-Mekong Cooperation Framework, established in 2016, primarily advances its own interests and does not adequately address concerns such as seasonal water flow regulation, ecological preservation, or equitable distribution.

China's Unilateral Action on the Brahmaputra and Mekong Rivers

China's control over the headwaters of critical transboundary rivers, including the Brahmaputra and the Mekong, has significant implications for downstream BIMSTEC nations. As the upper riparian state, China exercises considerable influence over the quantity, quality and timing of water flows into South and Southeast Asia. The country has pursued a unilateral approach on river management, prioritising large-scale dam construction, hydroelectric projects and water diversion schemes without consulting or securing agreements with affected downstream nations.

The Brahmaputra River, known as the Yarlung Tsangpo in China, originates in southwest Tibet at an altitude of approximately 19,750 feet, making it the highest continuously flowing river in the world. Spanning 3,848 kilometres, it crosses China, India and Bangladesh before merging with the Ganges and Meghna Rivers and emptying into the Bay of Bengal. The river serves as a vital lifeline for over 160 million people, primarily in India and Bangladesh, supporting agriculture, fisheries and hydropower. China has increasingly sought to harness the Yarlung Tsangpo's immense hydropower potential, initiating large-scale dam construction in Tibet. The completion of the Zangmu Hydropower Station in 2015 marked the beginning of this effort.[4] Since then, China has operationalised several dams on the middle reaches of the river and is now turning its focus to its lower reaches. Last December, China approved the construction of the world's largest dam near the Indian border, a project expected to generate 60 gigawatts of power—nearly three times the capacity of the Three Gorges Dam—at an estimated cost of USD 137 billion.[5] While the project aligns with China's long-term hydropower ambitions, it has sparked serious geo-political and environmental concerns, particularly in India. There are growing fears that China could manipulate water flows, exacerbating both droughts and floods downstream, while also gaining a strategic leverage over India, especially along the disputed Sino-Indian border.[6] The lack of legally binding water-sharing agreements further exacerbates these concerns, making China's unilateral control over the Brahmaputra River a critical challenge for regional stability and water security. As revealed already, China has been sharing hydrological data with India since 2006 and Bangladesh since 2008, but these measures, are limited in scope, seasonal in nature and do not provide long-term assurances against potential water flow disruptions or unilateral upstream interventions.

The Mekong River, the longest free flowing water body in Southeast Asia, also originates in the Tibetan Plateau and stretches approximately 4,800 kilometres, flowing through China, Myanmar, Laos, Thailand, Cambodia and Vietnam, before emptying into the South China Sea. As a vital artery of mainland Southeast Asia, it provides water, food and energy security for nearly 70 million people.[7] Since 1993, China has embarked on extensive dam construction along its section of the Mekong, known as the Lancang, and now operates twelve major dams, with plans for further expansion.[8] These dams periodically regulate water flow, increasing the chances of drought and reducing food production in downstream nations. Additionally, they cause erratic fluctuations in water levels, disrupting natural flood cycles, altering fish migration patterns and threatening bird and aquatic life. China's dam operations have increasingly raised concerns among lower Mekong nations, particularly regarding the lack of transparency and the absence of legally binding water-sharing agreements. Unlike downstream countries that coordinate their water governance through the Mekong River Commission, China has refused to become a full member, engaging instead through the Lancang-Mekong Cooperation Framework. Without better regional cooperation and transparency in water management, the Mekong River's ecological balance and the livelihoods of millions remain at serious risk.

Leveraging BIMSTEC for Collective Diplomatic Pressure on China

China's control over rivers originating in the Tibetan Plateau has become a growing concern for BIMSTEC nations, particularly regarding water security, food supply, and ecological stability. (Repetition). As China continues to expand its hydropower infrastructure and water control projects, the absence of legally binding agreements poses significant challenges for downstream BIMSTEC nations and underscores the urgent need for a unified regional approach on transboundary water governance.

BIMSTEC must serve as a vital platform for collective diplomatic engagement, enabling member states to take a united stand against China's unilateral water policies. A united bloc can amplify concerns, call for transparent water governance and maintain a stronger bargaining position with and against

China. BIMSTEC should establish a "Water Cooperation Mechanism" that aligns member state's positions, develops a common strategy and facilitates technical and policy coordination. Engaging with international legal frameworks such as the 1997 UN Convention on the Law of the Non-Navigational Uses of International Watercourses, could reinforce their demands for fair and transparent water-sharing mechanisms. Although China has refused to sign this convention, sustained regional pressure could push it for greater accountability.

Beyond diplomatic engagement, BIMSTEC countries can also leverage economic and trade ties with China, integrating water security concerns into broader economic and investment negotiations. Strengthening scientific and technical cooperation through independent hydrological research and satellite monitoring would reduce reliance on Chinese-provided data, enhancing regional preparedness for water-related risks. Additionally, the development of joint river basin management strategies and early warning systems for floods and droughts could improve resilience against water-related disasters and promote sustainable resource use. Despite existing challenges, a coordinated BIMSTEC approach has the potential to drive a more equitable and sustainable framework for transboundary river governance. By fostering regional unity, strengthening diplomatic engagement, and enhancing scientific collaboration, BIMSTEC can work towards securing long-term water security for its member states.

Conclusion

China's unilateral control over transboundary rivers originating in the Tibetan Plateau poses significant challenges for BIMSTEC nations, affecting water security, food production and ecological stability. The absence of legally binding agreements and Beijing's lack of transparency in water management have heightened concerns over unpredictable water flows, erratic flooding and long-term environmental degradation. As China continues to expand its dam building and water diversion projects, the need for a unified regional response has never been more urgent.

BIMSTEC offers a crucial platform for collective diplomatic engagement, allowing member states to amplify their concerns and push for greater transparency and cooperation from China. Establishing a Water Cooperation Mechanism, leveraging international legal frameworks, and integrating water security into broader economic negotiations can strengthen BIMSTEC's bargaining position. Additionally, enhancing scientific collaboration, independent hydrological monitoring, and joint river basin management strategies would improve resilience against water-related risks. While challenges remain, a coordinated BIMSTEC approach can help establish a more equitable and sustainable framework for transboundary water governance. By fostering regional unity and engaging China through sustained diplomatic and technical efforts, BIMSTEC can work towards securing long-term water security for its member states, ensuring the sustainable management of these vital shared resources.

NOTES

1 "Economics of Water Report: *Valuing the Hydrological Cycle as a Global Common Good." Global Commission on the Economics of Water*, n.d. 2024. https://economicsofwater.watercommission.org/report/economics-of-water.pdf.

2 Hangzo, P.K. Implications of China's Hydro-Hegemony on River Yarlung Tsangpo: Another Lever of China's Expansionist Tactics into India's East. VIF Paper. Vivekananda International Foundation. New Delhi. October 2021.

3 Walker, Beth. "China and India Ignore UN Watercourses Convention." *Dialogue Earth*, August 18, 2014. https://dialogue.earth/en/climate/7229-china-and-india-ignore-un-watercourses-convention/

4 Krishnan, Ananth. "China's first hydropower dam on Brahmaputra is fully operational." *India Today*, October 13, 2015. https://www.indiatoday.in/world/story/chinas-first-hydropower-dam-on-brahmaputra-is-fully-operational-267843-2015-10-13

5 Chik, Holly. "China Approves Tibet Mega Dam That Could Generate Three Times More Power Than Three Gorges." *South China Morning Post*, December 26, 2024. https://www.scmp.com/news/china/science/article/3292267/china-approves-tibet-mega-dam-could-generate-3-times-more-power-three-gorges

6 Hangzo, P.K. *Implications of China's Hydro-Hegemony on River Yarlung Tsangpo: Another Lever of China's Expansionist Tactics into India's East. VIF Paper.* Vivekananda International Foundation. New Delhi. October 2021. https://www.vifindia.org/sites/default/files/Implications-of-China-s-Hydro-Hegemony-on-River-Yarlung-Tsangpo.pdf

7 "Fisheries." Mekong River Commission, November 2024. https://www.mrcmekong.org/fisheries/. https://www.mrcmekong.org/fisheries/

8 "Averting Environmental Disaster along the Mekong." Asia Report No.343. *International Crisis Group*, October 7, 2024. https://www.crisisgroup.org/asia/south-east-asia/cambodia-thailand-china/averting-environmental-disaster-along-mekong. https://www.crisisgroup.org/sites/default/files/2024-10/343-mekong-environmental-catastrophe.pdf

PART V

Technology, Crime, and Non-Traditional Security

12

Energizing the BIMSTEC Counter-Terrorism and Transnational Crime Mission

Sudhir Saxena

Since BIMSTEC's creation, security cooperation has become an important gravitational point for its member states, with the agenda of Counter-Terrorism (CT) as the main driver. A large part of this shift has been influenced by developments that followed the regional grouping's inception, including an upsurge in terrorist activity that led to major events like the 9/11 and 26/11 attacks. These occurred parallel to the emergence of transnational terrorist networks with Al Qaeda in the lead, catalysing the emergence of affiliates and inspired entities in nearly all BIMSTEC nations. On the implementation side, the Counter-Terrorism and Transnational Crime (CTTC) work at BIMSTEC was affected by the US-led global war against terrorism, among other factors. The US-led effort eventually extended beyond military campaigns in Afghanistan and Pakistan, impacting global terrorist networks, financial flows, logistics, and supply chains, as well as radicalization.

In the period after 9/11, several CTTC-linked measures were undertaken by BIMSTEC member states to align with the US-led effort. The member states evolved their respective frameworks through domestic laws and via bilateral and multilateral cooperation. Some of these laws have comprehensively addressed the complex interplay between counter-terrorism aspects and those in the domains of narcotics, human trafficking, maritime security, and cyber security.

This paper attempts to analyse the status of the BIMSTEC CTTC Mission and offer suggestions on how it can further energize existing cooperation.

CTTC Framework

From 1997 onward, BIMSTEC leadership recognised that tackling terrorism and transnational organised crime was essential for ensuring growth and maintaining peace in the region. The leadership also recognised the need for cooperation among member states to address these problems. Based on deliberations at the First CTTC Summit, the Eighth BIMSTEC Ministerial Meeting, held in Dhaka, Bangladesh, on December 18–19, 2005, declared CTTC as one of the priority areas for deliberation and concrete proposals. The meeting also decided to create a Joint Working Group (JWG) on CTTC to enhance cooperation at both the policy and operational levels.[1]

Overall, BIMSTEC's CTTC objectives are addressed through a multi-tier mechanism, which includes interactions at the level of:

(a) Home Ministers
(b) National Security Advisors
(c) Senior Home Ministry Officials
(d) Joint Working Groups
(e) Sub-groups
(f) Expert Groups

Deliberations at the First JWG-CTTC Meeting, held in New Delhi from December 5–7, 2004, led to the creation of four sub-groups, with two more added in 2017. These are:

(a) Sub-Group on Intelligence Sharing
(b) Sub-Group on Legal and Law Enforcement Issues
(c) Sub-Group on Prevention of Illicit Trafficking in Narcotic Drugs, Psychotropic Substances, and Precursor Chemicals
(d) Sub-Group on Anti-Money Laundering and Combatting the Financing of Terrorism
(e) Sub-Group on Cooperation on Countering Radicalisation and Terrorism
(f) Sub-Group on Human Trafficking

The National Security Advisors, during their meeting in Goa on October 16, 2016, recognised the need for urgent measures and adopted a 16-point agenda of action, which included cooperation on terrorism and countering radicalisation.

At the Fourth BIMSTEC Summit held on August 30–31, 2018, in Kathmandu, Nepal, leaders expressed their determination to strengthen cooperation and coordination between their respective law enforcement, intelligence, and security agencies.[2]

Execution of the Counter-Terrorism Framework

India is the Lead Shepherd of the Sub-Group on Legal and Law Enforcement Issues. The First Meeting of the JWG-CTTC decided to establish this Sub-Group. Since its inception, it has deliberated on the legal instruments required to meet CTTC objectives. The Sub-Group has so far negotiated and finalised the following BIMSTEC Conventions:[3]

(a) **Convention on Cooperation in Combatting International Terrorism, Transnational Organised Crime and Illicit Drug Trafficking** (December 11, 2009, Nay Pyi Taw, Myanmar): Provides the widest possible measure of mutual assistance in preventing, investigating, prosecuting, and suppressing international terrorism, transnational organised crime, and illicit trafficking of narcotic drugs and psychotropic substances, including precursor chemicals.

(b) **Convention on Mutual Legal Assistance in Criminal Matters** (March 30, 2022, Colombo, Sri Lanka): Enables member states, subject to national laws, to provide the widest mutual assistance in criminal matters.

(c) **Convention Against Trafficking in Persons** (June 21–23, 2023, New Delhi, India): Addresses prevention and suppression of trafficking in persons, and protection and repatriation of victims.

(d) **Convention on the Transfer of Sentenced Persons**

(e) **Convention on Extradition**

While different member states have attempted to harmonise their CTTC-related frameworks with international commitments, variations in national responses were expected. Domestic political priorities and conflict situations have influenced the evolution of these frameworks. Differences have also emerged due to varying geographies—landlocked nations like Nepal and Bhutan versus maritime nations like India, Bangladesh, Myanmar, and Sri Lanka. However, responses to thematic issues like terror financing and radicalisation have generally been similar, albeit with different degrees of urgency.

Terror Financing and Money Laundering

Thailand is the Lead Shepherd of the Sub-Group on Anti-Money Laundering and Combatting the Financing of Terrorism. This sub-group aims to foster and strengthen cooperation, including information-sharing, to counter all forms of terrorist financing and money laundering. It has led to the exchange of best practices and information regarding these issues. Among other activities, the sub-group has specifically focused on Illicit Financial Flows (IFF) and has formulated an action plan to prevent them.[4]

Cyber Security

New-age terrorism has exploited cyberspace for operational coordination, propaganda, radicalisation, and managing logistics and supply chains. The availability of low-cost, software-driven, secure and agile technologies has significantly impacted the modus operandi of networks like Al Qaeda and ISIS. These groups have created and evolved mechanisms to strike targets and attract vulnerable youth to either join their networks or carry out attacks autonomously, including lone-wolf attacks. Over time, some terrorist entities, sometimes with state support, have also ventured into targeting cyber assets—reflecting an evolved level of expertise.

The First Meeting of BIMSTEC National Security Advisors, held in New Delhi on March 21, 2017, noted with concern the emerging cyber trends that facilitate online radicalisation, cybercrime, and threats to critical information infrastructure. It was decided to deepen cooperation among national cyber institutions. The First Meeting of the BIMSTEC Expert Group on Cyber Security Cooperation, held in New Delhi on July 14–15, 2022, discussed and updated the draft *Five-Year Action Plan for BIMSTEC Cyber Security Cooperation*. It also agreed to establish a BIMSTEC CERT-to-CERT (Computer Emergency Response Team) cooperation mechanism and to create a Cyber Crime Cooperation Framework for law enforcement agencies.[5]

Possibilities for Energising CTTC Cooperation

Although BIMSTEC acknowledges the need to address terrorism collectively, its response requires further evolution to address contemporary threats. Bilateral engagements between member states often proceed without alignment to the BIMSTEC CTTC framework. Some reasons for this less-than-energetic response, despite the global surge in CT activity, include:

(a) Domestic political priorities and internal conflict situations—Myanmar is a current example.

(b) Post-9/11 economic and financial fluctuations, which limited resources for regional efforts.

(c) Competing international policy and resource commitments that narrowed the execution space for BIMSTEC. Post-26/11 developments linking SAARC and BIMSTEC CTTC activity are a case in point.

(d) Technology and trained human resources were required to address complex transnational threats. While mechanisms were proposed, access to implementation tools remained limited.

(e) Although BIMSTEC member states share many similarities, domestic social and electoral priorities have constrained potential cooperation.

Technology cooperation is a key agenda item in the BIMSTEC framework. To further energise the CTTC effort, additional tech-driven initiatives can be considered, as outlined below. These suggestions acknowledge that CT cooperation is not starting from scratch but requires operational augmentation.

Intelligence Sharing

Success in missions linked to terror financing, money laundering, and cyber exploitation hinges on effective, timely intelligence-sharing. BIMSTEC nations have a history of bilateral and multilateral CT cooperation and are signatories to international conventions, including UN agreements.

BIMSTEC states share both land and maritime borders. For example, India shares land borders with four BIMSTEC countries. These are relatively less militarised than India's western and northern borders and have been exploited by terrorists and transnational criminals. Global CT developments have influenced BIMSTEC CTTC dynamics, creating momentum for enhanced intelligence sharing.

While member states already share intelligence bilaterally and via BIMSTEC nodal points, contemporary challenges necessitate an upgraded mechanism. A **dedicated secure Intelligence Sharing Communication Network** could be developed for BIMSTEC functions. India's Ministry of Home Affairs could lead this effort, linking its counterparts across the region. This network could host a data bank and archive to support query-based operational analysis. The system must be cyber-secure to ensure trust and facilitate confidence among cooperating agencies.

Such a network could allow multimedia briefings and data exchange, fostering a collective response mechanism to CTTC-linked challenges. While initial responses may vary due to differing domestic security situations, long-term benefits would accrue to all member states.

Information Acquisition & Data Processing Technologies

Member states already leverage technology in their CT missions. In addition to intelligence sharing, they could collaborate on **intelligence acquisition and data processing technologies**. As Lead Shepherd, India—drawing on its experience—could share relevant systems to foster interoperability and enhance the regional CTTC framework.

This would also open opportunities to **jointly train BIMSTEC personnel** to operate and optimise these systems. The benefits would spill over into related missions such as cybersecurity, narcotics control, anti-human trafficking, and maritime security.

NOTES

1 BIMSTEC. "Joint Working Group on Counter Terrorism and Transnational Crime." https://bimstec.org/joint-working-group-on-counter-terrorism-and-transnational-crime.

2 BIMSTEC. "National Security Chiefs Meeting." https://bimstec.org/national-security-chiefs-meeting.

3 BIMSTEC. "Sub-Group on Legal and Law Enforcement Issues." https://bimstec.org/sub-group-on-legal-and-law-enforcement-issues.

4 BIMSTEC. "Sub-Group on Anti-Money Laundering and Combating the Financing of Terrorism." https://bimstec.org/sub-group-on-anti—money-laundering-and-combating-the-financing-of-terrorism.

5 BIMSTEC. "Expert Group on Cyber Security Cooperation." https://bimstec.org/expert-group-on-cyber-security-cooperation.

13

Cooperation on BIMSTEC Cybersecurity Challenges and Emerging Technologies

Jiten Kumar Jain and Saroj Kumar Rath

Member states of the Bay of Bengal Initiative for Multi-Sectoral Technical and Economic Cooperation (BIMSTEC) are intensifying their collaborative efforts to address complex cybersecurity challenges and capitalise on emerging technological innovations. This central initiative focuses on identifying, monitoring and reporting cross-border fraudulent mobile numbers implicated in cyber scams, thereby enhancing regional protective measures for citizens. Concurrently, member nations are forging a unified framework for regulating Artificial Intelligence (AI), to mitigate the pervasive threat of deepfakes, which pose considerable security risks. To strengthen the regional cybersecurity infrastructure, nations like India and Sri Lanka are advancing their technical skill development and capacity-building initiatives.

These efforts notwithstanding, a critical challenge persists in the form of illicit call centre operations in Thailand and Myanmar, where BIMSTEC-based citizens are forcibly abducted and forced into executing digital arrest scams and financial frauds. The systematic dismantling of these illegal enterprises is essential to preserving BIMSTEC's reputation as a resilient, cyber-secure regional bloc. Such initiatives ensure a robust and secure digital ecosystem. In this paper, we aim to explore a) the development of a shared web platform for reporting cross-border fraudulent mobile numbers, b) a unified AI regulation framework to combat deepfakes and c) the transnational cybercrime networks exploiting abducted BIMSTEC citizens in Thailand and Myanmar.

A Note on Contextual Framework

The dot.com boom was in the offing and the computer-enabled world was about to commence, when four wise men from India, Bangladesh, Sri Lanka and Thailand met in Bangkok, Thailand, on June 6, 1997, to name an organisation.[1] They named it BIST-EC, which was the abbreviation of Bangladesh-India-Sri Lanka and Thailand Economic Cooperation. However, as time passed, these wise men were afflicted with a Shakespearean adage of "what's in a name."

In the drama *Romeo and Juliet* by William Shakespeare, Juliet professes her love for Romeo despite the ongoing feud between their families and questions whether Romeo's name should really stand in the way of their relationship.

> *'Tis but thy name that is my enemy.*
> *Thou art thyself, though not a Montague.*
> *What's Montague? It is nor hand, nor foot,*
> *Nor arm, nor face, nor any other part*
> *Belonging to a man. O, be some other name!*
> *What's in a name? That which we call a rose.*
> *By any other name would smell as sweet.*

The name BIST-EC was not a fascinating representative of member states. Therefore, the Bangkok gang met again in the same city on December 22, 1997, to invite three other members, Nepal, Myanmar and Bhutan to join their BIST-EC group. Only Myanmar responded to the call immediately and they renamed it as BIMST-EC, which was the abbreviation of Bangladesh-India-Myanmar-Sri Lanka and Thailand Economic Cooperation. It was only when Nepal and Bhutan joined the band on July 31, 2004, that the grouping was formally codified as the Bay of Bengal Initiative for Multi-Sectoral Technical and Economic Cooperation (BIMSTEC).[2]

Cybersecurity: Challenges or Opportunity?

The salience of technology and cybersecurity within BIMSTEC has undergone profound transformation, particularly in recent years, as the region experiences heightened digital interconnectivity. Cybersecurity has emerged as a foundational pillar of BIMSTEC's strategic framework, becoming an indispensable domain for multilateral cooperation due to the escalating dependence on digital infrastructures and proliferation of cyber threats. During the formative phase on cybersecurity, i.e. 1997–2005, BIMSTEC primarily concentrated on fostering economic, trade and technological collaboration between its member states.[3] However, with the advent of the Internet era, this accelerated digitalisation catalysed into concerns over cybercrime, data breaches and hacking activities. Therefore, in the subsequent decade, i.e., from 2005 to 2015, the grouping witnessed a paradigm shift. The widespread adoption of digital banking, e-commerce and mobile connectivity across BIMSTEC, led to an upsurge in cyber fraud, financial cybercrimes and digital vulnerabilities. Concurrently, terrorist entities accessed cyber tools for strategic communication, propaganda dissemination and ideological radicalisation, thereby intensifying security apprehensions among member states.[4]

In response to this evolving digital threat landscape, BIMSTEC formalised its commitment to cybersecurity by signing the Convention on Cooperation in Combating International Terrorism, Transnational Organised Crime, and Illicit Drug Trafficking in 2009, which integrated cybersecurity collaboration as a pivotal agenda. However, it was only in the post-2015 digital period, that BIMSTEC member states fully understood the need for cybersecurity. The unprecedented growth of ransomware attacks, sophisticated data breaches and state-sponsored cyber espionage operations underscored the exigency of regional cybersecurity cooperation.[5] The ubiquity of cyber threats made digital security a non-negotiable strategic priority, necessitating introduction of robust policy frameworks, intelligence-sharing mechanisms and collective cyber resilience strategies.

Responding to persistent cybersecurity threats, the 2018 BIMSTEC Leaders' Summit formally accepted cybersecurity as a critical security imperative, necessitating multilateral cooperation and coordinated strategic interventions between member states. Subsequently, on March 30, 2022, at the Fifth BIMSTEC Summit in Colombo, Sri Lanka, member nations ratified the establishment of the BIMSTEC Technology Transfer Facility (TTF), formally institutionalising a dedicated mechanism for technological exchange and cybersecurity enhancement. The same summit also adopted the BIMSTEC Charter that further consolidated regional cooperation in digital transformation and cybersecurity governance.[6]

Building upon prior deliberations, BIMSTEC has initiated structured engagements on cybersecurity cooperation, convening high-level expert meetings to formulate and implement a cohesive regional cybersecurity architecture. The First Meeting of the BIMSTEC Expert Group on Cyber Security Cooperation, held on July 14 and 15, 2022, in New Delhi, focussed on undertaking a comprehensive review and refinement of the draft "Five-Year Action Plan for BIMSTEC Cyber Security Cooperation." During this session, member states formalised agreements for the establishment of a BIMSTEC CERT-to-CERT (Computer Emergency Response Team) collaboration framework and the creation of a BIMSTEC Cyber Crime Cooperation Framework to enhance inter-governmental coordination in cyber law enforcement. Further advancing this initiative, the Second Meeting of the BIMSTEC Expert Group on Cyber Security Cooperation, convened on January 21, 2025, in New Delhi, extensively deliberated on the draft Concept Note for the BIMSTEC Cybercrime Cooperation Framework. These high-level engagements underscored BIMSTEC's resolute commitment to fortifying regional cybersecurity resilience, fostering institutionalised cyber defence mechanisms and enhanced transnational cooperation to mitigate cyber threats.[7]

Core Area: Practical Feasible Way Forward

The BIMSTEC is increasingly recognising the need for regional cybersecurity measures due to the surge in cross-border cybercrimes, including mobile-based frauds. One potential solution, as we painstakingly explored, is to create a "Live Shared Web Platform" for reporting fraudulent mobile numbers involved in scams. However, implementing such a system across BIMSTEC nations presents a complex set of challenges due to technological, legal and operational factors. Member states have varying levels of digital infrastructure and cybersecurity readiness. Countries with advanced cybersecurity ecosystems, for example, India and Thailand, may find it easier to integrate a real-time reporting system, whereas countries with weaker technological frameworks, like Bhutan and Myanmar, might struggle with implementation, interoperability and digital forensics.[8]

Each country has its own set of telecom service providers (TSPs) and mobile network operators (MNOs), making real-time data sharing and number tracking difficult. Some operators may lack the Application Programming Interfaces (API) integration capabilities needed to track real-time fraud and blocking of numbers automatically. A shared web platform would need to handle large volumes of fraud reports from millions of users, requiring cloud-based architecture with high-speed data processing capabilities. The real-time blacklisting of numbers across multiple jurisdictions would require AI-driven filtering to differentiate genuine complaints from false reports.[9]

Other than that, each member country has different data protection regulations. While India has the Digital Personal Data Protection Act and Thailand has the Personal Data Protection Act, countries like Sri Lanka, Bangladesh, Nepal, Bhutan and Myanmar have various privacy laws that might conflict with the cross-border sharing of mobile number data. A common regulatory framework is needed to secure data sovereignty and ensure privacy compliance.[10]

A fraudulent mobile number in Thailand might be operated by a scammer in Bangladesh and used to defraud a victim in India, thus raising questions of legal jurisdiction. Without harmonised cybercrime laws, investigating, prosecuting and blocking such fraudulent numbers across borders becomes difficult. Member countries currently lack a dedicated Mutual Legal Assistance Treaty (MLAT) for cybercrime cooperation. Without an MLAT, countries might delay their responses to scam reports due to diplomatic and bureaucratic procedures.[11]

Unlike the European Union's Agency for Cybersecurity (ENISA), BIMSTEC lacks a central cybersecurity governing body to oversee regional digital fraud prevention efforts. Without a dedicated cybersecurity agency, there is no clear authority to operate and maintain such a fraud-reporting platform. By overcoming these challenges, BIMSTEC can protect millions from financial fraud and foster a safe digital ecosystem across the region.

The rising use of AI and deepfake technology has created unprecedented threats to information integrity, national security and democratic institutions. Deepfake technology—AI-generated fake images, videos and audio have become a powerful tool for misinformation, financial fraud, cybercrime and even political manipulation.[12]

Achieving a harmonised AI governance structure between BIMSTEC nations presents significant legal, technological, geopolitical and operational challenges. India and Thailand are AI leaders, investing in deepfake detection and AI-based regulatory frameworks. Also, unlike the European Union AI Act, BIMSTEC lacks a comprehensive AI regulatory policy covering ethical AI development; liability frameworks for AI-generated harm and legal definitions of deepfake content.

Deepfakes have been weaponised for (a) election interference (fake speeches, voter manipulation); (b) diplomatic tensions (fake government statements causing regional instability) and (c) social unrest (deepfake-generated riots and protests).[13] Therefore, shared regulation of AI and deepfake technologies within BIMSTEC is an urgent yet highly complex challenge due to technological disparities, legal inconsistencies, geopolitical rivalries and cybersecurity risks. BIMSTEC must adopt a collaborative, phased approach to establish a regional AI framework that prioritises security, ethics and innovation.

Fraudulent call centres in Thailand and Myanmar (already mentioned above) employ various deceptive tactics to lure individuals with false job offers, and they eventually find themselves trafficked into scam centres, causing them immense suffering and economic loss. Upon entry into these scam centres, victims face inhumane conditions, including physical abuse, torture and threats, compelling them to participate in fraudulent activities. Reports reveal victims enduring beatings, electric shocks and illegal detention.[14]

In recent times, efforts to combat these operations have intensified. On March 10 and 11, 2025, India repatriated 549 of its nationals who had fallen victim to fake job offers and had been forced into cybercrime activities near the Myanmar-Thailand border. Similarly, on February 12, 2025, over 260 foreign nationals from countries, including The Philippines, Bangladesh and Kenya, were rescued from scam centres in Myanmar and handed over to Thai authorities. On February 6, 2025, Myanmar's Border Guard Force transferred 61 foreign scam call centre victims to Thai authorities.[15]

The financial ramifications are profound. In the first quarter of 2024 alone, Indians lost approximately Rs. 120.3 crore to digital arrest frauds. Notably, 46 percent of digital fraud cases, including digital arrests, trading scams and investment scams, were traced back to operators based in Myanmar, Laos, and Cambodia. The operation of fraudulent call centres in Thailand and Myanmar, exploiting abducted individuals from BIMSTEC countries, represents a grave challenge to regional security and human rights. Continued collaborative efforts between affected nations is imperative to dismantle these networks, rescue and rehabilitate victims and implement stringent measures to prevent such exploitation in the future.[16]

Conclusion

The advent of computers, as articulated in the provided prompt, represents a watershed moment in human history, catalysing a profound transformation across social, economic and political domains. Within BIMSTEC, this digital revolution presents both unprecedented opportunities and complex challenges, necessitating a sophisticated approach to technological integration and cybersecurity. The BIMSTEC, comprised of nations with diverse developmental trajectories, is witnessing a rapid proliferation of digital technologies. This surge, while fostering economic growth through enhanced connectivity and trade facilitation, simultaneously exposes the region to heightened cyber vulnerabilities. The "powerful machines" reshaping industries and communication, as noted in the prompt, translate within BIMSTEC to the digitisation of critical infrastructure, financial systems and governmental services. This digitisation, however, creates new vectors for malicious actors, and demands a robust and coordinated regional response.

It is interesting to note that India has a long history of providing solutions to complex scientific problems. Baudhayana, an ancient Indian scholar who lived during 800 BC, was one of the earliest known mathematicians to provide a statement in the *Baudhayana Sulba Sutra* on what was known as the Pythagoras Theorem *nearly* three centuries later. He is believed to have derived a rule for constructing right-angled triangles and laid the foundations of geometry in ancient India. The 600 BC Sage Manava, also known as Manu, is traditionally identified as the author of the *Manusmriti*, a text primarily focused on ethics, law, and social conduct. Though not primarily a mathematician, Manu provided early indications of arithmetic and geometry, and some scholars trace the roots of some of the basic principles of mathematics to his work. Apastamba, an ancient Indian scholar who flourished during 600 BC, highlighted geometric principles in his *Apastamba Sulba Sutra,* which included an early version of the Pythagorus Theorem. He made significant contributions to the construction of altars and the principles of geometry. Pythagoras, an ancient Greek philosopher and mathematician, who lived during 570–495 BCE, is best known for the Pythagorean Theorem, which states that in a right-angled triangle, the square of the hypotenuse is equal to the sum of the squares of the other two sides. His influence on mathematics and philosophy was profound and he is often associated with the development of mathematical concepts of harmony and proportions. In the 3rd century BC, Katyayana became one of the significant figures in the development of Sanskrit grammar. His work, *Katyayana Sutra*, focused on refinement and clarification of earlier grammar rules. Though his primary focus was language, he also contributed to early arithmetic and combinatorial ideas used in calculations for ritual purposes.

While ancient scholars Baudhayana, Manava, Apastamba, Katyayana and Pythagoras did not directly contribute to the invention or discovery of modern computers, their work laid the foundation for key mathematical and geometric principles, which are crucial to computing today. While they didn't foresee modern computers, their developing of early mathematical principles established the groundwork for later developments in mathematics and logic that eventually led to the creation of modern computing technology. The development of algorithms, number systems and geometric understanding all build on the foundation that includes the contributions of these early scholars.

The story of computers, therefore, begins long before the advent of the modern digital age.

The history of computers and artificial intelligence traces an extraordinary evolution from early mechanical inventions to the transformative digital technologies we rely on today. Beginning with Charles Babbage's Analytical Engine in the 19th century, often considered the first computer, the journey spans breakthroughs by pioneering figures like Alan Turing. Turing's contributions during World War II, particularly his use of computational machines for cryptanalysis, laid the groundwork for modern computing and theoretical computer science. His Turing Machine remains a cornerstone for understanding algorithms and computation. Post-war advancements, such as John von Neumann's development of the modern electronic computer, further accelerated the growth of computational power, which, during the World War II era, became pivotal in military applications like the Manhattan Project.

As computers advanced, researchers began to explore the potential of creating machines that could mimic human intelligence. This quest for artificial intelligence can be traced back to Turing's work, where he explored the possibility of machines that could think and reason like humans. In the 1950s, pioneers such as John McCarthy, Marvin Minsky and Alan Newell began formalising the field of AI, creating algorithms that could solve problems, play games, and perform tasks traditionally considered the domain of human intelligence. AI has progressed rapidly, driven by advances in machine learning, neural networks and deep learning. Today, AI systems are capable of performing several tasks, from diagnosing medical conditions to driving autonomous vehicles. The rise of AI is perhaps the most significant technological development of the 21st century, and its potential impact on society is profound.

The intersection of contemporary AI and ancient Indian mathematical wisdom, presents a unique opportunity for the BIMSTEC. This is particularly relevant in the context of AI, which heavily relies on algorithms and computational efficiency. The development of sophisticated AI models, particularly in areas like machine learning and data analytics, can be enhanced by drawing upon the algorithmic rigour and logical frameworks present in ancient Indian mathematical texts. For example, the precise geometric calculations and spatial reasoning found in the *Sulbasutras* can contribute to the development of advanced spatial AI applications relevant to BIMSTEC's infrastructure development and disaster management.

As we look to the future, AI is expected to play an increasingly central role in our lives. Automation, data-driven decision-making and intelligent systems will transform industries, economies and societies. However, this technological revolution also raises important ethical and philosophical questions about the nature of intelligence, autonomy and human-machine interaction.

The history of computers and artificial intelligence is a remarkable journey of discovery, innovation, and transformation. From the earliest mechanical devices to the rise of AI, computers have reshaped the world in once unimaginable ways. The future of history will be shaped by the continuing evolution of computing technologies. As AI and machine learning advance, we may be witnessing the dawn of a new era in human civilisation, one where humans and machines collaborate to solve the world's most pressing challenges. The future promises even more groundbreaking innovations in computers.

Against this backdrop, BIMSTEC's progress depends on a strategic approach to cybersecurity and emerging technologies. Robust regional cooperation is vital, moving beyond reactive measures to proactive investment in digital infrastructure. Prioritising cybersecurity is fundamental for meeting BIMSTEC's economic and social goals. A multi-layered framework is essential, addressing immediate vulnerabilities while integrating AI, drawing on ancient mathematical principles. Capacity building, data infrastructure, ethical governance and sustained collaboration are crucial for this holistic approach. It will help BIMSTEC navigate technological complexities. Effective cybersecurity ensures that digital evolution contributes to sustainable growth, regional security and cultural preservation. Balancing technological advancement with security and ethical considerations is the key to BIMSTEC's future.

NOTES

1 "Bangkok Declaration. 1997. Declaration on the Establishment of the Bangladesh-India-Sri Lanka-Thailand Economic Cooperation (BIST-EC)." Bangkok, Thailand. June 6, 1997. p. 1. https://bimstec.org/images/content_page_pdf/1705915065_Declaration%20on%20

Economic%20Cooperation%20-%2006.06.1997%20(Bangkok).pdf.

2 "Bay of Bengal Initiative for Multi- Sectoral Technical and Economic Cooperation. 2004." https://bimstec.org/history.

3 De, Prabir. *Twenty Years of BIMSTEC: Promoting Regional Cooperation and Integration in the Bay of Bengal Region*. KW Publishers. 2018. pp -21-28.

4 Raju, Adluri Subramanyam., and Chaudhury, Anasua Basu Ray. *New Futures for BIMSTEC: Connectivity, Commerce and Security*. Routledge Publication. 2021.

5 Xavier, Constantino, and Dhruv Banerjee. "BIMSTEC and Security Cooperation in the Bay of Bengal." *CSEP*, August 27, 2024. https://csep.org/blog/bimstec-and-security-cooperation-in-the-bay-of-bengal.

6 "BIMSTEC. Science, Technology & Innovation." https://bimstec.org/science-technology-innovation#:~:text=Accordingly%2C%20the%20MoA%20on%20the,for%20its%20entry%20into%20force..

7 "Second Meeting of the BIMSTEC Expert Group on Cyber Security Cooperation." Press Information Bureau, January 24, 2025. https://pib.gov.in/PressReleaseIframePage.aspx?PRID=2095700#:~:text= This%20Action%20Plan%20will%20cover, time%20frame%20of%205%20years.

8 Jain, Jiten., and Rath, Saroj. "Information Warfare: Why India needs to give Pak propaganda machinery a taste of its own medicine." DailyO. 2020.. https://www.dailyo.in/politics/india-pakistan-information-warfare-open-source-intelligence-ispr-isi-raw-33542.

9 Jain, Jiten. Securing BIMSTEC Region: A Pre-emptive Methodology. In The Book India's Cyber Security, edited by Saroj Kumar Rath. *Synergy Press*. 2015. p 94.

10 "The Digital Personal Data Protection Act." Ministry of Law and Justice. 2023. https://www.meity.gov.in/static/uploads/2024/06/2bf1f0e9f04e6fb4f8fef35e82c42aa5.pdf.

11 Rath, Saroj Kumar. *Fragile Frontiers: The Secret History of Mumbai Terror Attacks*. Routledge Publication. 2019. p -163.

12 Jain, Jiten. Securing BIMSTEC Region: A Pre-emptive Methodology. In The Book India's Cyber Security, edited by Saroj Kumar Rath. *Synergy Press*. 2015. p 95.

13 Rath, Saroj Kumar., and Jain, Jiten Kumar. Ban on Chinese Apps: Role and Scope for Indigenous Mobile Applications. *Employment News*. 2020.

14 Wongcha-um, Panu., and Thepgumpanat, Panarat. "Scams hubs on Thai Myanmar border still have up to 100,000 people, Thai police says." *Reuters*, March 18, 2025. https://www.reuters.com/world/asia-pacific/scam-hubs-thai-myanmar-border-still-have-up-100000-people-thai-police-says-2025-03-18/.

15 Goldstein, Leila. "Thousands rescued from illegal scam compounds in Myanmar as Thailand launches huge crackdown." *The Guardian*, February 19, 2025. https://www.theguardian.com/world/2025/feb/19/myanmar-scam-call-centre-compound-rescues-thailand-crackdown.

16 Head, Jonathan. Hundreds of foreigners freed from Myanmar's scam centers. *BBC*, February 13, 2025. https://www.bbc.com/news/articles/c2d3w90x86po.

14

The Nexus of Narcotics Trafficking and Organised Crime in BIMSTEC

Anurag Sharma

In June 1997, four nations along the Bay of Bengal established a sub-regional group called BIST-EC (Bangladesh, India [hereafter Bharat], Sri Lanka and Thailand Economic Cooperation). Later, following the inclusion of Myanmar, Nepal and Bhutan on July 31, 2004, BIST-EC was renamed as the BIMSTEC (the Bay of Bengal Initiative for Multi-Sectoral Technical and Economic Cooperation). It became a multilateral platform of seven South Asian and Southeast Asian nations, viz. India, Bangladesh, Bhutan, Myanmar, Nepal, Sri Lanka and Thailand. Among the 15 priority areas selected for bilateral and inter-regional cooperation, countering terrorism and transnational crime was declared most essential and urgent.

Among the BIMSTEC member nations, India is leading the "counterterrorism and transnational crime" group, where four sub-groups: (i) intelligence sharing, (ii) terror financing, (iii) legal, and (iv) law enforcement and narcotics, are led by Sri Lanka, Thailand, and Myanmar respectively.

The BIMSTEC region faces significant challenges from narcotics trafficking and organised crime due to its geographical positioning, porous borders and socio-economic vulnerabilities. This paper explores the current scenario of narcotics trafficking, the nexus between organised crime and terrorism and the policy frameworks in place to counter these threats.

The proliferation of narco-trafficking and organised crime in the BIMSTEC region has profound implications for national security, economic stability and public health. The interconnected nature of these illegal activities demands a coordinated regional and rational approach, yet disparities in national policies and enforcement mechanisms, hinder efficiency and effectiveness. This paper aims to analyse the multidimensional aspects of this issue and recommend actionable policy measures to counter its menacing impact.

The Venomous Nexus: Narco-Trafficking and Organised Crime in BIMSTEC Region

Narco-trafficking in the BIMSTEC region is deeply intertwined with organised crime that exploit the porous borders, the limited law enforcement capacities and socio-political vulnerabilities. The region's proximity to the "Golden Triangle", which covers large parts of Myanmar, Laos and Thailand, has long been infamous for opium production and narco-trafficking across BIMSTEC member states. In recent years, however, criminal organisations, predominantly based in Myanmar, have shifted their focus towards producing synthetic drugs, including methamphetamines.[1] According to the United Nations Office on Drugs and Crime (UNODC), in 2022, Southeast Asia witnessed seizures of nearly 151 tonnes of methamphetamine, underscoring the region's central role in global narcotic markets. Additionally, a record 27.4 tonnes of ketamine was confiscated, marking a 167 per cent increase on confiscations compared to 2021.[2]

In 2024, the UNODC Report highlighted a slight decrease in Myanmar's opium cultivation, with a 0.4 percent reduction to 45,200 hectares.[3] The decline followed three years of increased production linked to political instability after the 2021 military coup. Following a decline in the region's opium production, methamphetamine and crystal meth tablets have become more prevalent. Compared to the labour-intensive process of opium cultivation, synthetic drug production on an industrial scale requires less effort. It facilitates easier trafficking by land, sea, and air within Asia and the Pacific.[4]

Narcotic Production and Trafficking Routes

Given its geographical proximity to significant opium cultivation areas, such as the Golden Triangle, the BIMSTEC is highly vulnerable to narcotics trafficking and consumption. Myanmar (or Burma), one of the BIMSTEC members, is one of the largest producers of opium and its by-end products like heroin and other synthetic drugs[5], marking it as a narco-trafficking centre within the region. The political situation in Myanmar has resulted in a rise in the production of methamphetamine, which is trafficked through BIMSTEC nations using land and maritime routes. The large and unmonitored maritime spaces in the Bay of Bengal and Andaman Sea create opportunities for traffickers to smuggle significant quantities of narcotics.[6] As one of the case studies of maritime routes to smuggle narcotics, in February 2020, the Indian authorities seized two consignments of 371 kilograms and 1156 kilograms of methamphetamine from two vessels in the Bay of Bengal.[7] In December 2024, law enforcement authorities confiscated over 6,000 kilograms of methamphetamine from a Myanmar vessel near the Andaman and Nicobar Islands. The incident highlighted the use of advanced technology in narco-trafficking. In the first of its kind, traffickers utilised Starlink satellite internet devices to navigate international waters and avoid detection.[8]

The significant land-based trafficking routes originate from Myanmar and extend through India's northeastern states, Bangladesh and Thailand. These routes facilitate the movement of heroin and synthetic drugs into South Asia and other regions. "YABA" (a combination of methamphetamine and caffeine) tablets and other synthetic narcotic substances, including methamphetamine, are smuggled into the northeastern Indian states like Manipur and Mizoram, and then pushed to other areas.[9] The porous India-Myanmar border is a key transit point for large quantities of YABA tablets being trafficked into Bangladesh, where the demand is very high. The 2021 UNODC Report "*Synthetic Drugs in East and Southeast Asia*" indicates that East Asia and Southeast Asia reported a record methamphetamine seizure of 171.5 tons. Notably, the Lower Mekong sub-region, comprising of Myanmar, Thailand, Laos, Cambodia and Vietnam, accounted for 89 percent of these seizures.[10] In 2024, the UNODC reported that in 2023, the scale of methamphetamine production in the Golden Triangle area was substantial, contributing approximately USD 80 billion annually to the region's illicit economies. According to the report, the total amount of methamphetamine seized in East Asia and Southeast Asia, originating from the Golden Triangle, reached a record 190 tons in 2023. The number of methamphetamine tablets seized, totalling 1.1 billion and weighing 98.3 tons, was the highest ever reported for the region, as was the seizure of 90 tons of crystal methamphetamine.[11]

Maritime trafficking is also a growing concern in the BIMSTEC region, as narcotics traffickers and organised crime syndicates use sea routes to transport narcotics. The Bay of Bengal has become a vital conduit for heroin and methamphetamine shipments, with India, Sri Lanka and Thailand emerging as key transit points. In recent years, Indian authorities have intercepted several drug consignments originating from Myanmar and destined for international markets. In one notable instance, Indian law enforcement seized 1,156 kilograms of methamphetamine from a vessel in the Bay of Bengal, highlighting the increasing use of maritime routes for drug smuggling. Furthermore, Sri Lanka's strategic location along major maritime trade routes, makes it an attractive transit hub for narcotics smuggling between South Asia and Southeast Asia.

The shift from plant-based drugs like heroin and opium to synthetic drugs, particularly Amphetamine-Type Stimulants (ATS), is a notable trend in BIMSTEC's drug trade. Methamphetamine is the most produced and trafficked synthetic drug in the Golden Triangle region,[12] primarily manufactured in Myanmar's Shan State. Drug cartels exploit weak border controls and corrupt law enforcement agencies to distribute these narcotics across BIMSTEC nations. The Bangladesh Annual Drug Report - 2022 reveals a shift in the methamphetamine market, with a significant rise in crystalline methamphetamine, *also known as* ICE, seizures. Seizures of this form increased threefold from 36.8 kilograms in 2021 to approximately 105 kilograms in 2022.[13] As per the same report, YABA tablet seizures decreased by 13.75 percent during the same period, from around 5,30,000 tablets in 2021 to 4,37,000 tablets in 2022.[14] Efforts to curb narco-trafficking across BIMSTEC include international cooperation, enhanced border security and intelligence-sharing initiatives. The 2020 BIMSTEC Conference on Combating Drug Trafficking emphasised regional collaboration to dismantle trafficking networks. However, the persistence of narco-trade challenges highlights the need for stronger enforcement mechanisms and policy interventions to counter the distribution of narcotic substances in the region.

Linkages with Organised Crime Syndicates

The BIMSTEC region has witnessed an alarming rise in narco-trafficking activities since 2014 and its close intertwining with organised crime syndicates, which misuse porous borders, weak law enforcement and socio-economic vulnerabilities to operate drug networks across the region. Organised Crime Syndicates (OCS) carried out various illicit activities, including human trafficking, arms smuggling, counterfeit currency circulation, wildlife trafficking and cybercrime. Narco-trafficking remains prominent because of high demand and lucrative profits. Syndicates often use other illicit activities to facilitate narco-trafficking. Human trafficking is used to smuggle narcotic substances across borders. Women, children and illegal labour are deployed in narco-transportation, or as couriers/peddlers. Similarly, armed insurgent groups in the region, mainly in Myanmar, and organised crime syndicates, maintain a symbiotic relationship in which profits from narco-trade are utilised in illicit arms trade and insurgency, particularly in the Bharat-Myanmar border region.

WAR ON DRUG 2.0
ARREST & SEIZURE OF DRUGS BY MANIPUR POLICE DURING THE PERIOD FROM 20.03.2022 TO 13.05.2023)

Sl. No.	Particulars of drug	No. cases Regd.	No of persons arrested	Quantity of drugs	Local market (in Rs.)	International market (In Rs.)
01	No. 4. Heroin Powder	220	334	105.733 kgs	21,14,66,000	211,46,60,000
02	Opium	68	93	479.426 kgs	3,35,59,820	33,55,98,200
03	Spasmo Proxivon	06	07	34.6176 kgs	34,61,760	3,46,17,600
04	W.Y. Tablet	44	63	319.194 kgs	15,95,97,000	159,59,70,000
05	Brown Sugar	129	181	595.555 kgs	89,33,32,500	893,33,25,000
07	Cough Syrup	18	26	41,261 Bottles	41,26,100	4,12,61,000
08	Ganja	15	10	1072.945 kgs	10,72,945	1,07,29,450
09	Crystal Meth (Methamphetamine)	02	04	8.117 kg.	4,05,85,000	40,58,50,000
10	Pseudoephedrine	02	-	151 .175 kgs	7,55,87,500	75,58,75,000

Image 1: Arrest and Seizure of Drugs by Manipur Police between March 20, 2022, and May 13, 2023 [*Source:* Manipur Police]

Several insurgent groups in northeast India are known to fund their operations from narco-trafficking proceeds. Various factions within the Kuki and Zomi communities and some seasoned insurgent groups like the United National Liberation Front (UNLF) and the People's Liberation Army (PLA) have reportedly used money earned from narcotics to support their rebel activities.[15] From March 2022 to May 2023, as shown in Image 1, Manipur Police successfully carried out counter-narcotic operation "War on Drug 2.0", in which over 700 traffickers/peddlers were arrested, and around 2,767 kilograms of narcotic substances were seized worth Rs. 149 crore (local market price) or Rs. 1382.61 crore (international market price).[16] The People's Alliance for Peace and Progress (PAPP), one of the NGOs based in Manipur, reported that:

> "The **Kuki militants** and **drug mafias** are taking advantage of the shifting drug activities (poppy plantation and drug manufacturing) from the Golden Triangle, especially the Shan State in Myanmar, to the Indo-Myanmar border

> towards the Chin and Kachin States of Myanmar neighbouring India. The Kuki militants controlling these areas, as also the adjacent areas in Manipur and Mizoram, are emboldened by suspension of operations to indulge in illegal poppy cultivation and drug trade to raise huge financial resources".[17]

Myanmar's illicit drug trade serves as a significant driver of violence and conflict, both domestically and internationally. Armed conflicts frequently arise between insurgent groups and government forces due to competition over profitable drug markets and trafficking routes. The presence of organised crime networks in the areas is also associated with the manufacturing and trafficking of heroin. The UNODC report titled "*Myanmar Opium Survey 2018*" highlighted that as per the estimate by the Government of Myanmar, criminal activity in the country is likely to generate USD 15 billion per year.[18] In Myanmar, ethnic insurgent groups such as the Shan State Army (SSA) and the United Wa State Army (UWSA) have utilised the drugs trade as a significant source of revenue. The groups levy taxes on opium cultivators, processing facilities, and trafficking networks to generate funds for their activities.[19]

Initiatives against Narco-Trafficking

Since 2020, the BIMSTEC has taken significant steps to combat narco-trafficking in the region. In March 2021, the BIMSTEC Convention on Cooperation in Combating International Terrorism (CCIT), Transnational Organised Crime (TSC), and Illicit Drug Trafficking became operational after all member states ratified it. This convention aims to enhance collaborative efforts among member countries to address these pressing issues. In July 2024, addressing the fourth annual meeting of BIMSTEC Security Chiefs in Naypyidaw, Myanmar, India's National Security Advisor (NSA) Ajit Doval, highlighted the need for increased cooperation in counterterrorism, and stopping narco-trafficking, arms-smuggling and organised crime.[20]

In January 2023, the 10th Joint Working Group (JWG) meeting of BIMSTEC on Counterterrorism and Transnational Crime in New Delhi discussed regional threats and endorsed research reports from other sub-groups focused on narcotic and psychotropic substances and precursor chemicals. The Indian delegation from the Ministry of External Affairs (MEA), led by the Secretary (West), emphasised the necessity for collective efforts to counter terrorism and transnational crimes (CTTC), including steps to strengthen cooperation in working areas such as capacity building, information exchange, extradition and other forms of legal assistance.[21]

Table 1: List of Meetings of JWG-CTTC as of April 2025

Meeting	*Venue*	*Date*
1st JWG-CTTC	New Delhi, Bharat	09-10 December 2004
2nd JWG-CTTC	New Delhi, Bharat	04-05 May 2006
3rd JWG-CTTC	Nay Pyi Taw, Myanmar	16-17 January 2007
4th JWG-CTTC	New Delhi, Bharat	22-23 October 2008
5th JWG-CTTC	Kathmandu, Nepal	24-25 November 2011
6th JWG-CTTC	Colombo, Sri Lanka	07-08 May 2013
7th JWG-CTTC	Bangkok, Thailand	04-05 August 2015
8th JWG-CTTC	Dhaka, Bangladesh	13-14 August 2018
9th JWG-CTTC (Virtual)	Thimphu, Bhutan	25 November 2021
10th JWG-CTTC	New Delhi, India	12-13 January 2023

Source: BIMSTEC Secretariat.

Way Ahead: Challenges and Countermeasures

Tackling the nexus between narco-trafficking and organised crime in the BIMSTEC region is hindered by several factors, including diverse legal systems, land and maritime border issues, corruption, and socio-economic vulnerabilities. A well-coordinated approach and strong political will is required to address the above-mentioned challenges. Narcotics trafficking not only threatens a nation's security but also undermines regional economic growth and societal stability. The increasing use of sophisticated methods and technologies by traffickers requires BIMSTEC nations invest in modern surveillance and strengthen capabilities to counter this evolving threat effectively.

There is a need for synchronising legal **approaches**, while recognising narco-trafficking as a serious offence. For instance, Thailand has some of the strictest drug laws in the world, like the Psychotropic Substances Act 1975 and the Narcotic Act 1979, which includes capital punishment for large-scale trafficking.[22] India also has tough regulations under the Narcotic Drugs and Psychotropic Substances Act (NDPS). Countries like Myanmar, which has a history of illicit opium production, followed by narcotic manufacturing and trafficking, have struggled with enforcement of the law due to internal conflicts and lack of state control in certain regions.

(Repetition) The Indo-Myanmar border, which spans over 1,600 kilometres, is particularly vulnerable. Due to historical trade and ethnic linkages, trafficking routes have flourished across the porous border, moving heroin, methamphetamine and synthetic drugs into India.

Corruption within establishments and other institutions is another significant challenge coming in the way of countering narco-trafficking. Syndicates often use bribery and intimidation to ensure safe passage for their consignments. Countries with weak governance, lack of political will and ongoing internal chaos will open the doors of opportunity for cartels/syndicates to collaborate with corrupt officials to achieve their illicit objectives. Some BIMSTEC member nations struggle with political instability, economic challenges, or conflicting interests. For instance, political instability in Myanmar has made it challenging to enforce strict anti-narcotics measures, which is further helping narcotic cartels to expand their activities.

Furthermore, poor levels of cooperation and intelligence-sharing between BIMSTEC countries has impeded efforts to dismantle transnational narcotics syndicates. More efforts are a must to enhance transparency and commitment among member states. Strengthening the joint task forces and conducting regular high-level security meetings can also help build trust and improve collaborative enforcement efforts.

Additionally, drug abuse is becoming a growing public health crisis within BIMSTEC nations. The rise in supply vis-à-vis the demand for synthetic drugs, including methamphetamine and pharmaceutical drugs, has led to rising addiction rates, particularly among youth. This creates a huge burden on healthcare systems, increases crime rates and exacerbates social instability. India and Thailand have developed rehabilitation and de-addiction programs, but many BIMSTEC nations lack sufficient infrastructure to handle the scale of drug abuse within their populations. While BIMSTEC has moved positively towards narco-trafficking through its counterterrorism and transnational crime initiatives, some more concrete actions are required. Strengthening regional institutions, improving governance and fostering firm political will secure the region and ensure a narcotics-free future.

NOTES

1 Kang, Taejun. "South Korea, Interpol Confiscate Drugs Worth $1bn in Golden Triangle", *Radio Free Asia,* September 12, 2024. https://www.rfa.org/english/news/laos/korea-interpol-drug-crackdown-09122024064123.html

2 Doyle, Kevin. "UN Says Organized Crime Shifting Drugs Routes in Southeast Asia", *Al Jazeera,* June 2, 2023. https://www.aljazeera.com/news/2023/6/2/un-says-organised-crime-shifting-drugs-routes-in-southeast-asia

3 Peck, Grant. "UN Drug Experts say Opium Production has Levelled Off in Myanmar, But Instability May Trigger a Rise", *Associated Press,* December 12, 2024. https://apnews.com/

article/opium-heroin-golden-triangle-drug-trade-da7bd1347de918027324de05815dbf46

4 Ibid.

5 "Myanmar Remains A Leading Source of Opium And Heroin." *UNODC-Press Release.* December 12, 2024. https://www.unodc.org/unodc/en/press/releases/2024/December/myanmar-remains-a-worlds-leading-source-of-opium-and-heroin.html

6 "Navigating the Narcotics Network in the Indian Ocean." *The Geostrata.* January 28, 2025. https://www.thegeostrata.com/post/navigating-the-narcotics-network-navigating-the-narcotics-network

7 "Two days 'Conference on Combating Drug Trafficking' for BIMSTEC Partner Nations Concludes in New Delhi. - Ministry of Home Affairs, Government of India. February 15, 2020. https://pib.gov.in/PressReleasePage.aspx?PRID=1603292

8 Vengattil, Munsif and Aditya Kalra. "Indian Police to Query Starlink on Device Used In Huge Haul of Smuggled Drugs." *Reuters.* December 3, 2024. https://www.reuters.com/world/india/indian-police-query-starlink-device-used-huge-haul-smuggled-drugs-2024-12-03/

9 Chaudhury, Dipanjan Roy. "Mizoram Emerges As Major Drug Trafficking Route From Myanmar." *The Economic Times.* October 8, 2020.https://economictimes.indiatimes.com/news/politics-and-nation/mizoram-emerges-as-major-drug-trafficking-route-from-myanmar/articleshow/78553675.cms

10 Bhandari, Subel Rai. "UN: 1 Billion Meth Pills Seized In East, Southeast Asia Last Year." *Radio Free Asia.* May 31, 2022. https://www.rfa.org/english/news/myanmar/southeastasia-meth-05312022143430.html

11 Peck, Grant. "East, Southeast Asia had Record Methamphetamine Seizures Last Year: Profits Remain in Billions." *Associated Press.* May 28, 2024. https://apnews.com/article/crystal-methamphetamine-golden-triangle-shan-ketamine-cb5de08da123b150210793a667c0c149

12 "World Drug Report 2024." *United Nations Office on Drugs and Crime.* 2024. https://www.unodc.org/documents/data-and-analysis/WDR_2024/WDR_2024_SPI.pdf

13 "Table: Statistics on the Seizure of Drugs by All Agencies in Bangladesh." *Annual Drug Report of Bangladesh-2022.* https://dnc.gov.bd/sites/default/files/files/dnc.portal.gov.bd/annual_reports/37a9ace4_624d_4650_80ad_9f4041db6b2b/2023-05-10-07-21-ca4e1390829fc7f031c5df30419878f6.pdf

14 Ibid.

15 Pandit, Santishree Dhulipudi. "Northeast in the Middle of a Narco-Terror Crisis." *The Sunday Guardian.,* January 5, 2025. https://sundayguardianlive.com/opinion/northeast-in-the-middle-of-a-narco-terror-crisis

16 "FIR Manipur Police." October 2023. https://www.manipurpolice.gov.in/wp-content/uploads/2023/10/FIR-NO.-60872023-IMPHAL-PS.pdf

17 Mahapatra, Dhananjay. "Cross-Border Narco-Terror Root of Manipur Violence: PIL." *The Times of India.* May 31, 2023.https://timesofindia.indiatimes.com/india/cross-border-narco-terror-root-of-manipur-violence-pil/articleshow/100631644.cms ; Hazarika, Pulokjyoti. "Nexus between Insurgency and Narco-Trafficking: A Case Study of Manipur." *Vivekananda International Foundation.* April 26, 2024. https://www.vifindia.org/article/2024/april/26/Nexus-between-Insurgency-and-Narco-Trafficking

18 "Myanmar Opium Survey 2018." *UNODC.* https://css.unodc.org/documents/crop-monitoring/Myanmar/Myanmar_Opium_Survey_2018-web.pdf

19 Haider, Sarder Ali. "The Dark Nexus: Origins of Myanmar's Narcotics Trade and its Role in Fueling Insurgency and Regional Instability." *Southeast Asia Journal.* April 2023. https://southeastasia-journal.com/archives/7449

20 Seli, Yeshi. "Doval Talks Counterterrorism, Combating Drug Trafficking At BIMSTEC Meet in Myanmar." *The New Indian Express,* July 26, 2024. https://www.newindianexpress.com/nation/2024/Jul/26/doval-talks-counter-terrorism-combating-drugs-trafficking-at-bimstec-meet-in-myanmar

21 "BIMSTEC Meet Focuses on Collective Efforts to Counter Terrorism, Transnational Crimes." *The Print.* January 12, 2023, https://theprint.in/world/bimstec-meet-focuses-on-collective-efforts-to-counter-terrorism-transnational-crimes/1311563/

22 "Criminal Drug Offences in Thailand." *Pattaya Lawyers.* August 28, 2024. https://www.lawyerspattaya.com/criminal-drug-offenses-in-thailand.html

15

Tackling BIMSTEC's Non-Traditional Security Threats

Shubhamitra Das

The Bay of Bengal (BoB) region acts as a bridge between the Indian and Pacific Oceans as well as between South and Southeast Asia. Its geo-political and geo-strategic significance, therefore, cannot be undermined. Centred in the hub of the Indo-Pacific framework, it has the potential of institutionally binding the region with the sub-regional Bay of Bengal Initiative for Multi-Sectoral and Technical Cooperation (BIMSTEC) grouping, formed in 1997. Following the devastation caused by the Tsunami of December 26, 2004, Bangladesh, Bhutan, India, Myanmar, Thailand, Nepal and Sri Lanka realized the urgency for rejuvenating BIMSTEC for deeper cooperation and integration in trade, economic development, improved connectivity and fisheries management. BIMSTEC has the potential of emerging as a strong regional grouping that could further enhance broader Indo-Pacific regionalism. In fact, Indo-Pacific regionalism can only become successful, when sub-regionalism gets stronger. Sub-regionalism can leave a lasting impact on the political economy of countries, with implications on the geopolitics of the wider regional space. Sub-regional cooperation and partnership usually involves project-based connectivity initiatives that facilitate mutual economic growth, prosperity and encourage interdependence while helping with problem-solving mechanisms that further strengthen regionalism. This functional approach to regionalism is visible in initiatives like BIMSTEC, BCIM (Bangladesh, China, India, Myanmar Forum for Regional Cooperation) and MGC (Mekong Ganga Cooperation).

India is a leading member of BIMSTEC. In order to foster its "Look East, Act-East" policy and its "Neighbourhood First" policy, it has a special interest in strengthening the sub-regional grouping to counter traditional and non-traditional security (NTS) threats. The region is severely affected by the impacts of global warming, both natural and anthropogenic, frequent cyclones, Tsunamis, tidal floods, droughts and earthquakes, displacement and migration; transnational crime, Illegal, Unregulated and Unreported (IUU) fishing, all of which hamper sustainable economic growth. Another major issue is the Rohingya crisis, which needs to be addressed along with the consequences of increased human trafficking, crime, loss of identity and dignity. India has emerged as an exception in regional cooperative efforts and in directly providing humanitarian assistance[1] in the Indo-Pacific region. Issues related to NTS, and traditional security require a transboundary approach towards risk management.

India and her Regional Aspirations

Since independence, India's foreign policy has been to play a constructive role globally, with a focus on reviving Asian regionalism and the Asian identity. While regional efforts have been mostly bilateral in nature,[2] India has not shied away entirely from multilateralism. Its role in the United Nations and the Non-Aligned Movement (NAM) are testimony to that.

In the Post-Cold War period, it has increased its regional presence, keeping in mind China's aggressive stances on border disputes and its proximity to Pakistan. Disillusioned by the outcomes of the South Asian Association for Regional Cooperation (SAARC), India sought a broader regional identity and aspired for extending its understanding of the region beyond this geographical space. India's engagement is viewed from many angles, such as sub- regional, inter-regional, trans-regional and super-regional;[3] all of which highlight multi-dimensional and comprehensive regionalism. Apart from extended regionalism and the neighbourhood, India's pattern of cooperation experienced a facelift from non-alignment to multi-alignment. Within the framework of this new kind of diplomacy played by most Indo-Pacific countries, there exists a potential not only to make regionalism work, but also to paraphrase narratives on security, making it more accommodative.

Furthermore, being one of the founding members of NAM and working on the principle of non-interference, anti-colonialism and disarmament, India has emerged as one of the leading advocates of combatting NTS threats like global warming and climate change, disaster management and resilience, transnational crime, etc. During the G20, Prime Minister Narendra Modi announced that India wants to be the "Voice of the Global South" which further enhances India's role and responsibility with countries already affected by protracted internal warfare, or increased occurrences of natural disasters. The devastations caused by Cyclones Hudud (2014), Roano (May 2016), Vardha (December 2016), Mora (2017), Hamoon (2023) and Fengal (2024) are just a few mentions in a long list that requires a readiness to deal with them in the aftermath. The Indian Navy's Humanitarian Assistance and Disaster Relief (HADR) and the Search and Rescue (SAR) operations form a major part of its "Exercise Milan" along the Bay of Bengal.[4] BBIMSTEC has taken measures to counter transnational crime and terrorism in the region. While IUU fishing is another delicate issue that requires cooperation and stricter rules to prevent severe depletion of marine life and an existential crisis for communities making a living of marine produce.

Secondly, it severely hampers the marine ecosystem causing disturbance to biodiversity. Maritime Domain Awareness and Deep-Sea Domain Awareness is an important component of maritime security that requires cooperation and information sharing between countries of the region. India will need the help of Sri Lanka, Myanmar, Bangladesh, Thailand and Malaysia (if and when it becomes a member of BIMSTEC) to facilitate regular port visits, exchange and sharing of information and logistics, and more naval exercises to reduce IUU fishing and other NTS challenges.

BIMSTEC must note that the BoB region does not have a Regional Fisheries Management Organisation (RFMO)[5] that can regularise, record, monitor and organise search operations. The joint operations of the Indian Navy and Coast Guard need to be more inclusive and seen to be firmly tackling both human and drug trafficking, a rampant menace in the region.

The Rohingya issue needs more scholarship as well as strong political will to remove the tag of statelessness from them and allow them to return and survive in their own land.

Members of the sub-regional grouping are acutely aware of the myriad challenges hampering regional progress. Though Thailand initially proposed the creation of BIMSTEC for regional economic cooperation, today this grouping is dealing with issues that go beyond economic cooperation. It has become a key proponent for regional cooperation and integration. Disaster management is one of the most important areas for cooperation due to the severity and frequency of cyclones, earthquakes, tsunamis, floods and droughts.

India organized the BIMSTEC Leaders Retreat in 2016 and the BIMSTEC Disaster Management Exercise SAADMex in 2017 and 2020. The second such exercise involved the participation of Bangladesh, Myanmar, Sri Lanka, Nepal, besides India.[6] India's disaster management operations can be more effective when there is regional support and a strong political shown by member countries.

BIMSTEC: A Platform for Tackling NTS

BIMSTEC is a connect between South Asia and Southeast Asia. It also connects the Greater Himalayas with the Bay of Bengal. This geographical contiguity, sharing of similar history and economic complementarities[7] makes it easier to deal with issues. BIMSTEC is already functioning as a sector-driven organisation, with 14 sectors led by individual countries. India was to look into tourism and climate change. The latter is being looked into under the field of Environment and Natural Disaster Management and the nodal agency for this is the BIMSTEC Centre for Weather and Climate in India.[8]

BIMSTEC was meant to be a platform for India to boost its relations with Myanmar and Thailand[9] and is now seen as a replacement to SAARC[10] (but not actually so), where eight countries are members. Myanmar shares a land border with India, making India's northeast strategically important.

India's Act East Policy is aimed at strengthening the northeast to facilitate deeper engagement with Southeast Asia which share almost identical cultural, civilisational and linguistic ties. Moreover, the ethnic divide offers tremendous possibilities to develop borders and generate more knowledge on transborder identities to tackle transnational crime and improve trade and connectivity, which is a major BIMSTEC objective. Connectivity is the key to enhancing cooperation[11] both inland and through maritime cooperation. India's SAGARMALA and BHARATMALA Projects, Project Mausam, Neighbourhood First as foreign policy initiatives[12] and initiatives like Indo-Pacific Oceans Initiative (IPOI) and Security and Growth for All (SAGAR) interlink BIMSTEC to the Indo-Pacific region. Most importantly, BIMSTEC is required to improve disaster management programs. The earthquake that hit Myanmar and Thailand in March 2025 is a case in point. India activated "Operation Brahma" to provide aid and relief to Myanmar immediately. India again proved to be the first responder in a disaster relief operation.

To strengthen and institutionalise BIMSTEC, regional treaties, programmes, region-specific initiatives, capacitating member countries on land and in the maritime domain, identifying for trade and investment opportunities for regional cooperation, etc., has to be worked out between member countries. The BoB region can emerge as a zone of peace provided there is a check on regional militarisation, peaceful settlement of disputes and socio-economic cooperation of a reasonable and acceptable standard.... A strong, well equipped and well-trained secretariat would be an added bonus.[13] BIMSTEC must consider expanding its membership to Malaysia, which will help in governance, development, economic growth and disaster management and resilience on the one hand, and will be of benefit Malaysia on the other.

Conclusion

Member countries like Myanmar, Bangladesh, Nepal and Sri Lanka suffer from governance issues, civil strife and political upheaval and hence cooperation through BIMSTEC becomes all the more important. The economies of Myanmar and Thailand have been left shaken by last month's earthquake. To an extent, the April 2025 BIMSTEC Summit had its role cut out in that it had to emphasise more on disaster management and resilience mechanisms. Trust building between countries will have to be promoted to reduce transnational crime. India has to build a road map for its deeper engagement in the region and make the BIMSTEC work.

NOTES

1 Kanyon, Deon. "India Leading International HADR Cooperation in South Asia." *Daniel K Inouye Asia-Pacific Centre for Security Studies.* 2021.

2 Wagner, Christian. Bersick, Sebastian, Stockhof, Wim. And Paul Ven Der Welde (ed). "India's New Quest for Intra and Inter-regional Politics in Multi-regionalism and Multilateralism: Asian European Relations in Global Context." *Amsterdam University Press.* 2006.

3 Sridharan, Kripa. "India's Perspective on Regionalism in Asia. Collaboration under Anarchy: Functional Regionalism and the Security of East Asia." *S. Rajaratnam School of International Studies.* 2009.

4 Gamage, Rajini. "Bay of Bengal: What Implications for ASEAN" & "ASEAN and the Indian Ocean: The Key Maritime Links." *S. Rajaratnam School of International Studies.* 2017.

5 Faiyaz, Tarique and Balraj Kaur Siddu. "Tackling IUU Fishing, Transnational Organised Crime (TOC) and Maritime Security Threats in the Bay of Bengal." *The Journal of Territorial and Maritime Studies,* Vol. 11, No 1, pp. 43-64. 2024.

6 Kanyon, Deon. "India Leading International HADR Cooperation in South Asia." *Daniel K Inouye Asia-Pacific Centre for Security Studies.* 2021.

7 Naha, Alik. "India's Maritime Diplomacy in the Bay of Bengal." *World Affairs: Journal of International Issues,* Vol 27, No 1, pp. 46-61. January to March 2023.

8 Agarwal, Nitin. "The Re-Emergence of the Bay of Bengal." *Journal of Territorial and Maritime Studies,* Vol 7, No 2, pp. 49-73. 2020.

9 Wagner, Christian. Bersick, Sebastian., Stockhof, Wim. And Paul Ven Der Welde (ed) "India's New Quest for Intra and Inter-regional Politics in Multi-regionalism and Multilateralism: Asian European Relations in Global Context." *Amsterdam University Press.* 2006.

10 Subba Rao, S. "India's Paradigm Shift from SAARC to BIMSTEC." *World Affairs: Journal of International Issues,* Vol 24, No 1, pp. 90-99. 2020.

11 Subba Rao, S. "India's Paradigm Shift from SAARC to BIMSTEC." *World Affairs: Journal of International Issues,* Vol 24, No 1, 2020.

12 Gamage, Rajini. "Bay of Bengal: What Implications for ASEAN" & "ASEAN and the Indian Ocean: The Key Maritime Links." *S. Rajaratnam School of International Studies.* 2017.

13 De, Prabir. "The Expectations from BIMSTEC Summit." The Sunday Guardian Live, March 30, 2025. https://sundayguardianlive.com/investigation/the-expectations-from-bimstec-summit.

PART VI

Societal and Cultural Dimensions

16

BIMSTEC's Shakti: Shaping a Women Led Development Agenda

Cchavi Vasisht

The Bay of Bengal Initiative for Multi-Sectoral Technical and Economic Cooperation (BIMSTEC) unites seven nations—India, Bangladesh, Myanmar, Sri Lanka, Thailand, Nepal and Bhutan—into a regional bloc representing over 1.8 billion people. Women constitute nearly half of this population, playing critical roles in shaping the economies and societies of these nations. Yet, persistent barriers such as unequal access to education and health, limited economic opportunities, exclusion from leadership roles, sexual and gender-based violence (SGBV), and climate-related vulnerabilities hinder their full potential. The absence of a dedicated focus on women' agenda and development within the BIMSTEC framework and its fifteen sectors of cooperation represents a significant lacuna. This chapter posits that the formal inclusion of "women-led development" as a distinct sector of cooperation within the BIMSTEC framework has potential for transformative impact in addressing existing gender disparities and fostering inclusive regional progress.

Conceptualising Women-Led Development

The idea of women being active agents and leaders in development has its roots in the feminist movements of the 19th and early 20th centuries, which advocated for women's rights and participation in public life. The concept gained more prominence as a shift from earlier "Women in Development" (WID) approaches, which often focused on women as passive recipients of development processes, has over time, shifted to recognising women as active agents in both economic and social life. The concept of "women-led development" gained significant traction in the 1970s and 1980s.[1] From the First United Nations World Conference on Women in Mexico to being formally introduced as a strategy at the 1995 Fourth United Nations World Conference on Women in Beijing. The Beijing Platform for Action explicitly called for gender mainstreaming as a key approach to achieving gender equality.

Following the Beijing Conference, the concept of gender mainstreaming gained further traction and definition. The UN Economic and Social Council (ECOSOC) defined and endorsed gender mainstreaming as a strategy in 1997. Since then, it has been widely adopted by international organisations, governments and civil society as a central approach to promoting gender equality. More recently, the Sustainable Development Goals (SDGs) have emphasized gender equality and women empowerment within SDG 5 as integral to achieving broader development goals.

Within BIMSTEC, women-led dialogues/events are for pushing women-led development across BIMSTEC countries, such as the CII Dialogue on Women in Business and United Nations Office for Project Services (UNOPS's) discussion on women involvement in climate-related debates. In some countries, progress has been made. Over the past decade, the Indian government's interventions have focussed on building Nari Shakti and shifting them from "Women Development to Women-Led Development".[2] Statistical evidence reveals India's effort to increase women reservation through the Nari Shakti Adhiniyam, improvement in sex ratio to 1020 for the first time in 2024, increasing the representation of women within traditionally male-dominated sectors such as law enforcement and enrolment of women in Science, Technology, Engineering, and Mathematics (STEM) disciplines. Even while holding the G20 presidency in 2023, India specifically designated "women-led development" as a central focal point.

Examples across BIMSTEC states suggest the increasing participation of women in economic and political activities.[3] In Bangladesh, female entrepreneurs are transforming rural economies through microfinance programs offered by institutions like the Grameen Bank. Thai women entrepreneurs are driving innovation in tourism and small businesses, while promoting eco-friendly practices. With the high participation of the female labour force in Nepal, women are spearheading cooperative movements that enhance financial inclusion for rural communities. Sri Lankan women are contributing significantly to post-conflict reconstruction efforts through community-based organisations, whereas

Myanmar's women activists are participating in a civil war in the country. Bhutanese women are actively involved in preserving Bhutan's cultural heritage, while promoting sustainable tourism.

Despite advancements in specific domains, challenges stemming from socio-cultural norms, structural inequalities and diverse developmental stages among BIMSTEC member states continue to affect women differently. Notably, the expansion of BIMSTEC's sectors of cooperation from six to fifteen has not included gender equality or women-led development as a distinct sector of cooperation. This absence is further underscored by the lack of specific consideration for women's roles and needs within established sectors characterised by substantial female participation, such as agriculture and tourism. Similarly, salient transnational issues, including poverty and climate change, which disproportionately affect women, lack dedicated analytical or policy frameworks addressing their gendered dimensions within the BIMSTEC agenda.

Although, past dialogues and forums have occasionally addressed the involvement of women in business and the gender-specific implications of climate change, the formal integration of women-led development as a cross-cutting theme across the existing fifteen sectors, or its establishment as a distinct sixteenth sector of cooperation, would constitute a substantive step towards fostering more inclusive and equitable regional development within the BIMSTEC framework.

Nepal's President Bhandari's address at the BIMSTEC 2018 Summit, subtly hinted at a vision where women should not be considered as mere beneficiaries, but as active architects of BIMSTEC's future.[4] Her call to eradicate poverty and illiteracy, and her insistence on ending violence against women and addressing their socio-economic challenges, aimed to enhance dialogues and cooperation between BIMSTEC countries. The urgency to mitigate climate change necessitates tapping into women's traditional knowledge and community-centric approaches. In the next sub-sections, these challenges are elaborated in brief. To start with, let us look at the Gender Inequality Index (GII).[5] Thailand and Bhutan have a relatively lower GII (around 0.31 and 0.33), indicating less inequality compared to other countries in the region. In contrast, Bangladesh and Nepal have higher GII values of around 0.49, followed by Myanmar (0.47) highlighting significant gender disparities. Whereas India's GII value is approximately 0.43 and Sri Lanka is comparatively lower at around 0.37. These disparities are often rooted in cultural norms, gender biases and structural limitations that hinder women's access to education, economic opportunities and decision-making power.

Labour Force Participation: A Mixed Picture

Labour Force Participation Rates (LFPR) among women in BIMSTEC countries present a mixed picture. In 2023, Thailand and Bhutan had a relatively high female labour force participation rate at 59.3 percent and 56.6 percent respectively. In contrast, India and Nepal exhibited lower participation rates, 31.2 percent and 27.6 percent respectively. Other countries, including Bangladesh, Myanmar and Sri Lanka recorded rates of between 31.6 percent and 43.7 percent.[6] These variations highlight the influence of diverse socio-economic factors and cultural contexts with regard to women's labour market engagement.

In India, despite constitutional guarantees of gender equality, the economic empowerment of women is hampered by low female labour force participation. Moreover, Indian women continue to face significant challenges related to unequal pay for work of equal value and pervasive gender-based violence. In Nepal, women make substantial contributions to the agricultural sector, which remains a significant source of livelihood for a majority of the population. However, not having secure access to assets like credit and land ownership, limits their productivity and economic autonomy.

While Bangladesh stands out for the remarkable strides its women have made economically, particularly within the garment industry, this participation is often characterised by precarious working conditions and persistent gender-based wage gaps. Furthermore, rural women in Bangladesh continue to face significant limitations in accessing essential resources such as credit, land ownership and market linkages. Sri Lanka presents a seemingly paradoxical situation with its high female literacy rate exceeding 90 percent. This is due to prevailing social norms and expectations that often confine them to domestic roles. Political instability in Myanmar has adversely affected the women in terms of economic opportunities and securing jobs. While women play a vital role in the informal sector, particularly in agriculture and small-scale industries, they often lack security and benefits.

However, Thailand has highlighted a comparatively higher level of economic participation among women within the BIMSTEC region. They are significantly represented in key sectors like tourism and small businesses, demonstrating their entrepreneurial spirit. However, challenges related to wage inequality persist. In Bhutan, there are concerns about women's participation in higher-paying sectors. Therefore, we can conclude that women in the BIMSTEC region often engage in informal employment or low-paying jobs with limited job security. Even the COVID-19 pandemic led to widespread job losses among women, particularly in tourism-dependent economies like Nepal and Thailand. Additionally, structural barriers such as lack of access to financial resources and cultural norms such as gender biases remain significant barriers to women's economic participation across BIMSTEC nations.

Political Representation: Persistent Underrepresentation

Women remain significantly underrepresented in political leadership across BIMSTEC countries. As of 2023, Nepal stands out with the highest proportion of seats held by women in parliament at 33 percent, while Sri Lanka reported the lowest proportion, at around five percent. Other countries, including Bangladesh, Bhutan, India, and Thailand, fall somewhere in between 15 percent and 21 percent.[7] Similarly, women's representation in ministerial-level positions varies, with countries like Bangladesh and Bhutan reporting around 10 percent, while Sri Lanka had almost zero representation.[8] A comprehensive evaluation reveals a persistent pattern of underrepresentation and the continued influence of socio-cultural and structural barriers that impede women's full and effective political participation.

In India, despite constitutional guarantees of gender equality and the implementation of reservation policies at the local governance level (Panchayati Raj Institutions), women's representation in national political bodies, particularly in Parliament, remains significantly at 14 percent. Bangladesh presents a seemingly paradoxical scenario, where women hold prominent positions at the apex of political power, but this top-level representation does not necessarily translate into substantive political empowerment at the grassroots level. Similarly, Sri Lanka, despite its relatively high female literacy rate and advancements in other social indicators, exhibits a low level of female representation in its Parliament, consistently below six percent.

Myanmar faces a particularly challenging context for women's political empowerment due to prolonged periods of military dominance and civil conflict, lack of participation in the peace process and deeply entrenched societal norms that traditionally restrict women's roles in public life and leadership. The ongoing political instability further exacerbates these challenges and underscores the urgent need for democratic reforms that prioritise inclusive political participation.

Thailand and Nepal demonstrate a comparatively better record on women's political representation compared to some other BIMSTEC nations. In Nepal, the constitution mandates a minimum of 33 percent representation for women at all levels of governance, from local bodies to the national parliament. This affirmative action has led to a significant improvement in women's participation in political processes. However, challenges remain in ensuring that this numerical representation translates into meaningful influence and effective participation in policy formulation and implementation.

Building Capabilities: Education and Health

An overview of access to education and health care services for women across BIMSTEC countries highlights both progress and challenges. India's experience reflects the success of nation-wide campaigns like the "Beti Bachao Beti Padhao" and the "Pradhan Mantri Surakshit Matritva Abhiyan", besides increasing maternity leave to 26 weeks. However, the identified disparities between urban and rural areas underscores the need for more geographically targetted interventions and resource allocation. Challenges of increasing unpaid work performed by women in the domestic sphere also persists.

Bangladesh similarly demonstrates the positive impact of targeted interventions like stipends, which have helped achieve gender parity in primary and secondary education. Commendable strides have also been made in reducing maternal mortality rates, largely attributable to improvements in healthcare service delivery. However, the continued high dropout rates due to early marriage, reveals a complex interplay between educational access and deeply rooted socio-cultural factors. Whereas Nepal's progress in narrowing gender gaps through specific interventions like scholarships for girls from disadvantaged communities, offers a successful model for other member states. Nepal has also witnessed improvement in healthcare access, particularly through community-based health programs strategically targeting maternal and child health. However, geographical challenges and infrastructural limitations continue to impede consistent and comprehensive healthcare delivery in many remote areas of Nepal and Bangladesh.

Sri Lanka's high female literacy rate is a testament to sustained and effective educational policies. However, the skewness in access to higher education towards urban areas suggests a need to expand infrastructure and opportunities in rural regions. Sri Lanka has also established a relatively strong maternal healthcare system, often cited as a regional best practice. Additionally, Bhutan's achievement of equitable access to primary education for women is commendable, but the limited opportunity for higher education presents a challenge. Further, Bhutanese women benefit from a system of free healthcare services, underpinned by the national philosophy of Gross National Happiness. Despite this commendable framework, gaps remain in the availability of specialised medical care, requiring women to seek treatment outside the country, or face limitations in accessing advanced interventions.

Thailand's universal education and health care policies provide a strong foundation for women's education and health. The identified challenges related to vocational training opportunities suggest a need to align educational pathways with labour market demands. Challenges, however, persist, particularly affecting marginalised groups, including ethnic minorities and migrant populations, in accessing and utilizing available healthcare resources. Finally, Myanmar presents a particularly concerning situation where civil conflicts directly impede educational access and healthcare services for women, especially in ethnic minority regions. Even the healthcare infrastructure is weak due to prolonged political instability and underinvestment.

Sexual and Gender-Based Violence: Shadows of Patriarchy

A brief overview of Sexual and Gender-Based Violence (SGBV), across BIMSTEC reveals patriarchy's multifaceted nature and its role in perpetuating SGBV. In Bangladesh, nearly two-third of their women have faced SGBV. The government's initiation of a four-year National Action Plan on women, peace and security in 2019, represents a crucial policy response aimed at integrating gender perspectives into national security frameworks. India's low ranking (150 out of 153 countries) in the World Economic Forum's Health and Survival sub-index, attributed to violence, forced marriage and discriminatory health care access, highlights the profound impact of gender inequality for a woman's well-being. In response, India has launched the Mission Shakti Program and helpline number 181.

Thailand experiences a high incidence of violence against women, with over 20,000 reported annual cases. The establishment of the National Commission on the Policy and Strategy on the Improvement of the Status of

Women and the subsequent endorsement of measures on women, peace, and security in 2016 demonstrates a policy-level recognition of the issue. In Sri Lanka, the UNFPA report indicated that 90 percent of women have experienced sexual harassment in public transportation at least once in their lives. Bhutan grapples with significant concerns related to child marriage and domestic violence. Nepal also faces the intersecting challenges of gender-based violence and discrimination based on caste, ethnicity, disability and indigeneity. Lastly, Myanmar, despite being a signatory to various ASEAN declarations and the Convention on the Elimination of All Forms of Discrimination Against Women (CEDAW), has faced significant international scrutiny and condemnation for its failure to adequately protect women, particularly those from ethnic minority groups. The present civil war is adding further to it.

Climate's Gendered Impact: Vulnerabilities of Women in BIMSTEC

More recently, events like the UNOPS-BIMSTEC Roundtable on "Impact of Climate Change on Women and Girls" in Dhaka, drew attention to the often-overlooked intersection of climate change and gender inequality.[9] BIMSTEC nations, highly susceptible to climate change impacts like sea-level rise, cyclones, earthquakes and floods, exacerbate existing gender inequalities. For instance, water scarcity, intensified by droughts, increases the burden on women tasked with water collection, often requiring longer and more dangerous journeys. The climate-induced displacement also disproportionately affects women, making them vulnerable to trafficking, exploitation and gender-based violence within overcrowded shelters or during migration. Additionally, women with disabilities, face compounded challenges due to limited mobility and lack of access to resources during climate emergencies.

Similarly, the BIMSTEC side event "Integrating Gender and Poverty in Climate Finance," coinciding with the Beijing+30 Review, held immense significance in advancing equitable climate action.[10] It addressed the urgent need to move beyond gender-blind approaches, emphasising the necessity of integrating gender and social inclusion considerations into climate finance mechanisms. Here we can also look into the impact of the COVID-19 pandemic, which disproportionately affected women in BIMSTEC countries. Women employed in tourism-dependent nations like Nepal and Thailand, faced widespread job losses due to reduced travel demand. Similarly, female workers in the garment industry in Bangladesh and Myanmar, suffered income losses as global buyers cancelled orders.

Need for BIMSTEC's Initiatives for Women-Led Development

In a CII discussion focused on bridging the gender divide within BIMSTEC, Rumjhum Chatterjee, Chairperson of the Centre for Women Leadership, India, demanded a collaborative approach and emphasised the necessity of forging stronger partnerships and implementing forward-thinking strategies to expand economic opportunities for women.[11] She highlighted the commitment to "women-led development" within the broader BIMSTEC framework. Recognising the need for a proactive approach to empower women economically and socially, various initiatives have since been incorporated in the BIMSTEC framework.

First, creation of a BIMSTEC Chamber of Commerce as a dedicated platform for trade and investment focused on women's entrepreneurship. Such a chamber could facilitate networking opportunities and provide financial resources specifically tailored for women-led businesses. Women's economic participation in BIMSTEC countries is characterised by disparities in firm ownership and leadership roles as shown below.

Economy	*Percent of firms with women participation in ownership*	*Percent of firms with majority women ownership*	*Percent of firms with a woman top manager*
Bangladesh (2022)	6.7	2.5	3.6
Bhutan (2024)	31.3	18.6	21.4
India (2022)	3.9	1.8	6.8
Myanmar (2016)	35.1	33.5	41.1
Nepal (2023)	14.7	7.6	10.3
Sri Lanka (2011)	26.1	NA	8.8
Thailand (2016)	64.4	33.4	64.8

* According to the survey, this indicator is computed using data from manufacturing firms only.
Source: Enterprise Surveys (http://www.enterprisesurveys.org), The World Bank extracted in March 2025.

And entrepreneurship holds transformative potential for women-led development. This was highlighted during Women Leaders' Forum, an event, organised by the Indian Chamber of Commerce-Ladies Study Group and ICC National Women's Entrepreneurship Council (INWEC).[12] For this, financial institutions should develop tailored funding solutions for women entrepreneurs, programs should aim at enhancing business skills and financial literacy among women and establish platforms for women entrepreneurs to connect with mentors and peers.

Second, addressing the problem of climate change, which poses unique challenges for women, particularly in agriculture-dependent regions, is crucial. BIMSTEC can ensure climate adaptation policies are gender-responsive, safeguarding the well-being and empowering women and girls across the region. Third, the digital revolution presents both challenges and opportunities for women in BIMSTEC countries.[13] While technology can enhance access to information and markets, many women lack the necessary skills and resources to leverage these advancements effectively. Promoting digital literacy among women is vital.

Fourth, a Regional Network of Women Parliamentarians can be established where women can share best practices, advocate for gender-responsive legislation and mentor aspiring women leaders. One of the best ways to influence change is through demonstration. Here, showcasing stories of women and girls as positive role models and challenging stereotypes through social media will be useful. Addressing deeply ingrained socio-cultural norms and gender biases requires long-term efforts involving awareness campaigns, educational programs and community engagement.

Finally, despite the acknowledged importance of mainstreaming gender perspectives across its various areas of engagement, the BIMSTEC framework currently lacks a dedicated policy, or overarching vision specifically targeting women's empowerment. A foundational step necessitates the formal recognition of "Women's Empowerment and Gender-Related Developments" as a distinct sector of cooperation within the BIMSTEC agenda. This strategic inclusion would provide a dedicated platform for focused dialogue, policy formulation, and collaborative action.

Conclusion

Empowering women in BIMSTEC is not only delivering social justice but also imperative to achieving the goals of BIMSTEC, i.e., economic growth and social progress. With the greater emphasis on making policies, most of the individual governments have formulated gender-responsive policies. What is problematic is its implementation. Therefore, a regional framework with a dedicated policy and formal recognition of women empowerment or gender related development as a sector of cooperation can be the starting point. Women-led development is essential for achieving sustainable growth in BIMSTEC countries. While challenges persist, efforts to empower women through entrepreneurship, climate-linked finance, digital technology and regional cooperation offer hope for a more equitable future.

NOTES

1 "Women in Development". *United Nations*. 1992. Vol. No 1, https://www.un.org/womenwatch/daw/public/women%20in%20development%201992.pdf

2 "NARI SHAKTI: From Women Development to Women led Development." PIB. March 6, 2024, https://pib.gov.in/PressNoteDetails.aspx?NoteId=151861&ModuleId=3&reg=3&lang=1

3 "BIMSTEC: The Road Ahead." RIS, September 27, 2016. https://www.ris.org.in/sites/default/files/Publication/FINAL_Report%20BIMSTEC%20Agriculture.pdf. https://bimstec.org/images/publication_pdf_file/1696658122_BIMSTEC%20Report%20(3)%20(2).pdf

4 "BIMSTEC Summit: President's Emphasis to Ensure More Rights to Women. *Annapurna Express,* August 31, 2018. https://theannapurnaexpress.com/story/14669/,

5 https://hdr.undp.org/data-center/thematic-composite-indices/gender-inequality-index#/indicies/GII

6 "World Development Indicators Database." Estimates based on data obtained from the International Labour Organization (ILO) and United Nations Population Division. *World Bank.* March 2025.

7 "Proportion of Seats Held by Women in National Parliaments" *World Bank Gender Data Portal,* n.d. https://genderdata.worldbank.org/en/indicator/sg-gen-parl-zs.

8 "Proportion of Women in Ministerial Level Positions." *World Bank Gender Data Portal,* n.d. https://genderdata.worldbank.org/en/indicator/sg-gen-mnst-zs?view=trend&geos=BG D_BTN_IND.

9 "UNOPS-BIMSTEC Roundtable Discussion on Impact of Climate Change on Women and Girls." *BIMSTEC,* December 19, 2023. https://bimstec.org/event/118/unops-bimstec-roundtable-discussion-on-impact-of-climate-change-on-women-and-girls.

10 "Side Event on Integrating Gender and Poverty in Climate Finance." *BIMSTEC,* November 20, 2024. https://bimstec.org/event/219/side-event-on-integrating-gender-and-poverty-in-climate-finance.

11 "BIMSTEC Business Summit Report: Industry Partnerships for Deepening Regional Economic Engagement." *Confederation of Indian Industry,* August 2024. https://www.cii.in/International_ResearchPDF/BIMSTEC_BUSINESS_SUMMIT_ReportWeb.pdf.

12 Roy, Rajdeep Kumar "BIMSTEC Women Leaders' Forum: An Initiative by LSG and INWEC." The Telegraph, July 3, 2023. https://www.telegraphindia.com/my-kolkata/events/bimstec-women-leaders-forum-an-initiative-by-lsg-and-inwec-was-an-engaging-and-insightful-evening-for-women-entrepreneurs/cid/1949353.

13 "BIMSTEC's Digital Infrastructure: Paving the Way for Regional Economic Collaboration." *CII Blog,* August 23, 2024. https://ciiblog.in/bimstecs-digital-infrastructure-paving-the-way-for-regional-economic-collaboration.

17

Retracing Cultural Connect in BIMSTEC

Saudiptendu Ray

Cultures and civilisations that developed around the Bay of Bengal have used its waters as a pathway for trade, migration and cultural exchange for millennia. Cultural traits from the Indian subcontinent, which include language, script, ideas, stories, religion, tradition and architecture- travelled aboard ancient ships to cross vast seas to reach distant lands in Southeast Asia. The Indian subcontinent was also influenced by Southeast Asian cultural traits.

India's eastern coastline was dotted with ports like Palur (near the modern-day port of Gopalpur) that had trade linkages with Southeast Asia.[1] Other ports in the Bay of Bengal region, included Tamralipta (India), Bagan (Myanmar), and Ayutthaya (Thailand), and they served as cultural melting pots where merchants, scholars and artisans exchanged knowledge and traditions. The influence of Indian scripts, such as Brahmi and Grantha in Southeast Asian languages underscores the linguistic impact of these ancient trade connections. These ancient linkages have created cultures around the Bay of Bengal that today share common cultural traits.

In contemporary times, countries around the Bay of Bengal have formed the Bay of Bengal Initiative for Multi-Sectoral Technical and Economic Cooperation (BIMSTEC), which includes India, Bhutan, Myanmar, Thailand, Sri Lanka, Nepal, and Bangladesh. The chief purpose of BIMSTEC is to facilitate economic and regional cooperation between member nations. Along with that, the organisation also focuses on the historical linkages and the rich cultural heritage of these nations.[2] At the Fourth BIMSTEC Summit, held in Kathmandu, in August 2018, member countries said there was a need to enhance cultural exchanges to further strengthen historic cultural ties between the people of the region. They also underscored the importance of Buddhism as a connecting thread in the region's history.[3]

BIMSTEC nations share a deep connection with Buddhism, which originated in India and spread to different parts of the Indian subcontinent and later on to Southeast Asia and beyond. This outward movement of Buddhism played an important role in shaping Asian culture, history and social fabric. The article aspires to retrace this journey of Buddhism from India to other BIMSTEC nations, as well as to explore how Buddhism can be leveraged to strengthen regional ties, promote tourism, and preserve the cultural heritage.

The Birthplace of Buddhism

One of the most prominent debates that emerges in writing the history of Buddhism in the Indian subcontinent is accurately dating the life of Lord Buddha, or Siddhartha Gautama. According to the Pali tradition, his life is dated to 623–543 BCE,[4] though modern scholars, after studying the Ashokan edicts, suggest that Lord Buddha lived between circa 566 BCE and 486 BCE.[5] Siddhartha was born in the Sakya Republic in Lumbini, in the city-state of Kapilavastu in the modern-day country of Nepal.[6] Siddhartha spent his youth in luxury, but at some point, he became disillusioned with his comfortable and privileged life. He was troubled by the sufferings that, in the form of sickness, old age and death, sooner or later awaited him and everyone else.[7] The pleasures that he enjoyed seemed empty. Hence, he left home, adopting the life of a wandering ascetic. It is during this phase that Siddhartha travelled across the northern plains of India to attain knowledge.

The most important Buddhist pilgrimage sites associated with the life of Buddha are located in the Indo-Gangetic plain in northern India and the Tarai region in southern Nepal. These sites include **Lumbini** in Nepal (Siddhartha's birthplace), **Bodh Gaya** in Bihar (where Siddhartha attained enlightenment), **Sarnath** in Uttar Pradesh (where Buddha delivered his first sermon), and **Kushinagar** in Uttar Pradesh (where Buddha attained ***Parinirvana***). The significance of these sites can be understood from the fact that Buddha himself had mentioned them in the "Mahaparinibbana Sutta: The Great Discourse on the Total Unbinding"[8] and the "Mahaparinibbana Sutta: Last Days of the Buddha."[9] Buddhists from all over the world consider these ancient sites as sacred.

Lord Buddha's ashes were divided into eight portions. They were distributed to Ajatasattu, King of Magadha; the Licchavis of Vesali; the Sakyas of Kapilavastu (Nepal); the Bulis of Allakappa; the Koliyas of Ramagama; the Brahmins of Vemhadipa; the Mallas of Pava and the Mallas of Kushinagar.[10] Stupas were built over the relics of Lord Buddha across the Indian subcontinent.

The Spread of Buddhism in BIMSTEC Countries

After the Buddha's *Parinirvana* at Kushinagar, Buddhism remained a small sect in the Indian subcontinent until the third century BCE. It only gained momentum in India under Mauryan Emperor Ashoka (268-232 BCE). Under Ashoka, Buddhism spread not only across India, but also beyond the Indian subcontinent. The Third Buddhist Council was held at Pataliputra in 250 BCE.[11] The deliberations at this council resulted in the compilation of a Buddhist scripture called *Kathavatthu* (Points of Controversy). These teachings, approved and accepted by this council, became the basis of **Theravada Buddhism**. After the conclusion of the Third Buddhist Council, several Buddhist elders were sent to different parts of Asia to preach Buddhism. Emperor Ashoka sent Buddhist missionaries to preach Buddhism in Nepal[12] under Majjhima Thera after the Third Buddhist Council.[13] Emperor Ashoka also visited Lumbini and erected an inscribed pillar to commemorate the sacred birthplace of Lord Buddha.[14]

Mahendra (Mahinda) and Sanghamitra (Sanghamitta), children of Emperor Ashoka, carried the message of Buddhism to Sri Lanka and established a Sangha for monks and nuns in Sri Lanka.[15] One of the oldest Buddhist sites in Sri Lanka is the Mihintale mountain peak near Anuradhapura, which is associated with Mahendra. Multiple mountain caves like Mihintale that have survived in Sri Lanka, contain Brahmi script inscriptions.[16] According to ancient Sri Lankan chronicles like the "Mahavamsa" and the "Dipavamsa", Devanampiya Tissa of Anuradhapura (307-267 BCE) accepted Buddhism and helped in its expansion in Sri Lanka. The Buddhist Mahavihara in Anuradhapura was established under Devanampiya Tissa.[17] Within a few centuries, the Sinhalese adopted Buddhism after assimilating it with pre-Buddhist cults, rituals and ceremonies. Buddhism played a crucial role in the unification of ancient Sri Lanka.[18] Later on, Sri Lanka became a significant center for the practice of Theravada Buddhism. It also helped to spread Theravada Buddhism in Myanmar and Thailand.

Despite being a Muslim-majority country today, Bangladesh had a deep-rooted Buddhist past. Buddhism might have entered the modern-day Bangladesh during of Lord Buddha's lifetime, but like the rest of the Indian subcontinent, it remained a small sect. Buddhism gained prominence in Bangladesh under the Pala Empire in the 8th century CE. The Palas were patrons of Mahayana Buddhism and built monasteries like the Somapura Mahavihara in present-day Naogaon District in the Rajshahi Division of Bangladesh. Somapura Mahavihara was an important center for Buddhist learning in the early medieval period.[19] Buddhist artefacts have been excavated in Bangladesh, particularly in Wari-Bateshwar in the Dhaka Division, Mahasthangarh in the Bogra district and Mainamati in Comilla district.

The Chandra Dynasty (4th century CE to 11th century CE) of southeast Bangladesh and parts of The Arakan in Myanmar was one of the last Buddhist strongholds in the Indian subcontinent. This dynasty played a leading role in promoting Mahayana Buddhism in Southeast Asia.[20] These coastal kingdoms of the Bengal region had trade linkages with regions in present day Myanmar, Thailand, Indonesia and Vietnam. Buddhism in the Bangladesh region started declining after the Turkic invasions from the west in the 12th and 13th centuries CE.

In Nepal, the Kiratas (mountain people) were the first to embrace Buddhism, followed by the Licchavis and the Newar community,[21] The Kiratas, which includes the Limbu and the Rai people, adopted Tibetan Buddhism from their Buddhist neighbours in Tibet. The Newar people of the lower Himalayan region followed the Vajrayana tradition. Although the Licchavis and Newar tribes became Buddhist, they did not eschew altogether their ancient Sanatana Dharma. These hill tribes of Nepal continued to worship both Shiva and Buddhist deities.[22] Thus in Nepal, Sanatana Dharma and Buddhism absorbed elements from each other to such an extent that the distinction between them is not very clear. The two religions even share deities and places of worship.

Buddhism first arrived in Bhutan in the 7th century under Tibetan King Songtsen Gampo.[23] However, it was only in the 9th century that a Buddhist saint, Padmasambhava (Guru Rinpoche), firmly established Vajrayana Buddhism in the region, integrating indigenous beliefs like Bon religious practices into Buddhist practices. Later on, the Drukpa Kagyu School of Tibetan Buddhism was introduced in Bhutan in the 12th century. In the 17th century, Zhabdrung Ngawang Namgyal unified Bhutan under the Drukpa Kagyu School, shaping its governance and national identity.

Buddhism is believed to have arrived in Myanmar after the conclusion of

Third Buddhist Council in 250 BCE during Emperor Ashoka's reign.[24] The Mauryan Emperor sent two prominent Buddhist monks, Sona and Uttara, along with sacred Buddhist texts to spread Buddhism in *Suvarnabhumi* (somewhere in Southeast Asia, possibly Lower Myanmar and Thailand) across the Bay of Bengal. The earliest physical evidence of Buddhism in Myanmar is found in the Pali inscriptions of the Pyu Kingdom of Sriksetra in the lower Irrawaddy valley of Burma and the Mon Kingdom of Dvaravati.[25] The script used in these inscriptions found in Myanmar is similar to the South Indian Pallava script from the 5th-7th century.[26] These discoveries establish that cultural traits from the eastern coastline of India kept seeping into Myanmar through trade. The strengthening of trade relations ensured the growth of Buddhism in Myanmar. The Mon Khmer-speaking people of Myanmar from the Arakan region might have been the first group of people to accept Buddhism.

Myanmar became a centre of Theravada Buddhist tradition under the reign of Anawrahta Minsaw, who adopted Theravada Buddhism as the state religion of the Pagan Empire in the 11th century.[27] Changing the faith of the masses was greatly helped by the incoming flood of monks and sacred texts from the island of Sri Lanka. The construction of grand stupas such as the Shwedagon Pagoda in Yangon and the thousands of stupas in the ancient city of Bagan in the Mandalay region of Myanmar symbolises the deep-rooted Buddhist cultural identity.

Thailand's Buddhist heritage can be traced back to the 3rd century BCE, in the time of the Mauryans.[28] Others are of the view that Thailand received Buddhism much later, during the Mon kingdom of Dvaravati (6th to 11th century CE). Scholars base this claim on archaeological findings from sites like Nakon Pathom (Sanskrit: Nagara Prathama) of the Mon Kingdom. These archaeological findings include the Dharma Chakra (Wheel of Law), the Buddha's footprints and empty seat, and inscriptions in the Pali language, all carved on stone.[29] The first form of Buddhism introduced to Thailand was that of the Theravada School. The adoption of Theravada Buddhism by Thai rulers helped solidify its place in the kingdom's cultural and political structures. Thailand's deep connection with Buddhism has been an essential link in the regional Buddhist community, drawing connections with other BIMSTEC countries such as Myanmar, Sri Lanka, and India.

Thailand is home to numerous ancient Buddhist archaeological sites like Sukhothai Historical Park, Wat Mahathat and Wat Phra Si Sanphet from

Ayutthaya and Chiang Saen. The Sukhothai Historical Park, the former capital of the Sukhothai Kingdom, flourished in the 13th and 14th centuries and is often regarded as the birthplace of Thai art and architecture. In the north of Thailand, the ancient city of Chiang Saen, along the Mekong River, preserves relics of the Lan Na Kingdom, including ornate stupas and Buddha images. These sites, with their intricate carvings, grand stupas, and serene Buddha statues, offer insights into the evolution of Thai Buddhism.

Buddhism Unifying BIMSTEC

Buddhism, which spread through maritime trade routes and royal patronage, is the cultural and spiritual bridge that unifies BIMSTEC member nations. Most of them share a common reverence for sacred Buddhist sites and the holy relics of Lord Buddha. In contemporary times, this shared heritage offers immense potential for promoting cultural tourism, fostering mutual understanding and strengthening regional cooperation between BIMSTEC nations.

The Buddhist Circuit,[30] promoted by the Indian government, focuses on connecting key Buddhist pilgrimage sites across India to promote religious tourism. India, also called "The Land of Buddha", with historical sites like Bodh Gaya, Sarnath, Kushinagar, Nalanda and Ajanta, can help in attracting tourists from neighbouring BIMSTEC countries, especially from Sri Lanka, Thailand, Bhutan and Myanmar.

Buddhists from around the world visit the National Museum in New Delhi to get a glimpse of a relic of Lord Buddha. In February 2024, India strengthened its cultural ties with Thailand by sending these rare relics of Lord Buddha, along with those of his esteemed disciples, Arhanta Sariputra and Arahanta Maudgalayana, for a month-long exhibition there.[31] The relics travelled to Bangkok, Chiang Mai, Ubon Ratchathani and Krabi provinces in Thailand and drew more than four million devotees.[32]

The relics are classified as an 'AA' (rare) category of antiquities and are generally not sent for exhibitions outside India. But after a "special request" from the Thai government, the Indian Ministry of Culture happily agreed.[33] India has been making exceptions regarding the relics of Lord Buddha for the Buddhist countries. Previously, India had sent the relics of Lord Buddha to Sri Lanka in 2012.[34] These gestures from the Indian government have solidified India's relations with BIMSTEC neighbours. India also organised the First Asian Buddhist Summit in November 2024 based around the theme of the "Role of

Buddha Dhamma in Strengthening Asia."[35] The Prime Minister of India, in his recent visits to Thailand and Sri Lanka, visited Buddhist temples in both countries, further highlighting India's commitment to placing Buddhism at the forefront of India's foreign policy.[36]

The potential for economic cooperation in tourism, as well as joint efforts in preserving and promoting Buddhist heritage, has become a focus of regional collaboration. India has provided support for the restoration of Buddhist temples, pagodas and stupas in Bagan (a UNESCO World Heritage Site).[37] Similarly, Thailand is partnering India in preserving the Buddhist tangible and intangible heritage in India.[38]

Establishing scholarships and research collaborations on Buddhist studies among BIMSTEC universities and monastic institutions can help preserve and disseminate Buddhist teachings. Such initiatives would not only reinforce cultural ties but also contribute to intellectual and spiritual discourse within the region. The inauguration of the new Nalanda University in Bihar is an important step towards reviving the ancient learning that had made Nalanda an international center of knowledge.[39] This new Nalanda University will play a pivotal role in educating scholars from the BIMSTEC region.

Conclusion

From its birthplace in India to its widespread practice in Sri Lanka, Thailand, Myanmar and Bhutan, Buddhism unites these nations through shared values, teachings, and cultural heritage. However, the BIMSTEC region is not without challenges. The political, cultural and economic diversity of these countries presents difficulties in achieving full cooperation. Internal conflict in places like Myanmar and Bangladesh have created minor roadblocks to regional economic integration. Furthermore, there are also differences within the different Buddhist traditions (e.g., the difference between Theravada and Mahayana practices). Such sectarian differences within Buddhism, along with ethnic conflicts and political and economic instability in some member countries, have hindered deeper regional integration. However, a shared Buddhist heritage offers hope for overcoming these challenges. By focusing on common values of peace, compassion and non-violence, BIMSTEC countries can strengthen their cooperation and pave the way for greater socio-economic development, cultural exchange and mutual understanding.

NOTES

1 Patra, Benudhar. *Indian History Congress Proceedings*, Vol. 74 (2013), Ports and Port Towns of Early Odisha: Text, Archaeology and Identification, p. 54-63.

2 BIMSTEC Charter signed on March 30, 2022 in Colombo Sri Lanka. https://bimstec.org/images/content_page_pdf/1696679710_BIMSTEC%20Charter.pdf

3 Fourth BIMSTEC Summit Declaration, Kathmandu, Nepal, August 30-31, 2018. https://www.mea.gov.in/bilateral-documents.htm?dtl/30335/Fourth_BIMSTEC_Summit_Declaration_Kathmandu_Nepal_August_3031_2018

4 Harvey, Peter. *An Introduction to Buddhism: Teachings, History and Practices*. Second Edition. Cambridge University Press, 2013, p. 8.

5 Gethin, Rupert. *The Foundations of Buddhism*. Oxford and New York. Oxford University Press, 1998. p. 14.

6 Warden, A. K. *Indian Buddhism.* Motilal Banarsidass Publishers Private Limited, Delhi. p. 45.

7 Gethin, Rupert. *The Foundations of Buddhism*. Oxford and New York. Oxford University Press, 1998. p. 15.

8 *Maha-parinibbana Sutta: The Great Discourse on the Total Unbinding* (excerpt) translated from Pali text by Thanissaro Bhikkhu.

9 *Maha-parinibbana Sutta: Last Days of the Buddha* (excerpt) translated from Pali text by Sister Vajira & Francis Story.

10 David, T. W. Rhys. "Asoka and the Buddha- Relics." *The Journal of the Royal Asiatic Society of Great Britain and Ireland*. July 1901. pp. 397-410.

11 Willemen, Charles, Bart Dessein, Collett Cox. *Sarvâstivâda Buddhist Scholasticism.* Brill, Handbuch Der Orientalistik. pp. 44-45.

12 Beckwith, Christopher I. *Greek Buddha: Pyrrho's Encounter with Early Buddhism in Central Asia*. Princeton University Press, 2017. p. 234–235.

13 Seneviratna, Anuradha. *King Asoka and Buddhism: Historical and Literary Studies*. Buddhist Publication Society, Kandy. 1994. p. 46.

14 Ven. Murti. *A Historical Study of Pariyatti Sikkh in Nepal.* Mahachulalongkornrajavidyalaya University, Bangkok, Thailand. p. 10.

15 Crosby, Kate. Theravada Buddhism: Continuity, Diversity, and Identity. Wiley Blackwell, 2014. p. 2.

16 Bandaranayake, S.D. *Sinhalese Monastic Architecture: The Vihâras of Anurâdhapura*, p. 22

17 De Silva, K. M. *A History of Sri Lanka.* Second Edition. Penguin Books India, 2005. p. 12.

18 Ibid. p.12.

19 English, Elizabeth. *Vajrayogini: Her Visualization, Rituals, and Forms*. Wisdom Publications, 2002. p. 15.

20 Ghosh, Suchandra. "Locating Southeastern Bengal in the Buddhist Network of Bay of Bengal (C. 7th Century CE-13th Century CE)." *Proceedings of the Indian History Congress*. Vol. 74. pp. 148–153.

21 Dutt, Nalinaksha. "Buddhism in Nepal". *Bulletin of Tibetology*. 1966. pp. 27–28.

22 Ibid. p. 28.

23 Padel, Ruth. *Tigers in Red Weather: A Quest for the Last Wild Tigers*. Bloomsbury Publishing USA, 2006. pp. 139–40.

24 Seneviratna, Anuradha. *King Asoka and Buddhism: Historical and Literary Studies.* Buddhist Publication Society, Kandy. 1994. p. 46.

25 Skilling, Peter. "The Advent of Theravada Buddhism to Mainland South-east Asia." *Buddhism and Buddhist Literature of South-East Asia Selected Papers.* Journal of the International Association of Buddhist Studies. Volume 20, Number 1, Summer 1997. p. 105.

26 Ibid. p. 106.

27 Lieberman, Victor B. *Strange Parallels: Southeast Asia in Global Context, c. 800–1830,* Volume 1. Cambridge University Press, 2003. pp. 115-116.

28 Kusalasaya, Karuna. *Buddhism in Thailand: Its Past and its Present.* Buddhist Publication Society, Kandy. 2006. pp. 3-5.

29 Ibid. p. 4.

30 "Ministry of Tourism to organize conference on Buddhist circuit to promote potential of Buddhist tourism." Ministry of Tourism. October 5, 2021. https://pib.gov.in/PressReleaseIframePage.aspx?PRID=1761045

31 "India to Send 4 Relics of Buddha to Thailand.", *The Times of India.*, February 21, 2024. https://timesofindia.indiatimes.com/india/india-to-send-4-relics-of-buddha-to-thailand/articleshow/107862507.cms

32 "Sacred Relics of Lord Buddha Return to India After 25-day Exposition in Thailand.", *DD News.* March 20, 2024. https://ddnews.gov.in/en/sacred-relics-of-lord-buddha-return-to-india-after-25-day-exposition-in-thailand/

33 Divya A., "Buddha's Relics at National Museum to be on Display in Thailand.", *The Indian Express.* February 21, 2024. https://indianexpress.com/article/india/buddhas-relics-at-national-museum-to-be-on-display-in-thailand-9172154/#:

34 "Exposition of the Sacred Kapilavastu Relics in Sri Lanka." MEA, Government of India. August, 2012. https://www.mea.gov.in/photo features.htm?727/Exposition+of+the+Sacred+Kapilavastu+Relics+in+Sri+Lanka#

35 "First Asian Buddhist Summit has Reaffirmed India's Commitment to Buddhist Legacy: Experts." *The Hindu.* November 8, 2024. https://www.thehindu.com/news/national/first-asian-buddhist-summit-has-reaffirmed-indias-commitment-to-buddhist-legacy-experts/article68841818.ece

36 "How PM Modi Made Buddhism an Instrument of India's Foreign Policy for Global Harmony." *Firstpost.* April 4, 2025. https://www.firstpost.com/world/how-pm-modi-made-buddhism-an-instrument-of-indias-foreign-policy-for-global-harmony-13877277.html

37 "Myanmar Earthquake: Images from Bagan Historic Sites." *BBC News.* August 25, 2016. https://www.bbc.com/news/world-asia-37183943

38 "Gujarat Partners with Thai Institute to Preserve Buddhist Heritage Sites." *The Times of India.* December 10, 2024. https://timesofindia.indiatimes.com/city/ahmedabad/gujarat-teams-up-with-thai-institute-to-safeguard-buddhist-heritage/articleshow/116183916.cms

39 "A New Dawn for Nalanda: Reviving an Ancient Seat of Learning." *Hindustan Times.* June 19, 2024. https://www.hindustantimes.com/opinion/a-new-dawn-for-nalanda-reviving-an-ancient-seat-of-learning-101718783110495.html

ANNEXURES

Annexure 1
Sixth BIMSTEC Summit Declaration

04 April 2025
Bangkok, Thailand

"Prosperous, Resilient and Open BIMSTEC"

We, the Chief Adviser of the People's Republic of Bangladesh; the Prime Minister of the Kingdom of Bhutan; the Prime Minister of the Republic of India; the Chairman of the State Administration Council and Prime Minister of the Republic of the Union of Myanmar; the Prime Minister of Nepal; the Prime Minister of the Democratic Socialist Republic of Sri Lanka; and the Prime Minister of the Kingdom of Thailand; met in Bangkok, Thailand on 04 April 2025 for the Sixth BIMSTEC Summit, and

Reaffirming our firm commitment to the purposes and principles of BIMSTEC as contained in the BIMSTEC Charter and the 1997 Bangkok Declaration;

Recalling the First BIMSTEC Summit Declaration (Bangkok, 31 July 2004), the Second Summit Declaration (New Delhi, 13 November 2008), the Third Summit Declaration (Nay Pyi Taw, 4 March 2014), the BIMSTEC Leaders' Retreat Outcome Document (Goa, 16 October 2016), the Fourth Summit Declaration (Kathmandu, 30-31 August 2018) and the Fifth Summit Declaration (Colombo, 30 March 2022);

Expressing satisfaction on coming into force of the BIMSTEC Charter on 20 May 2024;

Recognizing the crucial role played by BIMSTEC in enhancing regional cooperation in agreed priority areas over 27 years of its existence and the need to revitalize BIMSTEC as an effective vehicle to fulfil the developmental aspirations of the peoples in the Bay of Bengal region;

Being convinced that geographical contiguity, plentiful natural and human resources, historical linkages and rich cultural heritage provide greater opportunities and complementarities to advance regional cooperation in identified core areas of BIMSTEC;

Also being convinced that now is the century of Asia and having achieved significant progress in recovering from the global economic recession, BIMSTEC is well-positioned to advance in growth and influence, harnessing strengths from our expanding demographics, great economic potential, and our collective capacity to harmonize our voices in pursuit of common progress and prosperity;

Acknowledging that the BIMSTEC Summit Declarations and BIMSTEC Ministerial Joint Statements including the recent institutional reform have provided our organization the directives to guide BIMSTEC cooperation in line with its noble vision and priorities to achieve tangible outcomes for the peoples of our region;

Noting with satisfaction that Member States have rebounded from the devastating effect of COVID-19 pandemic by boosting economic activities, sharing best practices, facilitating long term socio-economic recovery and contributing to peace, stability, prosperity and sustainability of the region;

Emphasizing on the need to make BIMSTEC more resilient against existing and future crises, including climate change, financial crises, pandemics, and other natural disasters as well as the necessity to develop mechanisms for coordinated response to such crises;

Being mindful of the need to work towards building a prosperous, resilient and open BIMSTEC through mutual collaboration, understanding and solidarity in the shared interest of the Member States;

Do hereby commit to:

1. ***Adopt*** the BIMSTEC Bangkok Vision 2030 for common aspiration towards a forward looking BIMSTEC region that is prosperous, resilient and open to tackle challenges and seize opportunities for the coming decade and ***agree*** to take appropriate measures on priority basis in the areas of mutual benefit to build a robust BIMSTEC to address the contemporary global challenges, expressed in the BIMSTEC Bangkok Vision 2030 (***included as Annexure***) as part of this Declaration.
2. ***Adopt*** the Rules of Procedure for BIMSTEC Mechanisms as recommended by the Ministerial Meeting and ***reiterate*** our commitment to timely holding of the Summit and meetings of all BIMSTEC mechanisms as mentioned therein.
3. ***Express*** deep appreciation to Thailand for initiating and hosting the First BIMSTEC Foreign Ministers' Retreat in Bangkok on 17 July 2023 and India for hosting the Second BIMSTEC Foreign Ministers' Retreat in New

Delhi on 11-12 July 2024, which provided a platform for Foreign Ministers to come together and provide substantive policy guidance. ***Appreciate*** the decision of the BIMSTEC Foreign Ministers to hold the Retreats and informal Meetings on regular basis, including on the sidelines of the United Nations General Assembly every year. ***Express*** deep appreciation to India for hosting the 1st Informal Meeting of the BIMSTEC Foreign Ministers which was convened in New York on 27 September 2024 on the sidelines of 79th Session of the UNGA.

4. ***Commend*** the Eminent Persons' Group (EPG) on the Future Direction of BIMSTEC for their Report and Recommendations, and ***emphasize*** on the early implementation of the recommendations, as appropriate. ***Task*** the Secretary-General of BIMSTEC to monitor and report the progress of implementation of the EPG's recommendations to the BIMSTEC Summit.
5. ***Emphasize*** that the Bangkok Vision 2030 will serve as a common aspiration for a BIMSTEC region that is Prosperous, Resilient, and Open by pursuing the following:

A. Building a Prosperous BIMSTEC by Accelerating Regional Growth Opportunities

6. ***Welcome*** the inclusion of Blue Economy, Mountain Economy and Poverty Alleviation under the purview of reconstituted Sectors and Sub-Sectors of cooperation and ***urge*** respective Lead Countries to develop the Plan of Action for each of these newly added Subsectors.
7. ***Reiterate*** our commitment to swiftly concluding the BIMSTEC Free Trade Area Agreement (FTA) and ***direct*** the Trade Negotiating Committee (TNC) and its Working Groups to finalize the constituent Agreements of the BIMSTEC FTA without further delay.
8. ***Acknowledge*** that several BIMSTEC Member States are poised to graduate from the LDC status, face structural constraints and challenges that hinder their competitiveness in external trade due to, among others, high trade and transit cost and ***commit*** to extend necessary support to the graduating and land-locked Member States in their development efforts, with a view to ensuring equitable benefits during implementation of the BIMSTEC FTA.
9. ***Underscore*** the need to accelerate trade facilitation measures within the BIMSTEC region and ***urge*** the Member States to finalize the Agreement on Trade Facilitation and the Agreement on Cooperation and Mutual

Assistance in Customs Matters on a priority basis. ***Further urge*** the Member States to explore the possibility of establishing BIMSTEC Mutual Recognition Arrangements of Standards to reap the benefit of trade facilitation measures within the region.

10. ***Encourage*** relevant officials of Member States to explore the possibility of establishing digital cross-border payment system and trade settlements with local currencies, noting that some Member States have already adopted the Unified Payments Interface (UPI).
11. ***Commit*** to continue to work towards shared objectives of closing digital divides, expanding the benefits of the digital economy, fostering an inclusive and secure digital space, and advancing equitable governance of data and emerging technologies to accelerate progress towards achieving the Sustainable Development Goals.
12. ***Appreciate*** the establishment of the BIMSTEC Expert Group on Fiscal and Monetary Policy and ***instruct*** the Expert Group to develop an action plan on Fiscal and Monetary Policy.
13. ***Reaffirm*** the importance of non-traditional security issues, especially Food Security, Energy Security, Environmental Security and Human Security that will support and drive productivity and sustainable growth in the region.
14. ***Stress*** on the implementation of "Plan of Action on Strengthening BIMSTEC Agricultural Cooperation (2023-2027)", as adopted by the Second BIMSTEC Ministerial Meeting on Agriculture and recognizing the importance of enhanced cooperation and sustainable use in fisheries and livestock, and their entire supply chain, and the use of science and technology such as precision farming, which has a great potential to make a significant contribution towards ensuring food security and improving livelihoods of people in our region, ***agree*** to deepen cooperation in this sub-sector.
15. ***Welcome*** the signing of the Agreement on Maritime Transport Cooperation, recognizing its potential to enhance regional maritime connectivity, facilitate cross-border trade, and spur investment in port infrastructure, logistics, and related sectors and therefore ***direct*** relevant authorities to expeditiously implement the Agreement.
16. ***Recognize*** that Connectivity is one of the most vital sectors of cooperation for regional integration. ***Stressing*** the importance of timely implementation of the BIMSTEC Master Plan for Transport Connectivity, we acknowledge the progress made in the India-Myanmar-Thailand Trilateral Highway, and

encourage our respective authorities to speed up their efforts to conclude the 'BIMSTEC Motor Vehicle Agreement'.

17. ***Emphasize*** the need for adopting appropriate policies and programmes for utilizing the youth force and for skill development to cater to the needs of the young population to develop into a workforce with adequate skills to cope up with the current and future challenges.
18. ***Express*** satisfaction at the formation of the BIMSTEC Expert Group on Blue Economy and ***instruct*** the Expert Group to formulate a Comprehensive Plan of Action to harness the enormous potential that the blue economy holds for our region.

B. Creating a Resilient BIMSTEC to Safeguard Against Future Shocks and Ensure Continued Progress

19. ***Call*** for further deepening of the Environment and Climate Change cooperation to safeguard the environment, mitigate climate change impacts and contribute towards achieving the Sustainable Development Goals.
20. ***Welcome*** the finalization of the Concept Note on Potential Areas of Cooperation and the BIMSTEC Plan of Action on Environment and Climate Change and ***underscore*** the importance of timely implementation of the Plan of Action.
21. ***Recognize*** the importance of regional security cooperation, especially in the areas of maritime security, cyber security, scams across digital and telecommunication channels, human & drug trafficking and other transnational crimes and ***underscore*** the need for strengthened and close cooperation between and among the law enforcement and criminal justice agencies of the Member States in combating these transnational crimes.
22. ***Welcome*** the formation of the BIMSTEC Home Ministers' Meeting mechanism and ***call*** for early convening of the First Meeting of BIMSTEC Home Ministers.
23. ***Decide*** to establish the BIMSTEC Health Ministers' Meeting mechanism.
24. ***Take*** note with satisfaction of progress being made in energy cooperation and ***instruct*** the relevant authorities for early conclusion and implementation of BIMSTEC Grid Interconnections with a view to promoting rational and optimal power transmission in BIMSTEC region.
25. ***Direct*** the officials of the Member States to develop a Plan of Action to improve preparedness and coordination for responding to natural disasters in the Bay of Bengal Region.

26. ***Welcome*** the signing of the Host Country Agreement between the Government of India and the BIMSTEC Secretariat for establishing BIMSTEC Centre for Weather and Climate (BCWC) in Noida, India and ***call*** for effective functioning of BCWC.
27. ***Welcome*** the launching of the BIMSTEC Energy Centre (BEC) in Bengaluru, India following the signing of the Host Country Agreement between the Government of India and the BIMSTEC Secretariat and ***call*** for finalization of all necessary procedures to ensure smooth operationalization of the Centre.
28. ***Welcome*** the initiatives to strengthen the efforts towards institution-building within BIMSTEC by establishing the BIMSTEC Centres of Excellence in Disaster Management, in Agriculture, and in Maritime Transport in India, and the BIMSTEC Centres of Excellence on Tropical Medicine, and in Public Audit in Thailand for expanding meaningful collaboration in respective fields.
29. ***Call*** for intensified collective action to explore avenues to widen and deepen cooperation in Science, Technology, and Innovation, including the pursuit of appropriate external partnership for achieving regional objectives, and in this connection, ***welcome*** the finalization of the BIMSTEC Plan of Action on Science, Technology and Innovation (20232027) and ***emphasize*** on its timely implementation.
30. ***Acknowledge*** the finalization of the BIMSTEC Plan of Action on Public Health (20232025) and ***emphasize*** on its timely implementation.
31. ***Welcome*** the finalization of BIMSTEC Plan of Action on Human Resource Development and ***emphasize*** on its timely implementation.
32. ***Appreciate*** the ongoing collaboration on traditional medicine within BIMSTEC, recognizing its contribution to public health and well-being and ***commend*** the BIMSTEC Task Force on Traditional Medicine for the "Traditional Medicine Systems of BIMSTEC Member States – 2023 Report" and ***encourage*** all Member States to leverage its insights to improve their traditional medicine systems and strengthen regional cooperation.

C. Fostering an Open BIMSTEC by Embracing People-to-People Connectivity and Exploring New Opportunities

33. ***Agree*** to take concrete steps to promote intra-BIMSTEC tourism, including through cross-border travel facilitation and sustainable tourism practices, leveraging the region's rich natural, cultural heritage, and historical sites,

which can help boost economic growth and employment. We ***underscore*** the critical importance to build on the progress made with regard to BIMSTEC tourism circuits, including the BIMSTEC Buddhist Circuits, BIMSTEC Temple Circuits, and BIMSTEC Eco-Tourism Circuits. We also ***encourage*** greater public-private partnership to enhance infrastructure, services, and innovation in the tourism sector.

34. ***Reiterate*** the commitment to foster cooperation in the culture; ***emphasize*** on the early operationalization of the BIMSTEC Cultural Industries Observatory as a repository for information on cultural industries.
35. ***Recognize*** the importance of further promoting people-to-people contact at various levels, in the areas of youth entrepreneurship, digital connectivity, tourism, culture, youth and sports.
36. ***Acknowledge*** the need of forging common positions on issues of mutual interest, including, in climate change negotiations, and seeking group recognition in various multilateral institutions.
37. ***Take*** note of the Secretariat's initiative to become observer at the United Nations (UN) and the United Nations Framework Convention on Climate Change (UNFCCC).
38. ***Welcome*** the signing of the Memorandum of Understanding (MoU) between the Indian Ocean Rim Association (IORA) and BIMSTEC, and the Memorandum of Understanding (MoU) between the United Nations Office on Drugs and Crime (UNODC) and BIMSTEC.
39. ***Express*** commitment to enhancing the visibility of BIMSTEC by organizing public awareness programmes on BIMSTEC, cultural events, sports, youth engagements and film festivals among the Member States.

D. Endorsement of Ministerial Decisions

40. ***Note*** the progress achieved in implementing directives given at the previous BIMSTEC Summits and ***instruct*** the Ministerial Meeting to coordinate implementation of our decisions and report to the next Summit.
41. ***Approve*** the Joint Statements of the Third BIMSTEC Energy Ministers' Meeting and Second BIMSTEC Ministerial Meeting on Agriculture as endorsed by the BIMSTEC Ministerial Meeting for implementation of the decisions and recommendations contained therein.
42. ***Approve*** the Joint Statement of the Nineteenth BIMSTEC Ministerial Meeting and Report of the Twentieth BIMSTEC Ministerial Meeting for implementation of the decisions and recommendations contained therein.

43. ***Welcome*** the deliberations of the Fourth Meeting of BIMSTEC National Security Chiefs as endorsed by the BIMSTEC Ministerial Meeting. ***Call*** for future meetings to discuss pertinent issues related to transnational organized crimes, in particular human trafficking and scams across digital and telecommunication channels.

E. Looking Ahead

44. ***Reaffirm*** the BIMSTEC Bangkok Vision 2030 as a vision that primarily propels the future of our region towards a Prosperous, Resilient and Open BIMSTEC by 2030, and ***task*** our Senior Officials to complete a comprehensive implementation plan for our consideration.
45. ***Welcome*** the appointment of Mr. Indra Mani Pandey of India as the Fourth Secretary General of BIMSTEC for the term 2024-2026 with effect from 4 January 2024 and ***express*** appreciation for his comprehensive Report.
46. ***Express*** our sincere appreciation to Mr. Tenzin Lekphell, former Secretary General of BIMSTEC from Bhutan, for his valuable contributions.
47. ***Express*** our deep appreciation to Thailand for its excellent leadership and valuable contribution during its Chairmanship of BIMSTEC.
48. ***Welcome*** and offer our full cooperation to Bangladesh as the next Chairman of the BIMSTEC.
49. ***Express*** our profound appreciation to the Government of the Kingdom of Thailand for the excellent arrangements made for the Sixth BIMSTEC Summit.

* * *

Annexure to the Six BIMSTEC Summit Declaration

BIMSTEC BANGKOK VISION 2030

A Prosperous, Resilient, and Open BIMSTEC by 2030 for our people and future generations

Remaining committed to BIMSTEC's principles and purposes as enshrined in the Bangkok Declaration 1997, we will achieve the BIMSTEC Bangkok Vision 2030 to build a Prosperous, Resilient, and Open BIMSTEC by 2030 by pursuing these following three key goals:

A Prosperous BIMSTEC, where poverty is substantially reduced and considerable progress towards sustainable development and viable growth are achieved. To achieve this goal, we will focus on:

- Strengthening regional supply chains for a steady post-pandemic economic recovery by enhancing transport and energy connectivity. This also includes the promotion of port and maritime connectivity, land connectivity, the implementation of the BIMSTEC Master Plan for Transport Connectivity, the conclusion of the BIMSTEC Grid Interconnection Master Plan study and its implementation, the Green Investment especially renewable energy, promotion of regional electricity trade, activation of BIMSTEC Grid-Interconnection Coordination Committee and BIMSTEC Energy Centre and linkages to other relevant regional cooperation groupings and countries with a shared vision of a secure and prosperous Bay of Bengal;
- Promoting trade, investment, trade facilitation, job creation, competitiveness of Micro, Small and Medium Enterprises (MSMEs), and inclusive and sustainable development. This also includes enhanced cooperation in digital economy, blue economy, mountain economy, sustainable tourism and corporate governance, as well as concerted efforts to implement the Framework Agreement on BIMSTEC FTA;
- Expediting the implementation of BIMSTEC Poverty Plan of Action (PPA);
- Identifying poor households and implementing targeted programs for the poor to gain resource accessibility, capacity development, job creation and fulfillment of human basic needs;
- Enhancing cooperation on food security including promotion of productivity in agriculture, livestock, and aquaculture.

A Resilient BIMSTEC, where crisis-preparedness, crisis-responsiveness and human security in various dimensions, including a steady post-pandemic economic recovery, are strengthened. To achieve this goal, we will focus on

- Promoting health security, and strengthening health systems to increase accessibility to quality health services as well as preparedness for future health challenges;
- Enhancing the cooperation on disaster relief, recovery, and reconstruction;
- Enhancing the cooperation on knowledge, skill and technology transfer,

and sharing good practices in development sector;

- Increasing maritime cooperation through the promotion of free and safe navigation, combating piracy, money laundering, financing of terrorism, Illegal, Unreported and Unregulated (IUU) fishing, as well as smuggling of narcotic drugs and illegal goods at sea;
- Promoting environmental protection, climate change adaptation/ mitigation measures, and the use of clean/renewable energy to build resilient economies and communities including through creation of the BIMSTEC Himalayan Science Council for scientific research.

An Open BIMSTEC which is inclusive, using multi-pronged and multi-stakeholder approach. To achieve this goal, we will focus on

- Promoting sustainable, environment-friendly, high-value, safe and purpose-driven tourism capitalising on shared heritage and historical, cultural and people-to-people ties, and the preparation for increasing cross-border and regional mobility of peoples;
- Fostering people-centred development;
- Enhancing the collaboration and networks of young entrepreneurs, innovators, expert groups, researchers, academia, students and professionals, as well as human resource development in Science, Technology, Engineering and Mathematics (STEM), arts and creativity.

To benefit from BIMSTEC's distinct characteristic as the only organization which links South Asia and Southeast Asia, we aim to achieve the BIMSTEC Bangkok Vision by 2030 with the spirit of cooperation, solidarity, equal partnership, shared responsibility, and mutual respect.

* * *

Annexure 2
BIMSTEC Charter

PREAMBLE

We, the peoples of the Member States of the Bay of Bengal Initiative for Multi-Sectoral Technical and Economic Cooperation (BIMSTEC), represented by the Heads of State or Government of the People's Republic of Bangladesh, Kingdom of Bhutan, the Republic of India, the Republic of the Union of Myanmar. Nepal, the Democratic Socialist Republic of Sri Lanka, and the Kingdom of Thailand:

Reaffirming the firm commitment to the principles and purposes of BIMSTEC as enshrined in the 1997 Bangkok Declaration;

Having recognized the Memorandum of Association (MOA) on the Establishment of the BIMSTEC Permanent Secretariat, done at Nay Pyi Taw, Myanmar on 04 March 2014;

Having recognized the Headquarters Agreement between the Government of the People's Republic of Bangladesh and the Secretariat of the Bay of Bengal Initiative for Multi-Sectoral Technical and Economic Cooperation (BIMSTEC) done at Dhaka. Bangladesh on 01 November 2015;

Being convinced that geographical contiguity, abundant natural and human resources, historical linkages and rich cultural heritage present great potentials for promoting deeper cooperation in identified core areas in the region:

Acknowledging that enhanced inter-linkages and inter-dependence within the economies and societies in the BIMSTEC Member States provide greater opportunity to advance regional cooperation;

Recognizing the special needs and circumstances of the least developed and land-locked developing countries in the region and underlining the necessity to provide meaningful support to their development process;

Reaffirming strong commitment to making BIMSTEC a dynamic, effective and result-oriented regional organization for promoting a peaceful, prosperous and sustainable Bay of Bengal Region through collective efforts, meaningful cooperation and deeper integration;

Stressing the need for a fair, just, equitable and transparent international order and reaffirming faith in the multilateralism with the United Nations at the centre and the rule-based international trading system;

Underscoring the importance of robust institutional arrangements to effectively steering the process of regional cooperation under BIMSTEC;

Having regard to all legal instruments concluded among the Member States since the establishment of BIMSTEC in 1997;

Having regard to the BIMSTEC Summit Declarations and BIMSTEC Ministerial Statements providing directives on vision and priorities of BIMSTEC cooperation and establishing rules, norms and practices for carrying out BIMSTEC activities:

Recalling the decision of the Fourth BIMSTEC Summit of 2018 to begin the process of drafting the Charter for the organization, building on the 1997 Bangkok Declaration, defining a long-term vision and priorities for cooperation, clearly delineating roles and responsibilities of different layers of institutional structure and decision-making processes:

Hereby decide to establish, through this Charter, the legal and institutional framework for BIMSTEC;

And to this end, the Heads of State or Government of BIMSTEC Member States, assembled in Colombo on the occasion of the Fifth BIMSTEC Summit, have agreed to this Charter.

CHAPTER I
PURPOSES AND PRINCIPLES

Article 1: Purposes

The purposes of the BIMSTEC shall be:

1. To create an enabling environment for rapid economic development through identification and implementation of specific cooperation projects in the already agreed areas of cooperation and such other areas that may be agreed upon by the Member States. Member States may periodically review the areas of cooperation.

2. To accelerate the economic growth and social progress in the Bay of Bengal region through joint endeavours in a spirit of equality and partnership.
3. To promote active collaboration and mutual assistance on matters of common interest in the economic, social, technical and scientific fields.
4. To provide assistance to each other in the form of training and research facilities in the educational, professional and technical spheres.
5. To cooperate more effectively in joint efforts that are supportive of and complementary to national development plans of the Member States which result in tangible benefits to the people in raising their living standards, including through generating employment and improving transportation and communication infrastructure.
6. To cooperate in projects that can be dealt with most productively on a regional basis among the BIMSTEC Member States and that make best use of available synergies.
7. To maintain peace and stability in the Bay of Bengal region through close collaboration in combating international terrorism, transnational organized crimes as well as natural disasters, climate change and communicable diseases.
8. To maintain close and beneficial cooperation with existing international and regional organizations with similar aims and purposes.
9. To endeavor to eradicate poverty from the Bay of Bengal region.
10. To establish multidimensional connectivity, promote **synergy** among connectivity frameworks in the region, as a key enabler to economic integration for shared prosperity.
11. To promote trade and investment as a major contributing factor for fostering economic and social development in the region.

Article 2: Principles

The BIMSTEC and its Member States, in the pursuit of the purposes stated in Article 1, shall observe the following principles in all the activities:

1. Cooperation within the BIMSTEC will be based on respect for the principle of sovereign equality, territorial integrity, political independence, non-interference in internal affairs, non-aggression, peaceful co-existence, mutual respect and mutual benefit.
2. Cooperation within the BIMSTEC will be complementary to and not be a substitute for bilateral, sub-regional, regional or multilateral cooperation involving the Member States.

CHAPTER II
LEGAL PERSONALITY

Article 3: Legal Personality of BIMSTEC

BIMSTEC as an inter-governmental organization is hereby conferred legal personality.

CHAPTER III
MEMBERSHIP

Article 4: Members of BIMSTEC

The Member States of BIMSTEC are the People's Republic of Bangladesh, the Kingdom of Bhutan, the Republic of India, the Republic of the Union of Myanmar. Nepal, the Democratic Socialist Republic of Sri Lanka, and the Kingdom of Thailand.

Article 5: Rights and Obligations

1. The Member States of BIMSTEC shall have equal rights and obligations under this Charter.
2. The Member States of BIMSTEC shall take all measures that deem necessary, including enactment of appropriate domestic legislations to effectively implement provisions of this Charter and to comply with all obligations of membership.

Article 6: Admission of New Members

1. The process for application and admission to BIMSTEC shall be prescribed by the BIMSTEC Ministerial Meeting upon the concurrence of all Member States.
2. The admission of new member shall be based on the following criteria:
   (a) The applicant State shall satisfy the conditions of territorial contiguity to and/or direct opening into, or primary dependence on the Bay of Bengal for trade and transport purposes and/or any other criteria agreed upon in the BIMSTEC Ministerial Meeting.
   (b) The applicant State shall agree to abide by this Charter.
   (c) The applicant State shall possess the **ability** and willingness to carry out the obligations of Membership.
   (d) Admission of the new Member shall contribute to unity and solidarity of the BIMSTEC.

3. The procedure for admission of new Member States shall be as follows:
   (a) Any State which desires to become a Member of the BIMSTEC shall submit an application to the Secretary General. Such application shall contain a declaration, made in a formal instrument that the State in question fulfils the criteria of this Charter.
   (b) The Secretary General shall, for information, send a copy of the application to the Members of the BIMSTEC and shall include the item in the agenda of the next available Ministerial Meeting.
   (c) Admission shall be approved by the BIMSTEC Summit, upon the recommendation of the BIMSTEC Ministerial Meeting.
   (d) The Secretary General shall inform the applicant State of the decision of the Summit regarding membership. Upon the approval of the membership application, the new member shall deposit the Instrument of Accession to the BIMSTEC Secretariat.

Article 7: Admission of Observers

1. The admission of an Observer shall be based on the following criteria:
   (a) The applicant State shall satisfy BIMSTEC Member States that the applicant for Observership has shown interest in. and is able to contribute to the activities of BIMSTEC.
   (b) The applicant regional/international organization shall satisfy BIMSTEC Member States that the applicant for Observership is in a position to contribute to the work programme of BIMSTEC.
   (c) The applicant State and regional/international organization shall bear in mind that granting of Observer status does not automatically qualify for the membership.
   (d) All decisions regarding the admission of observer states and regional/international organizations will be based on unanimity.
2. The procedure for admission of an Observer shall be as follows:
   (a) Any State, regional organization or international organization desiring to become an Observer of the BIMSTEC shall submit an application to the Secretary General. Such application shall contain a declaration, made in a formal instrument that the State or international organization or regional organization in question fulfils the criteria of the BIMSTEC Charter.
   (b) The Secretary General shall, for information, send a copy of the application to the Members of the BIMSTEC and shall include the

item in the agenda of the next Ministerial Meeting.

(c) All decisions regarding the admission of observer states and international/regional organizations will be made by consensus by the BIMSTEC Summit upon recommendations of the BIMSTEC Ministerial Meeting.

(d) The Secretary General shall inform the applicant State or international organization or regional organization of the decision of the Summit. If the application is approved, observer status shall become effective on the date on which the Summit takes its decision on the application.

(e) Roles and obligations for the Observer will be as agreed by the Member States in the relevant rules of procedures.

CHAPTER IV
ORGANS

Article 8: BIMSTEC Summit

1. The BIMSTEC Summit shall comprise the Heads of State or Government of the Member States.
2. The BIMSTEC Summit shall:
   (a) Be the supreme decision-making body of BIMSTEC;
   (b) Deliberate, provide policy guidance and take decisions on key issues pertaining to the realization of the purposes of BIMSTEC, important matters of interest to Member States and all issues referred to it by the BIMSTEC Ministerial Meeting and BIMSTEC Sectoral Ministerial Bodies;
   (c) Address emergency situations affecting BIMSTEC by taking appropriate measures;
   (d) Decide on application for admission of new Member States and Observers:
   (e) Authorize the establishment and dissolution of Sectoral Ministerial Bodies and BIMSTEC Centres/Entities.
3. The BIMSTEC Summit Meetings shall be:
   (a) Held once every two years, preceded by the Ministerial Meeting, and be hosted by the Member State holding the BIMSTEC Chairmanship; and
   (b) Convened, whenever necessary, as Special Summit to be chaired by the Member State holding the BIMSTEC Chairmanship, at a venue to be agreed upon by BIMSTEC Member States.

(c) The Chairman of BIMSTEC may, at his own initiative or at the request of a Member State, convene a Special Summit to address an important issue pertaining to the interest of BIMSTEC with the concurrence of all Member States.

(d) All decisions of the Summit Meetings shall be made on the basis of consensus.

Article 9: BIMSTEC Ministerial Meeting

1. The BIMSTEC Ministerial Meeting shall comprise the Ministers dealing with foreign relations of the Member States.
2. The BIMSTEC Ministerial Meeting shall have the following powers and functions:
   (a) Coordinating overall BIMSTEC cooperation;
   (b) Prepare the BIMSTEC Summit;
   (c) Coordinate the implementation of agreements and decisions of the BIMSTEC Summit;
   (d) Coordinate with the Sectoral Ministerial Bodies to enhance policy coherence, efficiency and cooperation with them;
   (e) Approve the budget of the Secretariat and BIMSTEC Centres/Entities as proposed by the Senior Officials' Meeting:
   (f) Endorse the deliberations of the BIMSTEC Sectoral Ministerial Meetings;
   (g) Appoint the Secretary General of BIMSTEC, with the rank and status of an Ambassador upon the recommendation of the Senior Officials' Meeting; and
   (h) Undertake such other functions as may be assigned by the BIMSTEC Summit.
3. The BIMSTEC Ministerial Meetings shall:
   (a) Meet annually, preceded by the BIMSTEC Senior Officials' Meeting (SOM), and to be hosted by the Member State holding the BIMSTEC Chairmanship;
   (b) Convene, whenever necessary, as special meeting to be chaired by the Member State holding the BIMSTEC Chairmanship, at a venue to be agreed upon by the Member States.
   (c) The Chairman of BIMSTEC may at his own initiative or at the request of a Member State, convene a Special Ministerial Meeting to address an important issue pertaining to the interest of BIMSTEC with the

concurrence of all Member States.

Article 10: BIMSTEC Sectoral Ministerial Meetings

1. The BIMSTEC Sectoral Ministerial Bodies shall comprise the relevant Ministers of line Ministries responsible for earning out the activities of the respective sectors.
2. The BIMSTEC Sectoral Ministerial Bodies shall have the following powers and functions:
   (a) Function in accordance with their respective established mandates;
   (b) Implement the agreements and decisions of the BIMSTEC Summit under their respective purview;
   (c) Strengthen cooperation in their respective fields in promoting BIMSTEC objectives;
   (d) Submit report and recommendations to the BIMSTEC Ministerial Meeting for the consideration of the BIMSTEC Summit; and
   (e) Assess and approve and take action on the deliberations of the BIMSTEC Sectoral Senior Officials' Meeting.
3. The Sectoral Ministerial Bodies shall meet as and when necessary to be hosted and chaired by the Lead Country of a particular sector. Each Sectoral Ministerial Body may have under its purview the relevant Senior Officials. Sectoral Working Groups and Sub-sectoral Expert Groups/Sub-groups etc., all to be hosted and chaired by the Lead Country of a particular sector or any other interested Member State.

Article 11: BIMSTEC Senior Officials' Meeting

1. The BIMSTEC Senior Officials' Meeting shall comprise the Foreign Secretaries/Secretaries/appropriate Senior Officials nominated by the BIMSTEC Member States.
2. The Senior Officials' Meeting shall have the following powders and functions:
   (a) Prepare for the BIMSTEC Ministerial Meeting;
   (b) Follow up and coordinate the implementation of agreements and decisions of the BIMSTEC Ministerial Meeting;
   (c) Coordinate with the Sectoral Bodies in Sectors where there is no Ministerial body;
   (d) Initiate proposals on all administrative and budgetary matters for the consideration of the Ministerial Meeting: and

(e) Undertake such other functions as may be assigned by the Ministerial Meeting.

(f) Assess and approve and take action on the deliberations of the BIMSTEC Permanent Working Committee.

3. The BIMSTEC Senior Officials' Meeting shall be:

(a) Held once a year, preceding the BIMSTEC Ministerial Meeting to be hosted by the Member State holding the BIMSTEC Chairmanship: and

(b) Convened, whenever necessary, as special session of the Senior Officials' Meeting to be chaired by the Member State holding the BIMSTEC Chairmanship, at a venue to be agreed upon by BIMSTEC Member States.

4. The Senior Officials' Meeting shall report to the BIMSTEC Ministerial Meeting.

Article 12: BIMSTEC Permanent Working Committee

1. The BIMSTEC Permanent Working Committee (BPWC) shall comprise the National Focal Point at appropriate senior level of each BIMSTEC Member State.

2. The BIMSTEC Permanent Working Committee shall have the following powers and functions:

(a) Deliberate on the administrative and financial matters of the Secretariat and BIMSTEC Centres/Entities;

(b) Prepare, in consultation with the Secretariat, schedule/calendar of BIMSTEC activities:

(c) Prioritize and rationalize BIMSTEC activities/projects; and

(d) Prepare for the BIMSTEC Senior Officials' Meeting.

(e) Undertake such other functions as may be assigned by the BIMSTEC Senior Officials' Meeting.

3. The meeting of BIMSTEC Permanent Working Committee (BPWC) shall:

(a) Be held at least twice a year, both to be hosted by the Member State holding the BIMSTEC Chairmanship;

(b) In addition, the Committee shall meet as and when necessary.

Article 13: BIMSTEC National Focal Point

1. Each BIMSTEC Member State shall establish a BIMSTEC National Focal Point (NFP) at their respective Ministry of External Affairs/Foreign Affairs.

2. The National Focal Point shall have the following powers and functions:
   (a) Serve as the national point of contact for all communications including e-mail with the BIMSTEC Secretariat;
   (b) Be the repository of information on all BIMSTEC matters at the national level;
   (c) Coordinate the implementation of BIMSTEC decisions at the national level; and
   (d) Coordinate and support the national preparations of BIMSTEC meetings.

Article 14: Secretary General and the Secretariat

1. The Secretary General of BIMSTEC shall be appointed by the BIMSTEC Ministerial Meeting, upon recommendation by the Senior Officials' Meeting, for a non-renewable term of office of three years, upon nomination by a Member State based on the principle of alphabetical rotation.
2. The Secretary General shall act as the Head of the Secretariat.
3. The Secretary General shall be of Ambassadorial rank.
4. The Secretary General shall have the following duties and responsibilities:
   (a) Carry out directives of the Member States through different mechanisms and coordinate implementation progress;
   (b) Coordinate, facilitate and monitor progress in the implementation of BIMSTEC agreements and decisions, and submit annual report on the work of the organization to the BIMSTEC Ministerial Meeting;
   (c) Participate in meetings of the BIMSTEC Summit. BIMSTEC Ministerial Meeting, BIMSTEC Sectoral Ministerial meetings and other relevant BIMSTEC meetings;
   (d) Represent BIMSTEC and participate in meetings with external parties in accordance with approved policy guidelines and mandate given to the Secretary General.
5. The BIMSTEC Secretariat shall comprise of the Secretary General. Directors and such other staff as may be required and approved by the Member States.
6. In performance of their duties, the Secretary General and the staff shall:
   (a) uphold the highest standards of integrity, efficiency and competence;
   (b) not seek or receive instructions from any government or from any other authority external to the Organization and government or external party outside of BIMSTEC; and
   (c) Refrain from any action which might not commensurate with their respective position as BIMSTEC Secretariat officials.

7. The Secretary General and the Secretariat will not comply with any instruction from any individual Member State other than through BIMSTEC collective mechanism to maintain the exclusive character of the Secretary General and the Secretariat.

Article 15: Other Subsidiary Bodies

Subsidiary bodies including BIMSTEC Centres/Entities, may be established through the signing of the specific Memorandum of Associations among the Member States and Headquarters Agreements with the Host Countries. Separate Agreements shall be signed for the establishment of each BIMSTEC Centre/Entity.

CHAPTER V
IMMUNITIES AND PRIVILEGES

Article 16: Immunities and Privileges of the Secretary General and Staff on deputation of the BIMSTEC Secretariat

1. The Secretary General and staff on deputation of the BIMSTEC Secretariat participating in official BIMSTEC activities or representing the BIMSTEC in the Member States shall enjoy such immunities and privileges as are necessary for the independent exercise of their functions.
2. The immunities and privileges under this Article shall be laid down in a separate BIMSTEC agreement.

Article 17: Immunities and Privileges of the Officials on BIMSTEC duties

The officials of the Member State participating in official BIMSTEC activities in the Member States shall enjoy such immunities and privileges as are necessary for the exercise of their functions.

CHAPTER VI
DECISION MAKING

Article 18: Consensus

All decisions in BIMSTEC shall be based on consensus.

CHAPTER VII
DISPUTE SETTLEMENT

Article 19: Peaceful Settlement of Dispute

Member States shall endeavor to resolve peacefully all disputes in a timely manner through dialogue, consultation and negotiation.

CHAPTER VIII
ADMINISTRATIVE AND PROCEDURAL MATTERS

Article 20: Chairman of BIMSTEC

1. The Chairmanship of BIMSTEC shall rotate on the alphabetical order of the English names of Member States. The changeover of Chairmanship shall take place during the Summit meeting in a manner whereby the Member State chairing BIMSTEC shall host BIMSTEC Summit and hand over the chairmanship to the Member State next in alphabetical order.
2. The Member State assuming the Chairmanship shall chair:
   (a) The BIMSTEC Summit and related summits and retreats;
   (b) The BIMSTEC Ministerial Meetings;
   (c) The BIMSTEC Senior Officials' Meetings; and
   (d) The BIMSTEC Permanent Working Committee.
3. The Member State holding the Chairmanship of BIMSTEC shall actively promote and enhance the interests of BIMSTEC through policy initiatives, coordination, consensus building and cooperation. The Chairman shall represent the organization to external partners.

Article 21: Working Language of BIMSTEC

English shall be the working language of BIMSTEC.

CHAPTER IX
BUDGET AND FINANCING

Article 22: General Principles

1. The BIMSTEC shall establish financial rules and procedures to ensure observance of sound financial management and budgetary discipline.
2. Financial accounts shall be subject to internal and external audits.

Article 23 Operational Budget and Finances of the Secretariat

1. The Secretariat shall be provided with the necessary financial resources to perform its functions effectively.
2. The operational budget of the Secretariat shall be met by the BIMSTEC Member States through annual contributions, as per the rate determined by the Ministerial Meeting, which shall be remitted in a timely manner.
3. The Secretary General shall prepare the annual operational budget of the BIMSTEC Secretariat for approval by the Ministerial Meeting upon the recommendation of the Senior Officials' Meeting.

4. The Secretariat shall operate in accordance with the financial rules and procedures determined by the Ministerial Meeting upon the recommendation of the Senior Officials' Meeting.

CHAPTER X EXTERNAL RELATIONS

Article 24: Conduct of External Relations

The BIMSTEC may conclude agreements with countries or sub-regional, regional and international organizations and institutions. The procedure for concluding such agreements shall be as laid down by the BIMSTEC Ministerial Meeting.

CHAPTER XI
FINAL PROVISIONS

Article 25: Signature, Ratification, Depository and Entry into Force

1. This Charter shall be signed by all BIMSTEC Member States.
2. This Charter shall be subject to ratification by all BIMSTEC Member States in accordance with their respective internal procedures.
3. Instrument of ratification shall be deposited with the Secretary General who shall promptly notify all Member State of each deposit.
4. This Charter shall enter into force on the thirtieth day following the deposit of the seventh instrument of ratification with the Secretary General of BIMSTEC.

Article 26: Amendments

1. Any Member State may propose amendments to the Charter. Proposed amendments to the Charter shall be submitted by the Ministerial Meeting to the BIMSTEC Summit for its decision.
2. Amendments to the Charter agreed by consensus by the Summit shall be ratified by all Member States in accordance with Article 25.
3. An amendment shall enter into force on the thirtieth day following the deposit of the last instrument of ratification with the Secretary General.

Article 27: Terms of Reference and Rules of Procedure

Unless otherwise provided for in this Charter, the BIMSTEC Ministerial Meeting shall determine the terms of reference and rules of procedure and shall ensure their consistency.

Article 28: Review

This Charter may be reviewed six years after its **entry** into force or as otherwise determined by the BIMSTEC Summit.

Article 29: Interpretation and Implementation of the Charter

1. Upon request of any Member State, the interpretation of the Charter shall be undertaken by BIMSTEC Secretariat in accordance with the rules of procedure determined by the BIMSTEC Ministerial Meeting with the concurrences of the Member States.
2. Parties to dispute may request the Chairman of BIMSTEC, to provide good offices, conciliation and mediation to settle any dispute arising out of the interpretation or implementation of the Charter.

Article 30: Legal Continuity

1. All treaties, conventions, agreements, declarations and other BIMSTEC instruments which have been in effect before the entry into force of this Charter shall continue to be valid.
2. In case of inconsistency between the rights and obligations of Member States under such instruments and this Charter, this Charter shall prevail.

Article 31: Original Text

The signed original text of the Charter in English shall be deposited with the Secretary General of BIMSTEC, who shall provide a certified copy to each Member State.

Article 32: BIMSTEC Assets

The assets and funds of the organization shall be vested in the name of BIMSTEC.

Article 33: BIMSTEC Flag

The BIMSTEC Flag shall be as shown in Annex-I.

Article 34: BIMSTEC Emblem

The BIMSTEC Emblem shall be as shown in Annex-II.

Article 35: BIMSTEC Day

The sixth of June shall be observed as BIMSTEC Day.

Article 36: Use of the Name of BIMSTEC

The name of "BIMSTEC" shall strictly be used only in respect of the meetings and events of the BIMSTEC cooperation sectors agreed by the Member States.

* * *

Done in Colombo on the Thirtieth Day of March in the year Two Thousand and Twenty-Two, in a single original in the English language.

For the People's Republic of Bangladesh

Her Excellency Sheikh Hasina
Prime Minister

* * *

Done in Colombo on the Thirtieth Day of March in the year Two Thousand and Twenty-Two, in a single original in the English language.

For the Kingdom of Bhutan

His Excellency Dr. Lotay Tshering
Prime Minister

* * *

Done in Colombo on the Thirtieth Day of March in the year Two Thousand and Twenty Two, in a single original in the English language.

For the Republic of India

His Excellency Shri Narendra Modi
Prime Minister

* * *

Done in Colombo on the Thirtieth Day of March in the year Two Thousand and Twenty-Two, in a single original in the English language.

For the Republic of the Union of Myanmar

His Excellency Senior General Min Aung Hlaing
Chairman of the State Administration Council and Prime Minister

* * *

Done in Colombo on the Thirtieth Day of March in the year Two Thousand and Twenty-Two, in a single original in the English language.

For Nepal

Right Honourable Mr. Sher Bahadur Deuba
Prime Minister

* * *

Done in Colombo on the Thirtieth Day of March in the year Two Thousand and Twenty-Two, in a single original in the English language.

For the Democratic Socialist Republic of Sri Lanka

His Excellency Gotabaya Rajapaksa
President

* * *

Done in Colombo on the Thirtieth Day of March in the year Two Thousand and Twenty-Two, in a single original in the English language.

For the Kingdom of Thailand

His Excellency General Prayut Chan-o-cha (Ret.)
Prime Minister

* * *

Annex 1

BIMSTEC FLAG

The specifications of the existing BIMSTEC Flag are as follows:

A. Type of Flags

There shall be following three types of flags for the BIMSTEC:

a. Table Flag
b. Car Flag
c. Outdoor/Venue Flag

B. Size of the Flag

The ratio of the Flags = Length: Width = 5:3

a. Table Flag: 10 in × 6 in (250 mm × 150 mm)
b. Car Flag: 12.5 in × 7.5 in (320 mm × 190 mm)
c. Outdoor/Venue Flag: 5 ft. × 3 ft. (1.52 m × 0.91 m)

C. Size and the Position of the Logo of BIMSTEC[1]

a. The centre of circle of the BIMSTEC logo shall be at the intersection point of the perpendiculars drawn from the middle of the length and the width of the flag.
b. Radius of the circle of the logo shall be $2/7^{th}$ of the width.
c. The height of the letters of the word "BIMSTEC" at the logo shall be $1/19^{th}$ of the width of the flag.
d. The height of lower edge of the word "BIMSTEC" at the logo shall be $4/9^{th}$ of the width of the flag.

D. Background of the Flag

The background of the flag shall be **white.** The shape shall be rectangular in the proportion of 5:3 with the existing Logo of BIMSTEC in the near middle of the Flag.

---

[1] All the specifications are calculated on the basis of the existing Logo of BIMSTEC

Annex II

BIMSTEC EMBLEM

Index